War and Human Nature

War and Human Nature

Stephen Peter Rosen

PRINCETON UNIVERSITY PRESS   PRINCETON AND OXFORD

Published by Princeton University Press, 41 William Street, Princeton, New Jersey 08540

In the United Kingdom: Princeton University Press, 3 Market Place, Woodstock, Oxfordshire OX20 1SY

Second printing, and first paperback printing, 2007
Paperback ISBN-13: 978-0-691-13056-9
Paperback ISBN-10: 0-691-13056-6

The Library of Congress has cataloged the cloth edition of this book as follows

Rosen, Stephen Peter, 1952–
War and human nature / Stephen Peter Rosen.
p.   cm.
Includes bibliographical references and index.
ISBN 0-691-11600-8 (cl. : alk. paper)
1. War.   2. War—Psychological aspects.   I. Title.

U21.2.R638   2004
355.02—dc22   2003065590

British Library Cataloging-in-Publication Data is available

This book has been composed in Sabon

Printed on acid-free paper. ∞

press.princeton.edu

Printed in the United States of America

10   9   8   7   6   5   4   3   2

Contents

Acknowledgments

THIS BOOK TRIES to show how work done in the neurosciences over the last twenty-five years can help us better understand how people make decisions, and, in particular, how they make decisions about war and peace. I hope this is the beginning, not the end, of the serious discussion of the biological dimensions of human international political behavior.

This is not a biological determinist argument. At each stage in the book, I try to show how the biological aspects of human decision making interact with the social and historical dimensions of human politics. Nor is it an attack on rational choice theory, though it does try to show how the neurosciences can help us better specify how people make calculations, and indicate when and how people will not behave in the ways predicted by economic theory. Because it is still early days as far as understanding the full complexity of the human mind, I make an effort to show the limits of my arguments, while trying to set out what I believe to be well-founded arguments based on the limited parts of human cognition that we do understand. The manuscript has been reviewed by neuroscientists and anthropologists working on the biology of violence, as well as political scientists. No errors in my presentation of work in the neurosciences were found. That does not mean that the reviewers agreed with my conclusions about human politics.

Because this has been and will be a contentious project, I am particularly grateful to the people who have helped me over the last six years. Andrew Marshall was, in this project, as in my intellectual life in general, essential. The help of Bob Jervis with this book was appreciated more than usual because I was working in a field in which he is a master. Allan Stam, Jon Mercer, John Mearsheimer, and Dick Betts all gave me a chance to present my work in its early stages, and to argue its merits, even though they had major disagreements with it. For this I am and will remain grateful.

War and Human Nature

Chapter One_____

Introduction

THE GREEK HISTORIAN Thucydides analyzed decisions about war and peace over two thousand years ago. People, he argued, were motivated by calculations of self-interest, but other factors mattered as well, factors like fear and honor, that were not quite the same as self-interest. If you asked a social scientist today what drives decisions about war, you would get the answer that people make decisions about the use of organized violence more or less in the same way that economists say people make economic decisions, that is, in a coherent, stable, and efficient manner. This book is an exploration of a more complicated understanding of human decision making. It does not reject the explanation of decision making offered by the economists, which is often a useful analytical tool. It does, however, argue that processes other than conscious calculation play a role in human decision making along with conscious calculation. Emotion, stress, and hormones such as testosterone are important players in human decision making. By understanding the role of these other cognitive mechanisms, we can often better specify the limits within which conscious, rational calculations are performed. We can also specify the ways in which human decision making may change as our bodily states change. This helps us understand why the behavior of decision makers may not be stable over time, though their behavior could be understood as rational at any one moment. These other nonconscious factors can enable rational decision making, but they do lead to decisions that we would not understand or predict if we did not take those factors into account.

The evidence for this argument comes from many sources. It includes data from college students who participate in psychological experiments. It includes data from people receiving medical treatment for mental disorders. In such cases, we must be very careful not to extrapolate directly from these findings to the behavior of leaders in the real world, who, after all, tend not to be college sophomores or brain-damaged. Yet those experiments and the data from the treatment of patients can help us understand the operations of the human mind. What happens when certain portions of the brain responsible for understanding human emotion, for example, are disabled? By answering this question, we can begin to see how the behavior of people who have not experienced brain damage may be affected by the operation of those portions of the brain. By understanding why nineteen-year-old men are different from average politicians, most noticeably with regard to their testosterone levels, we can begin to see how variations in testosterone levels can affect human decision making.

There will be a natural tendency to see the operation of these nonconscious cognitive mechanisms as producing "bad" decisions, while conscious calculations produce "good" decisions. While natural, this would be a mistake. To repeat, the nonconscious mechanisms often function in ways that make rational choice possible in complex settings. These nonconscious mechanisms exist because they played a positive role in human evolutionary history. For example, they make possible rapid decisions when there are severe limits on the amount of time available for deliberation. But they may lead to decisions that differ from what standard economic models would predict. As Daniel Kahneman and Amos Tversky demonstrated, people may overgeneralize from limited observations, impute characteristics to people on the assumption that they are representative of a group, and take more risks to avoid losses than to achieve gains.[1] This book will explore the ways in which emotional memories may affect rational decisions, how stress and distress may lead to depression and defeat, and how testosterone may affect the impulse to punish perceived challengers. All of these phenomenan could be judged, after the fact, to be "good" or "bad." The concern of this book, however, will simply be to understand how and why the decisions were made, without judging the outcomes. This issue will be explored, in particular, in chapter 2.

The argument of the book is, in its essence, reasonably simple. It includes biological issues, but it is not a biological determinist argument. Human beings have several mechanisms inside them that play a role in decision making. These multiple mechanisms exist as a result of our biological inheritance. Human beings are not exactly alike, and in a population of people there will be variations in their biological inheritance. These variations affect the mechanisms involved in making decisions about social problems, including war. These biological factors and the way in which they vary from person to person can affect the political behavior of states. But there is a social or organizational component to the argument as well. The behavior of states will depend on the nature of the social institutions that empower or weaken the influence of individuals with certain inherited ways of making decisions. The impact of the biological mechanisms analyzed in this book depends on the social settings within which people make decisions, social settings that are, in part, the result of human choice. In short, this book tries to make the case that there is a biological argument that Thucydides was right, that fear and honor play a role in human politics along with calculations of interest, but also that the other issues he analyzed, such as the nature of the political systems present in the ancient Greek world, matter as well.

Making that case takes some effort. This book uses the current scientific understanding of human nature, along with an understanding of social institutions, to explain human cognition as it is relevant to the issues of war and peace. Since the terms "human nature" and "cognition" are used in a variety of ways, they should be defined. In this book, cognition will mean the way in which information is selected, stored, recalled, and used, consciously or unconsciously, for decision making. Human nature will refer to the aspects of human cognition that are affected by biological inheritance, as those inherited factors are shaped by human interaction with the environment. This book argues that the two are linked. There are inherited parts of the brain and the endocrine system that function along with the parts of the brain that do perform conscious calculations. They affect rational calculation, and can facilitate rational calculation, but they can also push us toward decisions that are different from the ones we would make on the basis of conscious calculation alone. Indeed, it will be shown that conscious calculations by themselves may be insufficient to lead people to a decision, and other factors are important because they make possible rational choices in complex environments. Yet those other factors do complicate our internal decision-making processes. It is because of the coexistence of these other mechanisms, along with conscious calculation, that Thomas Schelling was correct when he stated that human behavior must be understood as the interaction between at least two conflicting selves within each person.[2]

The rest of this book is an elaboration of these ideas.

It helps to begin by looking at human nature and cognition in general, or the biologically affected ways of processing information that most people have in common. The biological sciences now give us a more detailed picture of how the human brain operates. While we do not have anything close to a complete understanding of human cognition, important elements of it are now better understood. For example, we know that the neocortex, the part of the human brain that is proportionally much larger than that found in any other animal, and which is responsible for conscious thought, does not treat all data equally. It is more sensitive to some kinds of data derived from sensory perceptions. In ways that can be reliably and empirically demonstrated, and for which evolutionary psychology provides plausible explanations, the neocortex is provided with, or preferentially selects, certain kinds of data. Certain memories, notably those formed at times of emotional arousal, and certain kinds of current data, notably the data associated with the expression of emotion in faces and voices, are more salient when we consciously and unconsciously consider what we should do. This selection of data is not done consciously, but it does shape conscious thought. The data selected for use by the human brain is not necessarily the selection of data that would lead to the choices that an economist would regard as optimal. For example, new information may not be given as much weight as an economist would think it should, if the new information conflicts with memories that have emotional associations.

The neocortex then processes that data within certain parameters, or constraints. Those constraints are not consciously chosen and may or may not be optimal in ways that economists would recognize. For example, rational decision making involves thinking about the future consequences of current actions. The act of considering the consequences of our actions before making a decision is a function performed by the neocortex. But *how far* into the future should we think? Should I care a great deal about the consequences of my actions ten years from now, or should I let the future take care of itself? In more technical language, what is the nature of our time horizons? How much do we discount costs and benefits that arrive sometime after our actions? These time horizons are not something that we always choose consciously. Our time horizons can be affected by human nature, as well as conscious decisions. Both human nature acting unconsciously and conscious calculation can affect what we consciously decide to do. By better understanding the biology of human cognition, we can better specify how people make decisions rationally, by specifying the biological mechanisms that supply the data needed for decision making and specifying the parameters, such as time horizons, within which decisions are rationally made.

To be more specific, there are parts of the human brain involved in decision making that are distinct from the neocortex. These are sometimes referred to as the evolutionary older parts of the brain, because they are also found in nonhuman animals. For example, the amygdala and the hippocampus, working together with portions of the endocrine system, react to information in ways that shape the decision making done by the neocortex. But there are also parts of the brain that perform an independent decision-making role, separately from the neocortex. When I am hungry and I see a doughnut, I may eat it, not because I consciously calculate that I should, but because something other than conscious calculations has decided that I will eat it. This form of decision making is not the same as conscious decision making and can affect social interactions. If I am challenged by my subordinate, I may lash out and punish that subordinate "without thinking," and in ways that may not be what I would, in calmer moments, refer to as being in my best interests. If I am subjected to prolonged stimulation from the environment that I cannot control, my stress response and endocrine system will respond in a way that will eventually create a state of mind equivalent to depression.

While depressed, I will make decisions that will be different from the decisions I will make when not depressed. At any particular moment in time, my biological state will affect my decision making. If you are aware of my immediate biological state, my decisions will be comprehensible, but my behavior will not be stable over time. My decisions may not be rational in the sense that they are not stable: the same information will lead to different decisions at different times.

In short, the human brain is not easily reducible to a unified, rational calculating machine. It has parts that support conscious calculation, parts that shape conscious calculation, but also parts that can run counter to conscious calculation. Because these characteristics of the human brain are to some extent determined by our heredity, they are resistant to changes that are motivated by conscious choice. I cannot decide, for example, not to be depressed. I can try not to be affected by traumatic memories, but I may not succeed. We are not unitary rational actors, though we can try, sometimes successfully, to make ourselves behave as if we were. Because certain decision-making mechanisms can be dominant at some times but not at others, we do not always make decisions the same way. This means that we may not display what is at the core of the economic model of human decision making, that is, consistent and ordered preferences that are stable over time. The nonconscious elements of decision making can and do change over time in ways that we cannot consciously control, and this can lead to inconsistencies in our behavior. For a variety of reasons, at some times we will behave as if we want A, and at others, we will behave as if we want not-A. Human beings have been known to want to have their cake and eat it too, or, in the case of international politics, to want peace, for example, but also want to lash out at challengers who hurt us.

Though there is much about human cognition that is shared by all people, human beings are not identical. Natural selection can operate only on a population that has variations, and human beings display variations in their inherited decision-making mechanisms. As a result, it is important to understand the way different people process information differently, because of their differing hereditary factors. With regard to many cognitive factors, people are not all the same. All people have some measure of intelligence, for example, but intelligence varies across individuals in ways that are affected by genetic inheritance, though we can argue about how big a factor genetic inheritance is compared with other factors.[3] Biological variations in cognition go beyond intelligence. A teenage boy reacts to a challenge from a peer in a way that is different from the reaction of a middle-aged woman. More subtle but important differences exist among mature adults, with regard to their sensitivity to status challenges, time horizons, or susceptibility to depression. The ability to specify the ways in which different people make decisions differently enables us to deal with one of the longstanding objections to the use of the results of experimental psychology to explain real-world political behavior. The objection is obvious: people who participate in lab experiments may not be like the people who are the heads of governments. In fact, they are very likely to be different. But we can now begin to understand this heterogeneity, and so distinguish and identify people with different cognitive profiles.

Up to this point, the emphasis has been on individuals and individual decision making, but individual human nature and the variations among individuals in their natures cannot, by themselves, explain the behavior of groups of humans. There may well be differences in individual cognitive profiles, but political decisions are seldom made and executed by single individuals. It may be the case that human nature affects human cognition, and that individuals are different from each other, but how do we go from that to an explanation of the behavior of governments? The argument of this book is that different social settings or institutions do not always randomly select people and give them political power. Instead, they may preferentially select people with particular cognitive profiles for positions of responsibility and then situate them in social environments that reinforce the decision-making tendencies that they have as individuals. To give one example discussed at length in chapter 5, turbulent political environments full of near-term dangers make it easier for people with near-term time horizons to rise to political power, and for them to gain tyrannical power. Once in a position of absolute power, such individuals will exist in a social environment in which their individual cognitive profiles will be of considerable political importance, and their individual predisposition to act in ways affected by near-term calculations will be reinforced by the social setting in which they exist. A different political system will select and empower a different kind of person. The institutions associated with oligarchic politics may select for people sensitive to social status and put those people together in an environment that tends to focus and magnify their status challenges to each other, reinforcing their predisposition to engage in challenge-response types of status politics. In other group settings, the stress-induced depression experienced by one individual will create behavior that others can observe, and which can trigger fear and depression in them. On the other hand, one can also specify social institutions that will tend to dampen or neutralize the effects of individual cognitive predispositions before they are translated into group behavior. Checks and balances are meant, among other things, to prevent individual tendencies to "act in the heat of the moment" from becoming actual. So the variations in human nature relevant to cognition will be important only when social conditions reinforce them.

Rationality and Nonrationality

This book is part of the debate about whether human actions reflect rational choice, so it is necessary to make clear what is meant by rationality. References to the concept of economic rationality have been made, but, to be explicit, rationality in this book will mean what economists mean by rationality: a microeconomic model of decision making that assumes not simply that people act purposefully, but that they have a stable, ordered, and consistent set of preferences, and that they have a stable way of making choices about how to use scarce resources in a manner that gives them the most utility from a given expenditure of resources. Rationality does not simply mean purposeful behavior or actions that are associated with goals. People are not rational in the economic sense if they want something and the opposite of that thing at the same time, or if they want different things at different moments in time, or if they use all their resources to get the most of their first choice while ignoring opportunities to get a lot of their second choice cheaply. People are not rational if, under one set of circumstances, they use information to make one decision and then later use the same information to make an entirely different decision. Economists define rationality in this way so that it can be used to generate specific, testable propositions about how actors will behave. An actor who makes purposeful decisions but makes them differently at different times, or who simultaneously wants contradictory things, is not an actor whose actions can be modeled or predicted, however familiar such individuals may be in real life.

The economic definition of rationality was a major improvement on the looser use of rationality, which looks at a decision and then reasons backward from the behavior to a set of goals. This kind of analysis then concludes that the actor was acting "rationally" to achieve his or her purposes. Hitler invaded the Soviet Union. Was this rational? It is possible to selectively focus on facts that Hitler might have known, and to so show retrospectively that his calculation of the costs and benefits of his possible actions must have led him rationally to decide to invade the Soviet Union. This way of analyzing the past has intuitive appeal, but it also has major problems. Suppose Hitler had not invaded the Soviet Union. We would then find facts to show why his decision not to invade was also "rational." A definition of rationality that explains a decision and its opposite is not useful. The economic definition of rationality is not loose. It is a tremendously powerful analytic tool in conditions in which its basic assumptions hold.

People often do make rational decisions, very often about economic issues. People almost always want to pay less for a particular refrigerator than more. But there are conditions in which the preferences of people are not stable and consistent. There are conditions in which their view of the future varies, or their use of information varies. In some circumstances, when confronting strong and basic human desires for food, sex, and safety, people often do want something and its opposite. They may want to lose weight and eat cake, or fight for their country but also not risk being killed. They may want to make money, but they may also want to punish a rival even though punishing the challenger does not increase their prosperity. They may calculate that their prospects for success are good at one time, but if they are depressed they may look at the same facts and decide that their prospects for success are low. These familiar kinds of inconsistent decision making can affect politics and, I will argue, are grounded in human nature.

Coming to Terms with Human Nature

Any effort to incorporate an understanding of human nature into our explanations of politics will be difficult and controversial. Why should it even be attempted? The short answer is that it cannot be avoided, and never has been. All theories of human politics have started, and must start, by talking about human nature. The question is not whether political analysis should investigate the subject of human nature, but whether one should use the best available information about human nature when analyzing politics. Limits on the available scientific evidence about human nature, of course, have not inhibited debates about politics based on alternative understandings of human nature. For example, Thomas Hobbes argued that men, by nature, were both inquisitive and fearful. They sought the causes of what they observed and invented invisible causes of events that had no visible explanations. They imagined the causes of things that harmed them and so became anxious and fearful about the sources of injury that they could not see. As a result, priests, whose domain was the unseen world, were powerful political figures, and their influence had to be radically circumscribed if there was to be a single sovereign, and domestic peace, in any political community.[4] From a terse characterization of human nature proceeded much of the political program of Hobbes. Rousseau, in contrast, argued that men, again by nature, were not naturally fearful, but predisposed to compare themselves, first to animals, and then to each other. Initially dispersed, they would be brought together by chance, and the propensity to make comparisons would then lead them to demand respect and appreciation; this was enough to launch a process of social envy and competition that would lead to human social misery.[5] Ultimately, men would have to be forced to be free, that is, they would have to be compelled to behave in ways that enabled them to escape the consequences of the human natures that they had inherited, according to Rousseau.

John Locke, who is in many ways the author who most influenced American political science, also wrote about human nature. In the field of human cognition, he is perhaps best known for his argument that the minds of people are blank slates, without any innate principles inscribed on them. While he did make this argument, the work, *An Essay Concerning Human Understanding*, is in fact a broader effort to say what the human mind was capable of doing, given the way it was, by nature, and what the implications were for human politics. Human beings, Locke noted, had a particular kind of mind and operated with a particular set of sensory organs, but other kinds of human minds were imaginable, with different kinds of senses. But given human beings the way they were, there were certain kinds of things they could never know and should, therefore, stop fighting about, most notably, all religious issues not resolvable by reason. Human nature also was such that people were driven by uneasiness and desires that resulted from the absence of some positive or negative good (the absence of pain, for example). But humans were not mechanical creatures driven by their desires, because they could suspend their decisions about whether to satisfy a particular desire. They could choose the moment when they would decide. They could, therefore, choose to decide when certain desires were dominant, as opposed to others. From this understanding of human nature comes Locke's argument for free will. From free will comes Locke's most famous political argument, that governments are legitimate only when people consent to them. Consent would have no special value if humans did not have free will, if their choices were simply the inevitable consequence of external conditions.[6] Here, too, the central political conclusion followed from a specification of human nature.

Hobbes, Rousseau, Locke, and other political thinkers had views of human nature that were, at least in part, correct, but they derived their views on human nature from thought experiments, introspection, and, perhaps, their prior views on politics. This book tries to proceed from the data amassed by the last thirty years of work in the biological sciences. That data has, to this date, not come close to giving us a full and complete understanding of how human beings make decisions. At best, we have partial understandings of human cognition. Though this book tries to use the best available data, at points simplifications of and extrapolations from the scientific evidence will be made in order to arrive at propositions about political behavior. The fact that the book begins from scientific data does not mean that its conclusions have the status of scientific truths. The conclusions, however tentative and preliminary, will be the subject of political debate, as have earlier efforts to discuss human nature and politics. An effort must be made to keep the debate constructive, and this can be hard to do when using data from the natural sciences to explain human behavior. The claim that a certain view of human nature is based on science has particular political force in our time. It is not subject to the common view that "you can have your view of human nature and I can have mine, and no one can say that one view is better than another." If something is said to be true, or possibly true, because it is based on the findings of modern science, we believe that we must take that claim seriously.

As a result, even modest efforts to advance tentative arguments using data from the natural sciences to explain human nature and political behavior immediately draw hostile reactions. If human nature is what we inherit, it is what we are given at birth. By the same token, it is not something we have chosen for ourselves, and so it is something that limits our freedom. The more substantive content we ascribe to human nature, the more we tend to limit the area of human choice and freedom. As a result, the effort to utilize a scientific understanding of human nature is controversial in ways that other efforts to understand human nature are not.

This problem has affected even the most apolitical biological scientists writing about human neuroscience. A prominent 1998 textbook on cognitive neuroscience began by summarizing past beliefs and theories about how the human mind processed information. It identified empiricism, the dominant strand in Anglo-Saxon psychology, before and after Freud, as the theory that all human ideas and knowledge came from our sensory experiences of the external world. Our minds were what our lives had made them. As far as our minds were concerned, we inherited very little. The textbook then noted, "This belief that environmental contingencies could explain all became welded into the very fabric of thought. After all, it reflected the American Dream. Anybody could become anything in the right environment."[7] The authors devoted the rest of the book to the demonstration that the empiricist view of the mind was not correct. The human mind has functions and structures that are the result of genetic inheritance, as well as its encounters with the environment. The authors realized, but did not dwell on, the fact that their scientific observations had political implications.

The fact that claims to scientific statements about human nature have this special status means that we must be particularly careful about how we make such statements. We should be careful not to claim too much. We must acknowledge, as all students of the brain now acknowledge, that the old debate between "nature" and "nurture" was improperly structured. Human cognition is the product of the interaction of inherited functions and structures with the environment. It is meaningless to talk about one in the absence of the other, and it is often difficult to separate the two, since the social environment can strengthen or weaken inherited mental predispositions, and inherited predispositions can shape the social environment. We can make some limited statements about certain inherited characteristics of the brain. But such statements about the inherited characteristics of the human brain could be true, or even obvious, and there might still remain important obstacles in the way of applying findings from the biological sciences to explanations of political behavior. We must acknowledge that we are nowhere near a comprehensive understanding of mental functions. One inherited mental predisposition might neutralize another, or reinforce it, depending on the circumstances. Hence, any statement about the impact of one particular brain function by itself may be misleading if all of the other brain functions, some of which are understood, most of which are not, are not taken into account.

If this is so, is it not simply premature to begin the effort to apply findings from these fields to the contentious world of international politics? Is this not particularly so since there are so many problems in taking findings from the laboratory and using them to explain social events in the real world? Do we not already have an adequate, if perhaps overly simple, model of human decision making, which assumes that human beings have preferences, use information rationally to evaluate the courses of action open to them, and choose the course of action that provides them most efficiently with what they want?

There can be no doubt that it is difficult to take what we know about the way individual human brains work and then use that understanding to explain how many human beings in complex social settings make political decisions. Political psychologists are more aware of these problems than most other people. Philip E. Tetlock catalogued many of the problems associated with using findings from psychology to explain international political events.[8] First, psychologists can explore whether, under specified laboratory conditions, people will display specified psychological characteristics. Even if psychologists cannot directly monitor everything that is going on inside the minds of people, they can run variations on the experiment in which they present subjects with different external conditions and then see if the subjects display different forms of psychological behavior. But we can never rerun political action in the real world, holding actors constant but varying conditions, so claims about the influence of psychological factors under certain conditions must always remain modest. Second, individuals may behave in ways that can be studied by psychologists in the laboratory, but groups of individuals will not behave the same way that isolated individuals behave. International relations is often about the behavior of groups of people. For those reasons, psychological studies of individual behavior, however interesting, may be poor guides to the understanding of international relations. Third, many events could plausibly be explained by reference to psychological factors, but they could be explained by reference to nonpsychological factors as well, and, in truth, we will never know exactly how much influence any one particular factor may have had by itself, since real-world events are unique, complex interactions of many factors. Finally, psychological experiments are performed most often using American college sophomores, who are likely to be cognitively different, say, from Otto von Bismarck.[9] Even more problematic is the fact that the current understanding of human cognition often emerges from clinical studies of sick people who needed treatment and who may, therefore, be very unrepresentative of government leaders who have not checked into mental hospitals. And so on.

There are at least two kinds of responses that can be made to these serious criticisms about transferring findings from the biological sciences to the study of real-world politics. First, many of the criticisms of the relevance of findings from the psychological sciences to politics can be leveled with equal merit at the relevance of rationalist theories. If we cannot put Bismarck into a laboratory to see if he has certain psychological predispositions, neither can we examine him to prove that he was rational in the sense that economists use. All we have, when developing either rationalist or psychological arguments about real-world political behavior, are historically recorded words and actions. In developing any theories about why people did what they did, the answer is to use both the rationalist model and the biological model to generate competing predictions about real-world behavior, and then go back and look retrospectively to see how those predictions hold up. If we cannot rerun history to show that a leader who is alleged to be nonrational behaved in a way that was different from the way a rational leader would have behaved, neither can we rerun history to prove that leaders were behaving rationally.[10] A rational explanation of decision making must begin with some inferences about what the leader in question wants. Since we cannot see inside the minds of dead leaders, we must infer their preferences, after the fact, by observing what they did. This kind of reasoning can easily turn into tautological statements about the rationality of leaders. The alternative is to assume that a particular leader wanted what leaders in general want, and then see if a given leader did what other leaders would have done. But, just as in the case of the critique of psychological theories, we cannot rerun history. Was Hitler acting the way any rational German leader would have acted, or was Hitler's decision-making process different from that of other rational leaders? We cannot rerun the history of the Hitler period with another German leader in power to find out what a "rational German leader" would have done. At any given point in history, what was the course of international political action that a rational actor would have adopted?

In the same way, the argument that factors other than psychological factors could have caused the observed behavior, even if that behavior was consistent with psychological theories, can be used to critique any explanation. The multiplicity of factors that could have affected the behavior we are studying, plus the complexity of real-world interactions among those factors, make it difficult to determine just what role each factor played in the real world, and how the outcome would have differed if one factor had changed, as Robert Jervis noted in his book, *Systems Effects*. It is hard to move from observations about the psychologically based behavior of individuals in isolation to the behavior of groups of people. But the same problem afflicts the rationalist approach. Arrow's theorem shows that groups of rational people will not display a consistent, transitive ordering of preferences, even if the individuals in the group are perfectly rational. Bargaining among rational actors can produce decisions that are not rational from the standpoint of the state. Of course, one can simply assume that governments behave the way an isolated rational actor would behave, but there is no theoretical reason to believe that this is in fact the case.

Extrapolation from studies of college sophomores and sick people to the behavior of national leaders is problematic essentially because we realize that people are different, and so we understand that we should not make conclusions about one kind of person by looking at very different groups of people. Political leaders may very well not be like the people studied in experiments. But if the argument is that people display heterogeneity of decision-making styles, why is it legitimate to assume that all leaders are equally rational and make decisions the same way? We can assume that only rational people will rise to the top of their government, but we can equally well assume that other kinds of people with different decision-making procedures will rise to the top of their government under different circumstances.

In the case of both rational choice explanations and explanations that make use of findings from the biological sciences, we should look to see whether the kind of decision-making process we see in controlled settings is also observable in real-world settings. In both rational choice explanations and cognitive explanations, we should avoid judging the outcomes of events and then reasoning back from outcomes assessed to be "good," after the fact, to rational decision-making processes, and from "bad" outcomes to irrational processes. We should characterize the processes themselves, and see whether those processes can be detected in the real world.

The assumption that states display economic rationality might be justified even if human brains behaved in the ways described by recent work in the neurosciences, if behavior conformed to predictions made on the basis of rationality—if states behaved "as if" they were making rational calculations. To make predictions about what rational decision making would be under a given set of circumstances, it is helpful to construct formal models, in which the effect of different factors on decisions can be clearly specified. The predicted outcomes of these models can then be empirically tested. The best-known work of this sort has been done by Bruce Bueno de Mesquita and David Lalman.[11] They found, using their own database, that states often went to war when their model, based on economic rationality, predicted they would. D. Scott Bennett and Allan C. Stam tried to replicate the finding that decisions to go to war empirically conformed to the predictions made by a model based on rational choice. Using data that referred to state interactions over longer periods of time and in regions other than Europe, Bennett and Stam found that in the largest set of cases, the model generated predictions that were "actually uncorrelated with the occurrence of mutually violent outcomes—not at all what the expected utility theory would predict. The situation with occurrence of war is even worse. The [model's] equilibrium of war is actually associated with the occurrence of peace." While behavior of states in the Middle East was often correctly predicted by the model, the behavior of Asian and African states was best predicted by taking the prediction of the model and then reversing it, because war occurred in those regions when the model predicted peace. In Europe, states that interacted with each other for thirty years did come to display rational behavior, but the reasons why they did not do so initially were not clear.[12] Bueno de Mesquita also used his model to predict the interaction between the People's Republic of China and Hong Kong,[13] but the prediction of the sharp and forceful suppression of Hong Kong autonomy by the PRC in the first years after the transfer of sovereignty has not been borne out by events in the real world.

These findings do not invalidate the rational choice model, which has some success in predicting behavior. One might take these findings and others and use them to make the rational choice model better. But why not take the same approach to models of human decision making based on the biological sciences? These models could be used to formulate hypotheses about what kind of behavior to expect in international relations, and then they could be tested, as best as possible given the limits on testing any social scientific propositions. They could become part of an ongoing project to refine our understanding of human behavior. Why would we not expect models based on the close empirical observation of human beings, which took into account the heterogeneity of human beings and the complexity of individual decision making, to provide a better intellectual starting point than models that assumed that all people made decisions the same way, and that individuals have simple and consistent decision-making processes?

Moreover, the criticisms of the application of experimental psychology to international relations ought to encourage us to incorporate our understanding of the biological elements of cognition into our psychological explanations of international politics. Recent work in the neurosciences and experimental psychology is the result of well-structured, replicable, falsifiable empirical scientific work that does get us part of the way inside what has been the black box of human cognition. This helps us escape the dilemma of having to infer mental mechanisms from behavior and then use those mechanisms to explain behavior. Unlike Freudian psychoanalysis, the recent work makes specific statements, for example, about memory formation, that can be and have been tested by specifying the biochemical pathways that operate selectively to form and recall memories, and then chemically blocking those pathways to see if memory formation is inhibited in the predicted ways. If knowledge about the unconscious cognitive mechanisms of the human brain, for example, is available, why should we not make use of it, instead of assuming what may not be true? If political science claims to be a science commensurate with other sciences, it should incorporate the same findings about the same phenomena that the rest of the scientific world accepts. That means, on the other hand, speculation about evolutionary pathways that might have created cognitive mechanisms must be treated as more or less interesting speculation that has to be confirmed. If, however, evolutionary models of human development generate propositions about human cognition that can be and have been tested, they should also be accepted.

The second general response to the criticisms leveled above goes beyond stating that rationalist and psychological theories often suffer from common problems. More constructively, the biological sciences may be able to help some of the problems that were identified above, which afflicted both rationalist and psychological theories. There is the possibility that the biological approaches to human cognition may help fix exactly the problems that have been leveled at the earlier efforts to use findings from experimental psychology to explain real world politics. If the biological sciences offer some ways of identifying and characterizing cognitive mechanisms that operate under some specified environmental circumstances, they may help us deal with the fact that human beings differ in the way they process information, by specifying the observable, measurable markers of different cognitive profiles. If the biological sciences offer us some limited insights into the variations in human cognitive types, ought we not use them, precisely because the assumption that all people are equally rational, or not, is unwarranted? If the biological sciences give us some understanding of human social behavior, how information is really exchanged in a group, or how fear develops and propagates in a group, for example, why should we not utilize this information?

In addition, standard models of rational decision making may be true but insufficiently specified to be useful, and the biological sciences may help us understand how to specify more precisely how people use information to make calculations to support their decisions. By being more specific and by looking inside the black box of cognition, we can begin to characterize the ways in which people may be cognitively different, and identify them in ways that are independent of their behavior. If the biological sciences can help us understand which kind of people have different cognitive profiles, under different circumstances, the cognitive sciences are not "overthrowing" rational choice, but filling in important blanks in the rational choice model. The cognitive sciences may have much to say about this subject and much to contribute, in general, to the improvement of our understanding of rational choice.

Puzzles and Human Nature

If you are interested in war, and begin the task of understanding human behavior in war by applying the standard model of rationality, you will find no end of puzzles. We have noted that a key assumption of models of rational choice is that people have stable preferences, and stable methods for making decisions: if they prefer A to B at one moment in time, they will prefer A to B later on. Yet it is one of the better-established findings in sociology that military organizations can routinely take groups of young people and change their preferences in relatively short periods of time. Armies recruit men and women who care very much about protecting their own lives, and who care nothing about each other in civilian life. They may even have been hostile to each other because they were members of groups that clashed in civilian life. Armies then put these young people through a training process such that they become willing to die for each other, even under circumstances where no superior officer can check up on their behavior and punish slackers. Thomas Hobbes was candid enough to admit that his model of human behavior that was based on the calculated avoidance of violent death could not account for the observable phenomenon of militaries, or, rather, that according to his theory, soldiers were justified in running away from battle. Yet they did not. What is going on? The rationalist account cannot give us an adequate explanation of one of the most basic facts about international relations, which is that states can get groups of people to die for each other.

There are more puzzles. Rational choice assumes that an individual has stable decision-making processes. Yet no one who has lived through such events would care to defend the proposition that people employ the same decision-making processes when they are safe, well fed, and have had enough sleep as they do when they are being shot at by an enemy force, or the survival of their country is at stake. Why is there this difference, and how does it affect the outcome of the decision-making process?

Rational choice models assume that people care about efficiently piling up the most of whatever it is that they want using a given amount of resources. They do not act, except under certain well-specified circumstances, as if they cared about how much they have compared with what other people have. Yet political leaders talk constantly about prestige and status in international relations. Is it just talk? Is such talk a mask for other goals? Or should we take heed of the fact that all primate communities form status hierarchies, and that status competition is a routinely observed characteristic of these communities? Might we not wonder if people who have unusually strong desires for social status might tend to rise to the top of social hierarchies, where they continue to be sensitive to status and prestige?

The decision to investigate the implications of the findings in the biological sciences for international relations would be justified simply by the availability of better information about human nature, but in the case of international relations, we have major outstanding puzzles that we have difficulty resolving using standard models of rational choice. This desire to do somewhat better in understanding these puzzles should lead us, at least, to look at the work being done in the biological sciences.

This book does not present a complete model of the mind. Such a model is not available, nor is it likely to be available for some time to come. With a complete model of the mind in hand, one could specify the cases where the predictions of economic rationality and the predictions of biologically affected decision making agreed, and where they disagreed. Then one could choose individual, real-world cases to see how biological factors functioned as, more or less, "independent variables." We could assess how much of real-world behavior was driven by "rational" factors, and how much by other factors. But we do not have this complete model of the human mind. Without such a complete model, one has to do something like what is done in this book, which is to focus on outstanding problems and apply, in an exploratory way, our limited understanding of aspects of human cognition. It may well be the case that subsequent work in the cognitive sciences will lead us to reconsider the arguments made in this book. But if we wait for a full and verified model of the human mind, we will wait a long time. While waiting we will be forced to resort to simplified models of decision making that we know to be flawed, instead of trying to incorporate pieces of what may be part of the model of the human mind, as they become available.

The Structure of the Study

Several ideas inform each of the following four chapters. First, and most importantly, the book will explore the implications of the possibility that the human mind has content-specialized functions for processing data about the external world that are inherited, in addition to the ability to consciously process data in the cerebral cortex. Those content-specialized functions are the result of our evolutionary history, involve the endocrine system as well as the brain, and are decision-making mechanisms that both operate independently and interact with conscious decision-making processes.

The human mind is not a *tabula rasa*, a blank slate on which the environment operates to create a decision-making process. Rather, following the work in evolutionary psychology, the book treats the mind as an evolved organ, with functions that have emerged as a result of our evolutionary history, and which interact with the environment in certain prescribed ways. This assumption runs counter to the dominant model of individual cognition central to modern social science. Emile Durkheim set out this model early in the development of modern social science in his *Rules of the Sociological Method*, first published in 1895:

> Collective representations, emotions, and tendencies are caused not by certain states of the consciousnesses of the individuals, but by the conditions in which the social group, in its totality, is placed. . . . [I]individual natures are merely the indeterminate material that the social factor molds and transforms. Their contributions consist exclusively in very general attitudes, in vague and consequently plastic predispositions which, by themselves, if other agents did not intervene, could not take on the definite and complex forms which characterize social phenomena.[14]

The human brain, according to this model, labeled by John Tooby and Leda Cosmides the Standard Social Science Model (SSSM), is unformed at birth. In the words of cognitive psychology, the brain has no content-specialized functions. It records sensations produced by external stimuli and notes what those impressions are associated with. It acquires functions, expectations, fears, and desires more complicated than the simple human physical appetites as a result of its encounters with the environment. The human brain is, if not infinitely malleable, so malleable that radically different environments can induce radically different habits of thought and behavior. In the SSSM, the question of what produces the social environment is answered by references to the social environment that preceded it, and so on back indefinitely. This begs the ultimate question of where social environments come from, but that question seemed sufficiently distant from operational questions as not to lead to major doubts in the SSSM. The SSSM is a model of the human brain as a very flexible, reprogrammable computer that learns in response to stimuli from the environment.

The major modern challenge to this model was first made by Noam Chomsky in 1957 in his book *Syntactic Structures*, and later in his more popular book *Language and Mind*.[15] He asked a very simple question. Given the infinite number of grammatical sentences possible in every human language, and given the brief and fragmentary exposure of children to sample sentences, how can children learn the rules of languages so easily in the short spans of time that we know to be sufficient for language acquisition? Why is it that children do not have to work their way through all of the possible meanings of any given verbal stimuli before learning what intentions lay behind the spoken words and sentences they hear? Language acquisition, which is rapid and easy in humans, is inexplicable if one assumes that the mind is a *tabula rasa*. Since, in fact, infants always and easily learn languages, Chomsky reasoned his way through to a view of all human language based on a universal grammar that all human beings share because it is not acquired from the environment but is built into their brains, and to an innate "Language Acquisition Device." People can learn languages because their brains do have content-specialized functions. They are built so as to be capable of giving only a certain set of interpretations to stimuli of a certain class. This view revolutionized and is now the dominant perspective in linguistics, though recent work has suggested that children learn different languages in different ways and respond to unconscious statistical analyses of what they have heard, perhaps without the need to assume a universal grammar or a specific language acquisition module.[16]

Did Chomsky's breakthrough have larger implications? Beginning in the 1970s, the view was developed that if the human mind has a built-in way of handling verbal stimuli, perhaps it has other innate cognitive structures to handle the equally complex and ambiguous stimuli it is constantly receiving. As developed by anthropologists, the question was raised, if these innate cognitive structures exist, where did they come from? The answer that emerged was that these structures emerged the same way that every other human structure emerged: through an evolutionary process that encoded evolutionary-valuable changes into our DNA. People do have brains with content-specialized functions in the way that they have other organs with certain specialized functions. Why might human brains have evolved with content-specific functions instead of with a generalized form of intelligence, equally useful for solving a broad range of problems? The answer might lie in the question, what forced the early primates that preceded humans to get smarter? In the 1970s and 1980s, Nicholas Humphrey, Richard Byrne, and Andrew Whitten suggested that human intelligence developed to handle the problems of human social interaction in increasingly large groups. Human intelligence emerged when early humans who had more capacity for processing information from social settings did better for themselves and for their kin in obtaining mates and forming coalitions against social rivals. Human intelligence, and the inherited components of the human brain, therefore, might have emerged in ways that were marked by the social and sexual selection process that drove the evolution of the human brain.[17]

This controversial view has been advanced by a growing group of anthropologists. John Tooby and Leda Cosmides have been in the forefront of articulating it. They have advanced another model of the mind that stands in explicit contradiction to the SSSM. It is best simply to present their own summary of their position as given in their edited volume, *The Adapted Mind*:

> The central premise of *The Adapted Mind* is that there is a universal human nature, but that this universality exists at the level of evolved psychological mechanisms, not of expressed cultural behaviors. . . . A second premise is that that these evolved psychological mechanisms are adaptations, constructed by natural selection over evolutionary time. A third assumption made by most of the contributors is that the evolved structure of the human mind is adapted to the way of life of Pleistocene hunter-gatherers, and not necessarily to our modern circumstances.

Hence the kinds of human behavior we are most familiar with, which make up the recorded human history of the last three thousand years,

> are all the novel products of the last few thousand years. In contrast to this our ancestors spent the last two million years as Pleistocene hunter-gatherers, and, of course, several hundred million years before that as one kind of forager or another. . . . For that reason, it is unlikely that new complex designs . . . could evolve in so few generations. Therefore, it is improbable that our species evolved complex adaptations even to agriculture, let alone to post-industrial society.
>
> . . . the human mind evolved in response to the demands of a hunting and gathering way of life. Specifically, this means that in relating the design of mechanisms of the mind to the task demands posed by the world, "the world" means the Pleistocene world of hunter-gatherers. That is, in considering issues of functionality, behavioral scientists need to be familiar with how foraging

people lived. We cannot rely on intuitions honed by our everyday experiences in the modern world. Finally, it is important to recognize that behavior generated by mechanisms that are adaptations to an ancient way of life will not necessarily be adaptive in the modern world.[18]

What are the content-specialized functions of the brain that we inherited and that still structure our cognitive lives? Learning language is clearly one because it seems to be impossible for a general purpose processor to cope with the problems of ambiguous symbolic communication. For the same reason, it is argued that both the capacity for understanding that human facial expressions are the manifestation of specific internal mental states and the social skills employed in acquiring mates are also embodied in our brain.[19] There is experimental evidence that supports this position. We know, for example, that damage to certain areas of the brain does not disrupt the learning of mathematics, but it does prevent adults from understanding social signals that undamaged adults can reliably extract from photographs.[20] Charles Darwin first made the argument that human facial expressions are evolved mechanisms for reliably communicating the interior emotional state of individuals, rather than arbitrary symbols that can be given any meaning. Although scholars adhering to the SSSM have criticized Darwin's argument, more and more data compiled by skeptics of the Darwinian position has only tended to confirm the view, at least for a short list of primary human emotions and expressions.[21]

There are some children who do seem to have minds that work in ways that resemble the SSSM. They remember events and consciously and painstakingly correlate the events with what subsequently happens, making corrections for mistaken correlations that lead to unfortunate predictions. They can see physical objects moving around them, making noises, and putting food near them, but they do not understand that those objects are human beings with minds and intentions. They do not understand that certain movements of the roughly spherical object on top of the larger bifurcated moving objects are expressions on the faces of human beings, indicative of interior mental states. These children are autistic. Most people have brains that are constructed so as to be particularly sensitive to patterns of light and dark that look like human eyes and follow the direction of the gaze indicated by the position of human eyes. They are predisposed then to make the inference that the direction of the gaze is associated with an internal mental state, that people are interested in what they are looking at. Children who are not equipped by nature to make that leap can learn to associate certain observations with certain behavior that tends to follow it. Such people do operate by means of a brain that is a general purpose processor, and their social lives are very difficult. They have to live in highly structured and simple social environments in order not to be confused. One autistic child who grew up to be a physical scientist commented that she stayed away from situations that might involve complex human behavior and kept and replayed in her head "videotapes" of human behavior so she could remember what kinds of behavior tended to lead to other behavior. She did not understand emotion. By repeated observation, she knew that some human behavior followed certain facial expressions. "I can tell if a human being is angry or if he is smiling."[22] This, it can be argued, is the pattern of human behavior associated with a brain that, for whatever reasons, lacks certain content-specialized innate functions. The capacity to infer from observations of a human being that this is another person like myself, with intentions that may be beneficial or harmful to me, is an extraordinarily powerful capacity. It is probably present in chimpanzees as well as humans, though not in the other great apes.[23]

The existence of content-specialized mental functions may not always be highly localized in the brain, and we are far from understanding all of them, and how they relate to each other. In the following chapters, we will review in detail the work that analyzes how several of these mechanisms operate: how they are equipped by human nature to respond to certain external stimuli, how they are linked to the production of hormones and are sensitive to levels of hormones in the body, and so on, in ways that are not fully controlled by conscious thought. The general point, however, is not that human beings are automata, hard-wired to behave in preprogrammed ways to external stimuli, but rather that these inherited predispositions operate at the same time as conscious information processing and decision making. At times, those inherited mechanisms operate in ways that produce impulses contrary to the actions indicated by conscious thought, and, under specified conditions, they drive decisions, leading us to strike back at a challenger even when we "know" that this would be counterproductive, or to give in to attractive, short-term temptations that we "know" are not good for us in the long run, or to despair and surrender even though we "know" that there are chances for success. In other cases, these inherited mechanisms support conscious decision making by selectively recalling and presenting information such that unconscious mechanisms for information retrieval affect the conclusions reached by conscious calculation.

This list of examples suggests that mechanisms lead to error. The question would then arise, how could organisms that had prospered in evolutionary history have survived with such faulty hard-wired decision-making processes? The speculative response has two parts. First, it tends to be the case that these hard-wired mechanisms produce clear-cut decisions very quickly, even in complex and ambiguous settings in which the conscious decision-making process would produce uncertain decisions after considerable delay. We can speculate that in human evolutionary history, the survival value of making some decision, any decision, and then action, as opposed to paralysis, was large and positive, although it may not be so today in the context of modern politics. Second, we can speculate that some human decision-making errors today are the result of the operation of mechanisms that evolved to solve problems very different from the problems we now actually encounter. As a result, these evolved mechanisms can now lead both to errors and to good decisions, depending on whether the structure of current problems resembles that for which we evolved content-specialized mental functions. Whether the evolutionary speculation is correct or not does not matter, because we can and should simply look for the presence or absence of observable mental mechanisms that incline us to behavior that is different from that indicated by conscious decision making, independently of whether the decision reached is "good" or "bad." If we focus on the processes, and not the outcome, we avoid the error of inferring a successful evolutionary process from "good" outcomes, or inferring a mismatch between our evolutionary heritage and current problems from "bad" outcomes.

The second major idea that the book explores is the proposition that although all human beings have inherited ways of using information about the world, there are variations across individuals in the extent to which these inherited mechanisms affect behavior. It is important to emphasize this because evolutionary theory has been interpreted to mean that a certain set of evolutionary conditions will lead to an "optimal" evolved type, or an optimal form of decision making, which completely displaces nonoptimal forms. The result is a cognitively homogenous population of humans. The general form of this argument is familiar from Kenneth Waltz's contention in his work, *A Theory of International Politics*, about how states in competition with each other would come to resemble each other or perish, and has been used to develop an argument about what kind of vision of the future, or time horizons, would be optimal for human beings under certain conditions.[24] This view, that competition produces homogeneity, is surely mistaken. Every species displays variations in its inherited characteristics. Evolution cannot occur without variations at the level of individuals that give them an advantage over other members of the species. Perfectly homogeneous populations optimized for one set of conditions would be very vulnerable to mass extinction if conditions changed. Mixed populations would be more likely to contain a variety of characteristics that were better able to respond to changing environments. Stephen Jay Gould has advanced the view that the evolutionary history we actually have observed is not the only evolutionary history that was compatible with the conditions that existed.

Evolutionary conditions were not so stringent as to make possible the emergence of one and only one population of species.[25] By the same logic, evolutionary history is not likely to have been so stringent as to produce total uniformity within species.

What might this mean? If there is a biological component that affects human decision-making behavior, and if it can be reliably measured, it should, in theory, be possible to identify the variations in human genetic coding that are associated with different, stable dimensions of personality. That is the theory. The practice has been much more problematic. There have been, for many years, studies that used comparisons of heterozygote (fraternal) and homozygote (identical) twins, as well as comparisons of child behavior within families, to measure the impact of variance in genetic inheritance on the variance of human behavior compared with the impact of environmental factors. Considerable debate and effort has been expended in developing better survey techniques for assessing the dimensions along which personality can vary.[26] Initially, personality was assessed by asking people to evaluate their own personality. Asking people about their own personality turned out to be full of risks, and determining the right words to accurately describe internal emotional states is very difficult. As a result, early "personality inventories" based on self-assessments were flawed, and made it difficult to search for possible genetic correlates of stable personality differences.[27] To this kind of difficulty had to be added the difficulties of studying human genetics. Progress has recently been made, but studies of human genetics are slow and hard. Conceptually, should we expect to find one personality type encoded on one gene? This approach, which has successfully identified the genetic basis of diseases such as Alzheimer's disease and some complex behavioral disorders such as schizophrenia, was given the label the One Gene, One Disorder (OGOD) approach. But after much work, it was determined that many human traits, including subtle variations in personality, were more properly understood as the result of a complex of multiple genes, not one of which is necessary or sufficient for the emergence of a personality characteristic.[28]

Work in this area of genetics and personality types has produced suggestive but inconclusive results. For example, a review of two independent studies published in 1996 summarized their findings as follows: "People differ greatly from one another in temperament—temperament being the dynamic organization of the psychobiological systems that regulate automatic responses to emotional stimuli. Individual differences in temperament are known to be moderately heritable and stable throughout life regardless of culture or ethnicity. . . . Now, two groups . . . have identified a specific genetic locus that contributes to variation in a human personality trait." Variants of D4 dopamine receptor gene were found to account for about 10 percent of genetic variation in the trait labeled Novelty Seeking, defined as "more exploratory, thrill-seeking, and excitable" versus "more deliberate, rigid, orderly."[29]

Subsequent studies have challenged and supported the particular findings of these two studies in roughly equal numbers.[30] The central point, that there is variation in the genetic inheritance of individuals that affects their decision making, remains a major hypothesis for investigation. With regard to some of the issues examined in this book, the propositions that are explored are the extent to which there are variations across individuals in their sensitivity to short- and long-term consequences of their actions, motivation to punish challengers, and inclination to give up when presented with uncontrollable circumstances.

Third, this book tries to understand the social mechanisms and institutions that select individuals of a particular character out of the heterogeneous pool of people available and give them political power. Not all human types rise to the top. It may be the case that different human types rise to the top in different societies. We know, for example, that some human societies in their internal organization are more oriented toward social status than others. We refer to them as more or less egalitarian. The people who rise to the top in those societies are sensitive to status, or status displays, and may remain so even if in some environments their behavior does not continue to produce rewards for them, because their behavior is the outcome of a biological process that influences their character and a social process that gives power and can also take it away. Kevin McAleer has written a history of dueling in Germany at the end of the nineteenth century. These duels were not relatively harmless, as is sometimes assumed by authors who argue that dueling was a relatively low-cost way of achieving social advantages.[31] By the early twentieth century, duels in Germany were being fought with Browning or Luger automatic pistols with rifled barrels, and five exchanges of shots at fifteen paces or less. The intent of the duel was to measure bravery, not marksmanship, so the duels were set up to produce a fatal exchange. The men who participated in such duels were members of the German political-military elite and included such men as Alfred von Kiderlen-Wächter, who fought, successfully it need not be said, three duels and became secretary of state for foreign affairs in the Wilhelmine Empire.[32] Dueling was a mechanism for insuring that the men who controlled German foreign policy had a certain well-established character, and it may have been the case that this character was not simply the result of an environment shaping the character of individuals but the social institution selecting out certain individuals who had a fixed, biologically based disposition. This is the argument that Kenneth Waltz makes when explaining the differences in the personality types that rose to the top in the Tory Party in the context of British parliamentary institutions and the personality type that rose to the top in the American presidential institution, though without the argument for a biological factor.[33]

But fourth, and finally, the inherited decision-making processes of individuals, even those who have been selected for political power, may not have anything to do with the political behavior of states engaged in international relations if the group or social setting in which they find themselves neutralizes or damps down the impact of the tendencies of those processes. We can easily think of situations in which people have deliberately constructed group settings that make it unlikely that individual impulses of one kind or another will turn into collective behavior. We know that people can get angry and make rash decisions, so we build cooling-off periods into discussions and negotiations. On the other hand, the environment or group setting in which individuals find themselves may reinforce or amplify the tendencies they have. A crowded, dark room will tend to turn the panic of one individual into group panic, for example. Because we cannot simply move from statements about the decision-making characteristics of one individual to the decisions taken by a group, we must try to specify the settings within which the decision-making characteristics of an individual will tend to create positive feedback loops that reinforce the tendencies of that individual. Timur Kuran, for example, has tried to specify the circumstances in which individual reversals of positions can lead to sudden group reversals.[34] In each of the following chapters, an effort will be made to specify the conditions under which individual cognitive behavior can affect group behavior.

These are the central arguments of this book. How can they be applied to particular issues? What follows is the effort to do so, with regard to emotion and memory, dominance and testosterone, distress, depression, and war termination, and time horizons and tyranny. In each of the following four chapters, emphasis will be placed not only on how the biological sciences may help us understand individual decision making, but on the nature of the social setting that must exist for these individual factors to affect group behavior. In each chapter, emphasis will be placed on explanations that differ from those produced by economic theories. This should not be taken as a statement that explanations based on economic rationality are never true, or do not coexist with noneconomic explanations. An effort is made in each chapter to specify the conditions under which the nonrationalist explanations might be important, but even in those cases, rational calculations almost surely were factors as well. I have emphasized the nonrational issues for the sake of exploring them, not to prove that people never display rational behavior. With these reservations in mind, let us begin.

Chapter Two

Emotions, Memory, and Decision Making

IN HIS BOOK *Strange Victory*, the historian Ernest May tried to explain the decisions of the French government in 1939 and 1940. He noted that "when Hitler or others in Germany made judgments about 'France' they were, for practical purposes, assessing decisions that would percolate through the mind of Edouard Daladier," the prime minister. How could one understand why Daladier made decisions the way he did? May went back to Daladier's first brief experience as prime minister in 1934, at the time of the Stavisky scandal that brought right-wing and left-wings gangs out onto the streets of Paris, killing eighteen people. In political circles, there was thought that the army should be called out. After deliberating, Daladier resigned rather than preside over what might become a civil war waged against the liberal forces in France. But civil war did not break out. The police quickly restored order. Daladier was denounced as a coward. May then concluded, "This experience scarred Daladier. After 1940, many would cite the episode as evidence that he had always been weak, indecisive, and inclined to avoid responsibility. If he himself had put into words the lessons it seemed to teach, he might have said that it showed the wisdom of being deliberate rather than precipitate. . . . But this may be a way of saying that it encouraged future indecisiveness." When May turned to the head of the French Army, General Gamelin, he also referred to crucial experiences that shaped Gamelin's way of making decisions: "Ever afterward, in moments of crisis, Gamelin's mind would go back to the days of 1914" when he had planned the Battle of the Marne.[1]

Why do we find it plausible that people who have lived through emotional experiences will later make decisions affected by their memories of those experiences? Even if plausible, is it correct to think of human memory and decision making in this way? How do people make decisions? In the account of decision making that economists give us, there is little or nothing said about the role of emotional experiences. Their account goes something like this: When presented with a situation that requires action, we think of alternative ways, or strategies, of getting what we want. We then use or search for information, which we use to evaluate each of the alternative strategies, one after another, to see which one will give us more of what we want for a given cost or, what is the same thing, what is the cheapest way of getting a given amount of what we want. As part of that process, we consider the probabilities of both the good and the bad things that might happen if we adopt a given strategy, and we take the value of those outcomes and their probabilities into account in our decision.

Although there is much about this model that fits with our experience, laying out the model indicates just how much time and information is needed if it is to operate as described. Economists recognize that the search for options and information is costly, so they acknowledge that we might decide to cut our searches short once we have found an option that is "good enough" relative to what we want. Herbert Simon called this behavior "satisficing." Even so, there is much about this process that is not completely clear. There is a great deal of information in the world relevant to our decisions. We may be perfectly rational, but we may make very different decisions if we rely on one set of data rather than another. If we cannot use all the data available, what determines what we look at first, or what data influences the most? How we search for information and what kinds of information we rely on, particularly if we cut our search short before evaluating "all" options, ought to be specified. It might reasonably be assumed that we would first use the information we found that seemed most "appropriate" or "obvious," again relative to our goals: when deciding whether to buy a car, we would look first at the size and reliability of several cars if we wanted to carry a lot of people on long trips, for example. In any case, the key is to use "obvious" information to perform some kind of calculation of what the alternative strategies are expected to get us.

But what makes some information come to mind more readily than others? This chapter will lay out what is known about the role that emotion plays in making certain data more "obvious" to us, and the role that emotion plays in pushing us toward a decision even when the available data is ambiguous. Emotion does not replace reasoning, but it affects what data is used when we reason, and it helps us act even when the rational basis for a particular action is open to question. Emotion helps us select data from the enormous amount of information available to us and reduces the cognitive problem to proportions that humans can handle. Emotion also can provide the motivation to act even when there is uncertainty. This is tremendously relevant to war and politics. International interactions, after all, are enormously complicated. Even with the time and money available to the governments of rich states, it is usually the case that there is considerable uncertainty about what outcomes will follow from any given decision. This is not just because it is difficult to acquire the information we might need, but also because the world is full of factors that interact with each other in complicated ways, such that we are not sure what will happen even when we know, more or less, what state the world is in now. We are often stumped when we try to predict the way in which a complex interactive system will evolve. This occurs for a variety of reasons, and Robert Jervis has summarized many of them. Several factors interact in ways that change over time. Small actions can have unexpectedly large consequences. Causal factors, when acting together, may produce results that we would not expect by adding together the effects they produce independently.[2] The point is that there is good reason to think that even well-informed people in government may not have much confidence in their ability confidently to calculate the outcome of particular actions. We might even expect people to be unable to make decisions under such conditions. There are, in fact, intelligent people with selective injuries to their brain who cannot make decisions. But most people not only make such decisions, they often believe quite strongly that their decisions are not only correct, but obviously correct. The role of emotion helps to explain this puzzle.

The role of emotion in decision making can be summarized in the following way. People can and do make decisions that are the result of the comparison of alternative expected outcomes. They do so when they have time and little experience handling that kind of problem. But when time is short, and people have had previous experiences in the area in question, an additional process affects their decisions. A situation, when encountered, is recognized, and a general course of action is associated with that recognition, all in one step. "I know what this is and I know roughly what to do." People adopt a general course of action in a way that seems "obvious" and necessary to them given what they observe. Further searches for information and rational analysis to develop more specific strategies can and do follow this initial recognition and reaction. But the initial decision is based on the information stored in the memory as it relates to the problem in question. A new situation, when encountered, will be seen as conforming to one of many patterns stored in the long-term memory of the decision maker. Those remembered patterns were formed at a time of emotional arousal through which the decision maker lived. In short, decisions are affected by emotion-based pattern recognition, a process of which the decision maker may or may not be consciously aware. Reason and conscious cognition will also be in operation and can reverse or modify the emotion-based decision, if time permits and compelling data is available. On the other hand, reason and conscious cognition can play a secondary role after a basic course of action has been highlighted by the emotion-based pattern recognition, helping to determine which specific actions to take that are consistent with the emotional reaction.

This way of decision making can be thought of as a severely compressed form of satisficing behavior, but one in which the decision maker may not be fully conscious of the cognitive mechanisms being engaged. In addition, the cognitive mechanisms involved in emotion-based pattern recognition are different from those employed in a conscious search that has been cut short. This way of making decisions has been distinguished from analytical searches and given the name "P-cognition" by Howard Margolis.[3] Antonio Damasio characterizes the process in which emotional experiences create a remembered pattern that shapes decisions as the "somatic marker" hypothesis.[4]

The hypothesized emotion-based pattern recognition aspect of making decisions has some obvious advantages compared with decision making on the basis of serial calculations of the outcomes associated with alternative strategies. Pattern recognition generates a decision with less new information because the patterns stored in the memory "fill in the blanks" when information is sketchy, to yield a complete picture. P-cognition also yields a decision much more quickly than the "analyze the situation, search for information, and evaluate options" process. P-cognition takes advantage of the fact that while the human brain has a large long-term memory that can retain many patterns, it is not good at processing large amounts of data in a short period of time. In computer language, the human brain has a large storage capacity but a small memory buffer (what we consciously hold in our working memory) and a slow central processing unit. It makes sense for the brain to use its large memory in ways that put less demand on its working memory and processing capacity. Emotion-based pattern recognition produces a decision that subjectively "feels right" and is confidently acted upon. It is therefore likely to become the dominant solution in a group setting in which others have weak commitments to alternative solutions. Emotion-based pattern recognition has some obvious weaknesses as well. Emotional experiences may create mental patterns that may readily spring to mind, and which may lead to policy success, but which may also lead to an incorrect characterization of the problem at hand. It may lead to a decision that is not the best available, and it may even lead to the application of a completely inappropriate pattern to a given situation, and to policy failure.

When emotion-based pattern recognition produces satisfactory results, it will be hard to prove that rational search mental mechanisms were not at work. Since the outcome was "good," it will be argued that the decision-making mechanism that should produce "good" results must have been at work. It will be somewhat easier to assert the operation of emotion-based pattern recognition when policies have failed. This kind of decision making, it might be said, is not likely to produce success in foreign policy making. Indeed, it might even be a recipe for error. Under some conditions, this may be true. However, although the explanation or theory I will be exploring can be an explanation of failure, it should also explain success by showing how this kind of decision making can, under certain circumstances, yield satisfactory foreign policy decisions. Policy failure does not prove the operation of emotion-based pattern recognition, but neither do good results prove the operation of rational search mechanisms. Both modes can yield good and bad outcomes. A better way to determine which mechanism is at work is to identify observable behavior associated with the processes involved in each mechanism, behavior that is independent of the decision, and then to see whether that behavior is present in cases of policy failure and success.

The processes associated with emotion-based pattern recognition can be specified, and some of them are observable and different from that predicted by the model of alternative strategies analyzed one after another. Specifically:

1. Memories of perceived external patterns that are formed at times of emotional arousal are preferentially stored and retrieved by the brain. These memories form the basis of emotion-based pattern recognition. They are persistent and slower to change than unemotional lessons learned. At the level of the brain and body mechanisms, this form of learning is associated with the operation of a sensory organ-thalamus-amygdala-endocrine pathway, as opposed to the sensory organ-thalamus-cortex pathway associated with conscious decision making, and operates more quickly than conscious decision making.

2. When activated, these memories strongly predispose the person having the memories toward certain broad categories of action, such as like/accept/trust or dislike/resist/distrust, but do not select detailed courses of action.

3. In practice, the process of decision making based on emotion-based pattern recognition is distinguishable from standard expected-utility calculations by producing decisions very early in the decision-making process, before there is a need to decide, before much relevant information has arrived, and before alternative strategies have been evaluated or even formulated. Alternative courses of action that are not consistent with the general emotional response are not considered with the same level of time and effort as the preferred decision.

4. The variations in individual behavior associated with this form of decision making are caused by variations in the different experiences that induced emotional reactions in the histories of the individuals.

5. In social settings, individual behavior driven by individual memories can become group behavior when cohorts of people have had the same experiences and so have the same reactions based on emotion-based pattern recognition.

6. Alternatively, in small-group settings, the individual memories of the dominant individual can be transformed into group behavior when the predis-

position of the dominant figure shapes the nature of the options and information presented to him or her by subordinates in ways that confirm his or her predisposition.

What follows is a review of what we know about the role of emotion-based pattern recognition in the way people make decisions, at the level of the brain, then in experimental settings, then in complex real-world settings, about which we have only limited, second-hand data concerning the behavior of decision makers. The argument will be made that what can be observed at more basic levels is consistent with and can be used to understand what is observed in more complex settings. This is not a proof that what is observed at basic levels is actually happening in complex settings, but it is a way mentally to begin formulating questions and tests that would prove the argument, tests that may have to attend the development and application of new measurement devices, techniques, or experimental opportunities. As such, it is more a plan of research than a conclusion, but not, I hope, without value as such.

What Does the Brain Know?

We can start with a very basic question that seems far from the issue of emotion and pattern recognition, but which is in fact central to it. If we use information to help us make decisions, what information do we use? At one extreme, do we use all of the information we have ever been exposed to? Clearly not. At the other extreme, we usually do not use only the information that we are consciously working with in our mind. When we do an arithmetic problem in our head, for example, we use only the information we can immediately recall. If we forget it, we have to start over. Most of the time, however, we can work on a problem and pause to retrieve additional information that is in our memories. If we selectively reach into our memories for information, which memories, of the billions that we have, will we use? How many memories can we process in sequence, if we cannot have an indefinitely large number of memories in mind at a given moment? Can we use information of which we are not consciously aware? We may know how to swim or ride a bicycle or catch a high fly ball, but we are not conscious of the information we use. Could this be true in decision making not related to physical activities?

These are issues with which experimental psychology has grappled for many years—in some cases, for almost a century. Let me first present the outline of the account of what is currently hypothesized about emotion and cognition, and then present the confirming data. The story, in its most simple form, is that the brain acquires far more information than we can or do hold in our conscious mind at any moment. This stored information is referred to as our implicit memories. If these implicit memories are to be useful, the mind needs ways of rapidly acting on the basis of that knowledge. We retain vast amounts of information of which we are usually unconscious. It would be a waste of scarce energy (the brain has first to call on the supply of blood and energy in the human body and takes about 20 percent of our metabolic budget) to acquire and hold large amounts of information that are useless, so there is reason to suspect that the brain does have ways of using that massive amount of information, even if we are not consciously aware of much of it at any one time. If in life-threatening situations we had to deal with our environment by reviewing, in sequence, all of the details of that environment, and then sequentially searching our memory to see which details matched our memories, and then summing up the results of the matches, we would never have enough time to deal with the threat. Instead, the brain has ways of marking some information for retrieval under certain circumstances, and of processing blocks of information without looking at each data point individually.

The brain can process data in two ways. In the first way, the brain can sequentially become aware of and process discrete pieces of information. Because this kind of processing is sequential, the more data is presented, the longer the brain will take to review it. This process has been studied closely in vision. Subjects, for example, are given a page with many images or "distractors" on it and are asked to find the item that does not fit. For example, a page is filled with even numbers, with one odd number embedded in the matrix. The more distractors, the longer it takes to find the element that is different, if, as is likely in this example, the item to be found does not "stand out." But the brain can process data in another way as well. Sometimes we search for items and do not need to look at each item in sequence. Sometimes the thing being looked for "stands out." One green item in a field of red distractors can be found without looking at each distractor in turn until the green one is processed. Under some circumstances, recognition "pop-out" will occur because the brain can process many data points in parallel. These are "easy" problems for the brain. Behaviorally, the observable difference between serial processing and processing that produces "pop-out" is that the amount of time needed to process many data points in parallel does not increase with the number of distractors, up to some limit in the number of data points. In vision, this constitutes the basis of visual pattern recognition, and much work has been devoted to understanding what kinds of vision can and cannot be understood in terms of pattern recognition.[5]

Pattern recognition appears to occur when the brain aggregates discrete items of information into blocks or chunks. This happens in many ways in addition to vision. When we listen to human speech, we do not hear individual letters or sounds, but entire words. Indeed, if we had to process each individual sound of which words are composed, we would not be able to understand normal language, because if we hear more than sixteen sounds a second, we hear a tone and not the individual sounds. We can fill in the blanks when letters are left out of words we read because we know the pattern and can recognize it even when data points are missing. Patterns can contain much information, as in the case of stories we can remember because we know the pattern of the story, or, in plain speech, the plot. We can clearly remember visual images with many features that we can recall because they are "about" something. The pattern then is one chunk of information that can be held in mind, even if there are too many constituent parts for us to remember individually.

The question then becomes what forms patterns and activates pattern recognition in ways that are associated with decisions. Animals and to some extent humans have been studied to see what happens when multiple stimuli in the environment are presented at the same time that an event triggers an emotional response. We normally use emotional response to mean a state of mind. There is another way of thinking about emotion that focuses on the arousal of the body—increased heart rate, release of stress hormones, and so on. This does not deny the existence of mental states but is more easily observed than mental states and exists in animals that may not have the mental states that we associate with emotions such as fear, though we could agree that the animals displayed fear. This kind of physical, or somatic, arousal is not the result of prior experiences, but of the way the mind is organized from birth. Loud noises, bright flashes of light, pain, and human faces expressing hostile emotion are unconditioned stimuli to which babies respond, and which continue to elicit emotional responses throughout life. But those unconditioned stimuli create emotional arousal that can subsequently produce responses to stimuli more complicated than unconditioned stimuli themselves.

The idea of unconditioned and conditioned responses is, of course, old. But even early behavioral, "Skinner box" types of experiments produced surprising results. When one stimulus was presented along with a noise or shock, animals learned to associate the two. This was the expected formation of conditioned responses. What was unexpected was that the animals also took into account many of the specific details of their box. When the animals were put into a physically different box, the same stimulus could be presented and the animals would not react. The noise plus other information about the physical environment constituted a complex pattern of stimuli associated with emotional arousal, and it was that pattern that was recalled and that provided the basis for conditioned responses. The brain looked outward at the world and inward at its own state, and tagged those memories of the outside world that occurred at the same time that the body was aroused. Multiple external sensory data were stored as a pattern associated with the memory of emotional arousal, and when that pattern was again presented, it triggered an emotional response.

What was the function or value of the emotional response? *Pattern recognition of events associated with past emotional arousal radically reduced decision-making time.* The brain did not have to look through each facet of its environment in sequence before becoming aroused, and it did not have to review all of its memories of patterns before reacting, but only those associated with emotional arousal. When this kind of pattern was recognized, it triggered an internal reaction that quickly elevated the heart rate and other functions. It is a way of minimizing the amount of time the organism needed to prepare generally for action of any kind. Once ready for action, more time could be taken to assess the situation and to decide precisely what to do—typically in animals, flight, freeze, or fight. The emotional response is not a detailed plan of action, but it both highlighted certain memories for retrieval and predisposed the organism toward certain actions. People, can, of course, override these predispositions. Even if we act on these predispositions, we may need to think before we can decide what specific course of action we should take: if we flee, which route should we take, and so on. In other cases, the emotional reaction may create a general aversion or attraction to a person or object. What we then do must be resolved, but those decisions take place within the broad category of our initial emotional response.

What evidence is there for these hypotheses? The account I presented made claims about limits on the amount of information that people can store, the rate at which they can process information. Statements were made about mental mechanisms for forming data into patterns and marking those patterns on the basis of emotional response. These claims must be supported. Because we are concerned with human cognition, let me begin with a review of studies of human behavior. However, because live, conscious, human brains cannot be experimented with, under most conditions, I will also turn to brain functions in animals, which have been more intrusively studied. The animal studies can be used to refine hypotheses about human mental behavior. On rare occasions created by disease or accident, these hypotheses can be tested by study of ongoing human brain functions, and I will present the evidence from these studies. The account to support the argument made above, therefore, jumps from simple studies of human mental activity, to animal models, and then back to human behavior.

Human Data Processing

What do we know about the rate at which people can process data? First, we can calculate with some precision how much information the brain receives by counting the number of sensory inputs into the brain. The number of sensory nerve endings in the eyes, ears, skin, and so on has been estimated. There are approximately ten million visual cells in the eyes, a million more in the skin, one hundred thousand each in the ears and nose. Further studies on (volunteer) patients who needed brain surgery revealed that patients who were awake during the surgery did not consciously perceive sensory inputs directly to the brain that lasted less than roughly half a second, so a maximum of two bits per second could be consciously received by particular areas of the brain when they were stimulated directly, bypassing sensor organs. A paradox immediately emerges. The number of sensory impulses that the body sends to the brain is on the order of 10^7 bits per second, but the ability of the brain consciously to handle sensory impulses appears to be much less.

Second, the part of the brain that produces conscious awareness of the external world is able to process only a trivially small part of the data the sensory organs receive. Beginning in the 1950s, spurred by the demands of communications theory, experimental psychologists worked to establish the maximum amount of data the human brain could consciously process in a given amount of time. The answer, which was replicated across different experimenters using different methods (math problems, written and aural word comprehension, listening to notes on a piano), suggested that the upper bound was 50 bits per second. These experimental results were refined by an elegant insight, which was that when humans were presented with pulses of sound, they could hear them as discrete pulses up to the rate of 16 per second, after which time they were perceived as a low tone. The same was true for visual images, since 16 images per second represents the threshold at which the brain transforms discrete images rapidly following each other into the perception of continuous motion, and the images lose their status as individual pieces of data. The effective limit on data processing therefore seems to be somewhere in the range of 16–50 bits per second. This is a severe limit on how much information we can consciously be aware of, and how brief an exposure to sensory data we can be conscious of. A standard textbook on physiology summarizes this body of knowledge by saying, "What we perceive at any moment, therefore, is limited to an extremely small compartment in the stream of information about our surroundings flowing from the sense organs."[6]

If we are not consciously aware of sensory data to which we are briefly exposed, if our data processing rate is 16–50 bps, what do we do with all that extra data? Is it just lost? The answer to that is clearly not. The amount of data we can work with at a given time is closely related to short-term memory, but our long-term memory is available to be utilized selectively. At any given time, we can selectively turn our attention to different streams of data, current or recalled, so that we can quickly use our limited data processing capacity sequentially for different purposes. To some extent, we can redirect this capacity at will, and this is what some scientists have called the "searchlight" nature of consciousness. This term is evocative, but it is still true, as Charles Darwin wrote, "by what means attention—perhaps the most wonderful of all the wondrous powers of the mind—is effected, is an extremely obscure subject."[7] Since we can clearly draw on a store of far more sensory data than we can be aware of at a given time, people began to hypothesize that discrete pieces of data were processed into aggregates before we became conscious of them. The key issue is that we process information in ways of which we are not conscious. Human cognition or data processing, on the one hand, and awareness or consciousness, on the other, are thus not coextensive.[8] The process seemed to involve three related but different phenomena: selective memory retrieval, data chunking, and implicit memory. Understanding the first phenomenon requires an understanding of how we selectively recall information from our long-term memory as the result of brain activities of which we are not aware. The second requires that we understand how we connect pieces of data into patterns so that we can deal with small numbers of chunks of data, rather than many bits, in ways that reduce the enormous amount of information available so that our short-term memory can use that information without being overloaded. Again, it appears that we do this compression without being aware that we are doing it, or how we do it, though we are aware of the output of the process. The third phenomenon involves an understanding of the unconscious, or rather, the different kinds of implicit memory.

What Do We Remember? Emotion and Memory

Why do we consciously recall some things more readily than others? It is not hard to come up with examples of things that are vivid in our memories. While we often have trouble recalling information we want and need to recall, we find ourselves easily recalling things that occurred when we were emotionally aroused. Psychologists have studied this phenomenon to help treat people who had involuntary and debilitating recollections of violent crimes and battlefield experiences. One set of studies found that "the most predominant feature of Post Traumatic Stress Disorder (PTSD) is that memories of traumatic experiences remain indelible

for decades and are easily reawakened by all sorts of stimuli and stressors. Despite this fact, there has been relatively little research on the accuracy of traumatic memories in patients with PTSD." Some aspects of
PTSD were straightforward. The length of exposure to combat was correlated with development of PTSD. Trauma that was repetitive increased
the likelihood of PTSD, as in the case of Israeli soldiers who served in
two successive wars. The memories themselves, while vivid, were narrow, with extremely sharp memories of details that were at the center of
vision, while peripheral events were obscured. Studies of patients with
physical brain trauma revealed that areas of the brain could be destroyed
and, with them, the conscious, declarative memories of traumatic events.
But flashback memories would still occur, indicating that declarative
memory (memories that we are able to articulate) and PTSD memories
are handled separately by the brain. Finally, after the trauma, traumatized individuals were observed to be sensitive to trauma-related verbal
cues and were more distracted by these cues than nontraumatized people. The author of this study advanced the hypothesis that a psycho-
evolutionary approach would argue that "the interaction of cognition
with emotion allows emotional behavior to be an adaptive response to
biologically significant events." In this argument, human cognition
evolved as individuals were selected out for their ability to learn about
evolutionarily important events, particularly those events that were life
threatening.[9]

Extreme emotional experiences may create traumatized individuals
who need medical help in order to function, but that does not demon-
strate that people without PTSD necessarily have vivid memories associated with emotions, though it may suggest that they might experience a
less intense version of the same phenomenon. What would be valuable is
a study of emotional arousal and memory in ordinary people. Such studies have been performed. In laboratory settings it has been found that
students will better remember stories with high emotional content than
emotionally flat stories. In the real world, events with high emotional
content (e.g., for Californians, the Loma Prieta earthquake; for British
citizens, the resignation of Margaret Thatcher) produce clear short-term
memories of where people were and what they were doing at the time of
the event. When the same people were tested again a year later, they had
memories that were very consistent with their initial responses to questions about the event. It is important to note that these clear memories
were not always accurate, and remembered events were conflated in
time, although subjects were sure they were accurate. A separate study
also showed that the three most vivid memories of individuals queried
tended to be personal events with great emotional significance.[10]

This is of clear importance for decision making. Of all the information we have in our memories, those memories with high emotional content may be preferentially, if inaccurately, recalled. There is additional evidence to support this hypothesis. If emotional arousal enhances memory, and we can specify the mechanism that links emotion and memory, patients in whom this mechanism is damaged should not show enhanced memory for emotional events or stories. This has also been confirmed by experimental studies. In one study it was found that in humans, temporary chemical suppression of the activity of the amygdala has the effect of blocking the formation of long-term memories of an emotionally arousing story. In a separate study, a patient was examined who was cognitively normal but who had a hereditary disease that damaged only the amygdala. This patient was presented with a story, accompanied with pictures, about a boy who had been in a terrible traffic accident. The patient showed no preferential memory of the parts of the story concerning the injury, whereas control subjects did. Most interesting, the diseased subject reported that his emotional reaction to the story was strong and of the kind reported by the controls, suggesting that he did experience an emotional reaction, but that the amygdala could not operate to interact with parts of the brain that performed cognitive tasks, such as the formation, retention, and activation of memories.[11] Further studies showed that the amygdala was crucial in animals and humans for conditioning, the production of an autonomic nervous system (ANS) response, to stimuli. Patients with damage to their amygdala were presented with a loud noise and a picture. They showed no increased sweat response to the noise and did not sweat when later shown the picture by itself, though they could recall having seen the picture before. Patients with damage to another part of the brain, the hippocampus, did show an ANS response to the picture after conditioning, but could not recall having seen the picture. The experimenters concluded that "the amygdala is indispensable for emotional conditioning and for the coupling of extroceptive information concerning somatic states."[12] That is, the amygdala is involved in turning perceptions of the external world associated with the bodily arousal and felt emotions into memories that are easily recalled, and which themselves trigger an emotional response, again, in the sense of physical arousal, when recalled or when presented with an external stimulus that triggers the recall of the memory.

While not conclusive, a coherent argument can be extracted from the work reviewed so far. It has two components. Strong emotional experiences that activate our ANS and change the internal state of our bodies enhance our ability to remember events associated with the experience. This enhanced memory can take two forms: those explicitly recalled and of which we are conscious, and those that produce bodily reactions but not conscious awareness. The two forms of memory associated with these two responses are called explicit and implicit memories. In the case of explicit memories and emotion, we can more easily recall to our conscious mind the events associated with the event when presented with cues that suggest the event. We may not be aware of the cues that activated our explicit, emotional memories. We may also have an involuntary, ANS reaction to those cues—our skin will sweat, our hearts will beat rapidly, and so on—without an explicit recollection of the circumstances that created this memory or conditioning. A simple example is a situation that makes us feel "nervous," though we cannot say why, or though we know that we should not be nervous. Because of the therapeutic origins of many of these studies, there is less study of the cases where a situation makes us feel good, though, again, we cannot explicitly say why.

These phenomena could be of considerable cognitive importance. If we react to external events by recalling to mind an emotionally arousing event while we simultaneously find our bodies in a state of pleasant or unpleasant arousal, or if we have the ANS reaction without consciously recalling the event that formed this response, we might tend to adopt or reject a proposed course of action because of the interaction of present cues with past emotional experiences, without an attempt to look at alternatives to the proposed course of action. The emotional reaction would have more weight in decision making when the objectively analytical factors were indeterminate. "It was a toss up. I had to go with my gut." Or "Look—who knows what choice might have been best. I just knew that this was the right thing to do. Don't ask me why."

Though plausible in the form just presented, would such decisions really be different from a learned, cognitive response? If I live through a war and the war was bad for me, is it not possible to characterize this as conscious, cognitive learning, without dragging in all the additional elements of emotion and implicit and explicit memories? The answer appears to be no, for two reasons. First, if the existence of learning on the basis of "past experience" is acknowledged, it is still necessary to specify exactly what we learn from all of the experiences we have. From which past experiences do we learn, out of the uncountable experiences we have had? Arguments based purely on conscious cognition have problems specifying which experiences teach us lessons. The account that utilizes our emotional responses, on the other hand, specifies which experiences will be the basis of cognitive learning, assuming we can specify what causes emotional arousal. Second, as will be discussed below, people who have brain injuries that impair their ability to form emotional memories do, in fact, have difficulty making decisions in unstructured situations. Conscious learning appears not to produce conclusions forceful enough for real-world decision making. The emotion-based account of memory formation explains why we may have strong reactions to external events, and may lean strongly toward certain decisions, even when information is incomplete or ambiguous. The emotion-based argument explains why we can and do make decisions, when the objective data are inconclusive, about what option is best. This account does not suggest that conscious reflection plays no role, only that emotion-based memories narrow the range of options that are more closely examined, and the character of the information that is used initially in conscious deliberations.

This account hinges on an adequate specification of what happens in the brain and body to trigger an emotional arousal. If emotional arousal followed conscious cognition, then emotion would add little to our understanding of decision making. I may avoid war simply because I have thought about the experiences of past wars and learned what the costs of war are. If I am then confronted by the prospect of war, the fact that I then become angry or sad does not make my decision any different. If, however, I react emotionally to events in ways that are prior to conscious cognition, or if emotional reactions interact with conscious cognition, then my emotional response may lead me to react in ways that would not be predicted by a model of conscious evaluation that ignored the role of emotions.

So what do we know about what triggers an emotional response? The short answer is that people do display emotional responses in ways that do not simply reflect conscious cognition, though in complex settings conscious cognition does interact with emotional responses. Emotional reactions can be prior to conscious cognition and can affect human decision making in social settings.

The path to that answer is long. To study the causes of emotional responses, we must first identify when an emotional response occurs, and then see if that response takes place in ways that are independent of conscious cognition. To determine the occurrence of an emotional response, we can ask people how they are feeling, or we can monitor their internal physiological states associated with emotional experiences, for example, in the case of fear, elevated heart beat rates, elevated adrenaline, and depressed testosterone levels in the blood. These responses are not triggered by conscious acts of will, though they may be related to how we consciously understand a situation, and are part of our autonomic nervous system. Experimental studies suggest that reports of mental states and ANS responses do not always agree. Could the aspects of human physiology associated with the ANS produce changes in the reports people give about their emotional state? For example, if we induce an increase in the heartbeat rates of people, do we make them "feel" afraid, at least insofar as they report their feelings? In one influential experiment, some students were injected with adrenaline, while others were not, and then both groups watched pleasant and unpleasant scenes from a movie. The emotions of the subjects, as reported by students about themselves, were correlated with what they were watching, not with their artificially elevated hormone levels. Pleasant, soothing scenes elicited reports of pleasant emotions, even when subjects were injected with adrenaline.[13] This suggested that mood or emotion did not have an involuntary, physiological component but was instead the product of conscious cognition: the students watched something, interpreted it, and then reacted emotionally. For many years this study and others like it suggested that emotion followed conscious cognition.

Other experiments, however, suggested that we did react emotionally, before we engaged in conscious cognition. Beginning in the 1950s, multiple experiments by independent researchers showed that people could be exposed to stimuli/information so briefly that they would state that they had no memory of observing anything—subliminal perception. They would later have preferences for and display ANS responses to the drawings or patterns of words to which they were exposed. In another experiment, students were shown one number very briefly (the so-called masked number), followed by a number (the "target" number) that was displayed for a longer period of time. They were then asked to move one hand if the number was greater than five, the other if it was less than five. The students had no memory of the masked number, but their response was significantly delayed when the masked number and the target number led to conflicting responses.[14]

John Kihlstrom also did research that showed how priming, that is, showing people images so briefly that they did not consciously perceive them, not only activated the ANS, but also acted as an aid to social decision making.

> Such information-processing activity would be non-conscious in a double sense: neither the stimuli themselves, nor the cognitive processes that operate on them, are accessible to phenomenal awareness. Such doubly non-conscious processes nevertheless exert an important impact on social interaction. Through the operation of routinized procedures for social judgment, for example, we may form impressions of people without any conscious awareness of the perceptual-cognitive basis for them. . . . A large number of social judgments and inferences, especially those guiding first impressions, appear to be mediated by such unconscious processes.[15]

This kind of research led one scholar, R. B. Zajonc, to write, "How fully and completely must subjects be cognized before they can be evaluated? I argue . . . that to arouse affect, objects need to be cognized very little—in fact, minimally." People assume, Zajonc wrote, "that if a decision has been made, then a cognitive process must have preceded it. Yet there is no evidence that this is indeed so."[16] Metastudies of the work done in this field confirmed that subliminal exposure to stimuli could shape preferences in what was called subliminal emotional priming.[17] Other scientists in the field objected that even though people might not be aware of the subliminal stimuli and the way in which they had learned from it, this did not mean that cognition had not taken place, only that the cognition had not been conscious. Richard Lazarus wrote that while rabbits might react to the sight of a fox without cognition, people needed to react to much more complex stimuli, which they then had to process. This processing is cognition, and so cognition must be involved in emotional response. This cognition would take in many pieces of information at once. The information would be evaluated, after which there would be an emotional response. In this view, emotional responses did not take place independently of cognition, but followed cognition. Lazarus's argument, however, had one important point that might be overlooked. People assume that cognition is a process of conscious appraisal that takes in information in a serial fashion. Lazarus's interpretation of the data was that some forms of cognition were neither conscious, controllable, nor logical. While emotion followed appraisals, it was not the case, he wrote, "that such an appraisal is necessarily deliberate, rational, and conscious." Cognition need not be objectively correct, but could distort reality. "Finally, cognitive appraisal does not necessarily imply awareness of the factors in any encounter on which it rests."[18] Although a fierce academic battle ensued between Zajonc and Lazarus, both accepted the fundamental point: stimuli could be processed and recalled without the subject being aware of it, could be processed unconsciously in ways very different from the way we processed data consciously, and could lead to conditioned emotional responses that we neither chose nor desired but which affected our behavior and preferences. As Zajonc subsequently wrote, "I selected some examples in which deliberate, rational, or conscious processes could be shown to be clearly unnecessary for the generation of affect. If Lazarus and I could agree that these forms of cognition are not necessary for an emotional arousal, then part of our problem would be solved."[19] This level of agreement clearly does exist in the written positions of the two men. What is important to note is that the generation of emotional responses does not generate a specific course of action, but only a broad predisposition toward or away from certain objects or events.

The experiments done by Zajonc and others were conducted by observing the external observable aspects of human behavior connected to memory and decision making. By themselves, they could not specify how the brain was internally processing information, but could only note that certain kinds of stimuli generated some unexpected behavioral results. It

would be difficult to reject standard models of conscious, rational cognition unless one somehow could look inside the brain to show that it was
processing information unconsciously for decision-making purposes in
ways that were different from the ways it consciously processed information. The effort to look inside the brain led scientists to ask the following
question. Did the brain have two internal decision-making mechanisms,
one based on emotional reaction to the stimuli, and the other on conscious cognition? If so, the two could produce the same decisions, but
they might also interact, leading people in directions other than those expected by a model based only on deliberate, rational cognition. This
question led to a speculative answer, that there were areas of the brain
that were physically separate and that had different "evolutionary" ages.
There were parts of the brain that were, for example, responsible for the
unconscious regulation of breathing, heartbeat, and similar automatic
functions. But, in addition, might there be another part of our brain that
responded independently and emotionally to stimuli? This part of the
brain would have been evolutionarily "conserved" from the parts of the
brains of earlier or simpler animals that produced automatic fight or
flight responses to stimuli. The part of our brain that performed conscious cognition was evolutionarily "newer" and not well developed in
nonhuman animals. It was hypothesized that the older system was located in a precise area of the brain called the limbic system. The brain as
a whole, with three physically and evolutionarily separate components,
was called the "triune" brain by Paul McLean.

This proposition echoed Freud's assertion that "in the realm of the
mind . . . what is primitive is so commonly preserved alongside the transformed version which has arisen from it that it is unnecessary to give in-
stances as evidence."[20] Unlike Freud's assertion, McLean's hypothesis
was specific enough to be tested experimentally, largely on animals. The
parts of this hypothesis that posited physically and evolutionarily separate sections of the brain did not stand up to experimental investigation.
Some parts of the limbic system turned out to be directly wired into the
portions of the brain that were involved in conscious thought, while others were responsible for not only emotion, but also short-term, conscious
memory. Given this evidence, it was hard to argue that emotional responses were processed in a particular place in the brain that had its own
evolutionary history. Further research showed that "simpler" animals
also had areas of the brain that corresponded to those parts of the
human brain responsible for conscious thought, and, in general, the notion of earlier forms of life being "simpler" was questionable.[21]

What did stand up to investigation in animal models was the idea that
at least one emotional response, that of fear, did operate in part through
pathways that were different from those involved in conscious thought.

A series of experiments were performed to find out why, in animals, the link could be cut between the parts of the brain that first received sensory data (auditory or visual thalamus) and the parts that were involved in animal learning (auditory or visual cortex), but the animals could still be conditioned to display ANS responses to stimuli that had been associated with (auditory) shocks to them. That is, the animals whose brains were altered could not learn to avoid activating an audible tone that preceded a shock, but they would still react reflexively with fear (their ANS would be activated) when they heard the tone. The experiments operated by tracing individual neural pathways by the use of chemical tracers that migrated only down those neural links that were activated, and stained them for study in subsequent autopsies. What was found was that sensory inputs indeed went to the thalamus and then to the cortex, as implied by a model of the brain that asserted that the parts of the brain responsible for cognition and learning directly received data from the outside world. However, sensory inputs *also* proceeded from the thalamus to the amygdala, the part of the brain that regulates the ANS and the release of hormones, heartbeat rate, and so on, without first going through the cortex. *The thalamus-amygdala link functioned twice as rapidly as the thalamus-cortex link.* Fear responses could be created without the involvement of the parts of the brain that took part in learning. The function of fear conditioning appeared to be that it prepared the body for some general kind of response but did not trigger any specific course of action. It got the body ready to respond while the part of the brain responsible for learning decided what to do, if anything.

Other links were also identified. It was observed that mice that had been fear conditioned to react to an audible tone in one lab setting would also show fear when simply placed in that lab setting. They had learned about the general context in which they had been afraid, not just the specific stimuli. However, mice in which the part of the brain called the hippocampus had been severed did not show the ability to learn contextually, though they still responded with fear to the sound of the tone. The hippocampus appears to receive inputs from the transition cortex, the part of the brain to which signals from many sensory inputs are sent before going to the hippocampus itself, where the formation of long-term memory takes place. In ways that are not yet understood, the transition cortex appears to "bundle" sensory inputs and transmit them to the hippocampus in ways that form long-term memories about contexts, which are not a single stimulus, but collections of many stimuli taken together. The hippocampus also receives stimuli from the amygdala. This is significant because long-term memory now seems almost certainly connected to the Long Term Potentiation (LTP) of synaptic pathways. LTP makes it easier for a neuron to trigger a response across a synaptic gap. LTP occurs when a neuron receives stimuli from more than one input at the same time. A stimulus from a single neuron to another neuron will not trigger that neuron to fire across a synapse before LTP has occurred but will activate the neuron to fire across a synapse after LTP has occurred. "Cells that fire together, wire together" is the casual formulation of this observation. The conjecture is that stimuli to the hippocampus from the amygdala that are received while inputs are being received from the transition cortex will cause LTP and the formation of long-term memories of contexts, or what might equally well be called patterns. This is the argument at the level of brain cells about how *emotional arousal, which occurs at least in part independently of conscious cognition, may enhance the formation of memories of patterns*. This argument has been tested and validated by means of experiments in mice and monkeys.[22]

Emotional Memory, Pattern Recognition, and Human Decision Making

So much for animal brains. What about people? Were emotional responses and memories formed in humans in ways that were not simply explained by conscious cognition? Did this affect human behavior? The motive to investigate this question was originally clinical. Patients with various forms of brain injury had some common characteristics. They displayed normal or above average intelligence as it is conventionally measured, and they had good or even above average memories when tested on paper or when asked specific questions. But they showed no emotion, or they displayed emotion at random and then acted as if they had never displayed emotion. They seemed insensitive to the emotions of others, showing no embarrassment, for example, when viewing other people who were placed in humiliating circumstances. They had no reactions to pictures of emotionally charged situations. What is most interesting for our purposes is that they also could not make decisions. If set at a task, they would continue it indefinitely, or interrupt their activity when distracted by trivial events. They would deliberate endlessly about how to do something, without coming to any conclusion. They could make no plans for the future.[23] After further study, it was found that what these patients had in common was damage to portions of the brain that included the amygdala, but which was not confined to the amygdala.

Could the links observed in animals between the amygdala and emotional responses be observed in humans? Could its impact on the human ability to make decisions be established? Experiments in which the physiological components of emotional response were altered were conducted to study the effects on the formation of memories. Students were injected with chemicals that blocked the operation of the amygdala-ANS link and then asked to read stories with high emotional content. These students did display a reduced ability to form long-term memory relative to students receiving placebos.[24] Other experiments were conducted that studied the way in which learning was inhibited in cases where injury to portions of the brain, the amygdala in particular, was observed. Six patients were identified who had brain lesions that interfered with the links between the amygdala and the rest of the brain. Their intelligence as measured by tests was in the normal range, but they had been hospitalized because they had been unable to manage their lives, having squandered money, drifted in and out of marriages, and been generally unable to make decisions about their life. They, along with ten subjects who did not have these lesions, were presented with specially structured sets of cards and allowed to flip through them. Some decks of cards had cards that, when drawn, gave the player a hundred dollar payoff, but also cards with penalties of several hundred dollars. Other decks had modest payoffs, but disproportionately smaller penalties. After being allowed to flip through and examine the decks, the subjects were wired to measure their skin conductance responses (SCR) and given the decks to play with for real money. Undamaged subjects would display elevated SCR when they drew penalty cards, while the patients with lesions would not. More interestingly, after playing with the different decks a few times, the normal patients would begin to sweat after they drew about ten cards from one of the risky decks that included cards with large penalties, even before drawing a penalty card. When asked if they noticed anything about the structure of the game, they would reply that they had *not* noticed anything special about the decks. After drawing twenty cards, the undamaged subjects would still say that they noticed nothing that gave away the structure of the game. By card 50, all of the normal subjects would say that they had a hunch that some decks were riskier than others. By card 80, seven of the ten undamaged subjects could explicitly formulate a proposition about how the decks differed. The subjects with brain lesions would continue to draw from the risky decks, even when they had explicitly formulated hypotheses about the differences among the decks. This lead the researchers to suggest that in humans there may be "two parallel but interacting" decision-making chains of events, one in which sensory knowledge "activates neural systems that hold nondeclarative disposition knowledge related to the individual's previous emotional experience of similar situations." These in turn activate "autonomic and neurotransmitter nuclei (such as those that deliver dopamine to selected cortical and subcortical forebrain regions). . . . The ensuing non-conscious signals then act as covert biases on the circuits that support processes of cognitive evaluation and reasoning." The other chain involves conscious recall of pertinent facts regarding various options and their outcomes, and the application of reasoning strategies to these facts. The nonconscious biases act as aids to calculation by highlighting or marking salient data. Or, more briefly, "The results suggest that, in normal individuals, non-conscious biases guide behavior before conscious knowledge does. Without the help of such biases, overt knowledge may be insufficient to ensure advantageous behavior."[25] The biases or emotional responses do not dictate a precise course of action but predispose those experiencing them, in this case, toward risk aversion.

What is the link between the emotional reaction to events and the ability to acquire information subliminally, that is, without being conscious of having been exposed to the information? One can formulate a hypothesis consistent with the earlier logic about the advantages of cognitive mechanisms that operate more quickly but produce behavior that is less specifically related to the stimuli. If consciousness depends on the nonconscious processing of sensory data to render it into a form of which we are consciously aware, consciousness might well lag behind the arrival of sensory data. Neural mechanisms that reacted to sensory data without the need for such processing might be able to respond more quickly, and lead to action more quickly, before we were consciously aware of the sensory data. This is intuitively true to anyone who has played sports. If we stop to think about how to handle a ball, we become clumsy. If we react without conscious thought, we act more quickly and appropriately, if we have enough experience in the game. Does information enter our brain more quickly if we are not aware of it? Scientists have tested that hypothesis and have found that the answer is yes. People were put in experiments in which their reaction times were measured. When presented with a stimulus, they would move their finger. They were asked to say when they decided to move their finger. Elaborate tools were developed to refine the ability to time the subjective moment of decision, but they did not affect the findings. Working with electrodes placed on the outside of the brain, experimenters consistently found that the brain activity associated with moving a finger (the Readiness Potential or RP) peaked about half a second before people made the conscious decision to move their finger. The brain reacted to sensory data and readied itself to act before the conscious decision to act was made. Then, in a series of experiments on patients requiring brain surgery, Benjamin Libet specified more precisely what was occurring. By placing electrodes directly into the sensory areas of the cortex, he was able to show that electrical stimulation that lasted less than half a second was not consciously perceived by the patients, who were under local anesthesia. However, stimuli applied directly to the thalamus (which has independent links to the amygdala) could generate unconscious memories that produced conditioned responses, without the prior involvement of the areas of the brain responsible for cognition.[26] Subliminal perception works so that we can be aware of and remember sensory data that we do not have time to be consciously aware of. These perceptions create unconscious or implicit memories that, when stimulated by sensory inputs that fit the context (pattern) associated with the formation of the emotion, trigger the brain and body responses associated with emotion.

Emotional responses may help form memories, and they may then be the product of subliminally formed memories. Is there anything special about certain sensory inputs that make them more likely to evoke an emotional response? In the experiments above, a conditioned stimulus (CS) is a stimulus, such as a musical tone, that a subject is conditioned to associate with something called an unconditioned stimulus (US), something the subject will react to without prior exposure, such as pain, loud noises, or bright flashes of light. Are there unconditioned stimuli other than pain and such to which people react without learning, and which might be a particularly strong way of forming conditioned stimuli? Scientists working on what is called "preparedness theory" have found some evidence that humans form more persistent fear-related responses more quickly when exposed to things that might be expected to have posed threats to human beings for periods of time relevant to evolutionary changes in our brain. A readiness or predisposition to become afraid of heights is one example. It is not that we are instinctively afraid of heights, or snakes, or spiders. Rather, we are prepared to learn more easily that heights and such are dangerous.[27]

All this might be true and could be relevant to some situations. It might explain why we remember being injured as victims of crime. However, it still might not be relevant to the kind of politics in which we are interested. After all, in political behavior, leaders are now rarely taken to the edge of a cliff by an adversary, or receive physical pain as a consequence of their actions, and they might no longer be expected to develop emotional responses that affect cognition. However, this view must be modified by the observation that people are also unusually sensitive to the stimuli they receive from human social interaction, which should not be surprising given the evolutionary advantages to being able to manage and learn quickly from human social experience.[28] Hardwired predispositions to learn from human social stimuli would enable people to learn quickly and nonconsciously what kinds of behavior elicit positive social responses and the reverse. And that is the case. Human beings respond to the emotional tone of a human voice when it is so soft that they can no longer make out the words, or when the voice is electronically garbled. Subjects who were asked to interpret the meaning of statements they heard read aloud displayed a variance in their response that was affected twenty-two times more by the tone of the voice than by its verbal contents.[29] The same is true of faces. Normal subjects can reliably identify fear in photographs of faces that they see. Patients with brain damage that severs the links to the amygdala cannot.[30] Because of the role of the amygdala in the formation of emotional memories, it is suggested that the amygdala also plays a role in assessing facial expressions in ways that form emotional memories. This was confirmed by other experiments. Patients with damage to the amygdala were admitted to hospitals because they had displayed an inability to choose which people to approach physically and engage intimately in social situations. They were presented with verbal descriptions of people, and with pictures of people displaying various emotions. They showed no difficulty assessing people on the basis of the verbal descriptions, but they showed reduced ability to make judgments about trustworthiness and dangerousness of people on the basis of the photographs. The deficits were most severe in the cases of photographs showing people with extremely negative facial expressions. In the words of the scientists, "The findings suggest that the human amygdala triggers socially and emotionally relevant information in response to visual stimuli. . . . The retrieved information might be either overt or covert [explicitly or implicitly remembered] or both."[31]

What does this all mean? Faces are not just single data points. Faces and facial expressions are patterns. The study varied single data points in the photos, such as the shape of the nose or mouth. Those changes had no impact on the ability or inability of normal and injured patients to make judgments about the expected behavior of the people in the photos. In the experiment with risky and safe card decks, subjects did not make judgments on the basis of individual or discrete data points, but on the basis of a series of events. They were making a judgment on the basis of a comparison of patterns presented in an immediate situation with implicit memories of a pattern. Making that judgment was connected to the ability to react emotionally to patterns. Pattern recognition associated with the emotional arousal, or somatic markers, was in operation.

Emotion, Pattern Recognition, and International Relations

Can all this, finally, be related to decision making in international relations? Under what circumstances might we expect to find emotion-based pattern recognition in operation? The account presented above would suggest that pattern recognition that rests on emotion-based learning would play a role and affect the decision-making process when decisions were made under severe subjective time pressures, and at times of emotional arousal. It would also be plausible that this form of decision making would become more important when serial search-and-analyze modes of decision making yielded no clear answer.

People have, for many years, made the case that pattern recognition takes place in international relations. It has been labeled analogical reasoning. Yuen Foong Khong made use of the literature in cognitive psychology that refers to cognitive structures or schemas, and the argument that because the human brain can hold only seven (plus or minus two) "chunks" of data in its working memory at a time, "human beings have to rely on some sort of simplifying mechanism to cope and to process— to code, store, and recall—the massive amount of information they encounter in their daily lives. . . . these simplifying mechanisms are to be found in knowledge structures stored in memory." These schema, in Khong's account, fill in missing information when we encounter complex situations that are imperfectly understood. Analogies play a role in foreign policy decision making that is very similar, if not identical, to cognitive schema. Khong provides an impressive and convincing account of the number of times decisionmakers referred to historical analogies in making decisions about the Vietnam War. But, relying on the best experimental psychology available at the time, he had difficulty answering what he acknowledged to be the crucial question: "From where do policymakers get their historical lessons?" Which experiences form the dominant schema? Different policymakers learn different lessons from history, and even one policymaker has many different experiences on which to draw. Again, relying on the available experimental psychological literature, Khong argued that policymakers have a repertoire of analogies, and, in a given situation, they apply the "availability heuristic" and draw upon the analogies "that come most readily to their minds," or that are "superficially" similar.[32]

This does not explain which memories are recalled but is simply a statement that the memories that are recalled are the ones that are recalled. It is not false, but it does not help identify ahead of time which memories will form the pattern used to characterize a new situation and identify the one course of action to be adopted or rejected. By adding the accounts of brain functions related to emotion and the amygdala, however, we can make a more specific statement about which memories will emerge, implicitly or explicitly, to shape decisions. They are the memories of external sensory inputs that were processed by the hippocampus at a time when the amygdala activated the ANS. That is, the memories of experiences that were associated with severe emotional arousal will tend to be recalled whether the new stimuli closely resemble the remembered, emotion-linked pattern or not. Those recalled memories may be explicit—"I think of Munich when I see Vietnam"—or implicit—"I feel nervous in this situation in which I am called to acquiesce in the results

of aggressive military activity." Some looseness remains—everything I
see may not remind me of Munich if I lived through it, only things involving international politics, things involving concessions to foreign
leaders. Some conscious processing of the current situation appears to be
necessary but is left unspecified. But the range of memories from which
analogies will be selected can be greatly narrowed, because most leaders
will not have had many experiences that aroused in them personally
great fear.

This explanation also suggests that historical episodes will mark most
clearly the men and women who lived through them. The emotional
force of historical events will ordinarily not be transmitted to people
who did not live through them, though it is possible to imagine exceptions in which historical lessons are transmitted in emotionally arousing
ways. History can be recounted in ways that arouse emotion in the students. If the teaching experience is itself highly emotional, so that the historical data is transmitted to students who are emotionally aroused by
their teachers, analogies can span generations. Hearing parents recount
wartime suffering can be an emotional experience for children. This effect can be deliberately amplified by social mechanisms. In France, for
example, mutilated veterans of World War I were sent to visit elementary
school children to tell them about the horrors of the war through which
they lived.[33]

Modern studies of the changes in the cognitive styles of individuals as
they age strongly suggest that Aristotle was correct when he argued in
the *Rhetoric* that young people are more quick to react emotionally with
anger, are less easily frightened, and have a greater ability to approach
problems analytically rather than by applying memories. Old people
have many memories of the past, but new short-term memories are not
formed as easily as when young.[34] Young people will not be generally
afraid, but when they are afraid, they will react very strongly, and so they
will be capable of forming new memories easily. Aristotle claimed the
body was at its peak at the age of thirty to thirty-five, and the mind was
at its peak at the age of forty-nine, his approximate age when writing the
Rhetoric. Youths old enough to have their first experiences of the world
presumably would be younger than that, in their twenties through early
forties. The implication is that emotional memories of international relations would tend to be formed in people in that age group. This sugges-
tion is consistent with the work on generational memories that found
that the group that identified World War II or the Vietnam War as the
most important event of their lives was fifteen to twenty-four and sixteen
to twenty-seven, respectively, when those events occurred. The same was
found for generational memories of the Iranian hostage crisis and the assassination of John Kennedy.[35]

It is also consistent with the finding of Gideon Rose that the most salient cognitive consequence associated with the end of wars in the victors' camp was the subsequent desire to avoid war termination policies that had caused the decisionmakers emotional pain in the last war that they had fought. Americans who had participated in the end of World War I tended to be determined to avoid the policy failures of 1918. As Roosevelt said in a radio broadcast in 1943, "After the Armistice in 1918, we thought and hoped that the militaristic philosophy of Germany had been crushed; and being full of the milk of human kindness we spent the next twenty years disarming. . . . The well-intentioned but ill-fated experiments of the former years did not work. It is my hope that we will not try them again. No—that is putting it too weakly—it is my intention to do all I humanly can as president and commander in chief to see to it that these tragic mistakes shall not be made again."

The policy of unconditional surrender was perhaps overdetermined in 1943. But what of the American decision to go on fighting in Korea, solely because negotiations had stalled on the issue of whether or not communist Prisoners of War in UN hands would or would not be forced to return to China and North Korea? American public opinion was indifferent to or very ambivalent about this policy, but Harry Truman was not. He recorded in his diary his horror at what had happened to POWs returned to the Soviet Union, and his determination not to repeat that error. Soldiers who had been personally involved in the forcible repatriation of Russians and East Europeans at the end of World War II had severe emotional responses to their experiences. Rose found that compared with the available alternative theoretical arguments—bureaucratic interests, balance of power, and domestic public opinion—the negative emotional lessons of history were the best predictor of American war termination policy.[36]

These accounts are suggestive but are perhaps exceptions or marginal cases. However, larger statistical studies confirm that negative experiences of the kind that could easily lead to severe negative emotional arousal have reliably led nations to turn against the policies that led to the negative emotions. Dan Reiter has studied the pattern of alliance behavior of small countries in the aftermath of world wars. Reasoning from some of the same social psychological literature that Khong used, he developed a hypothesis about learning in international politics based on the importance of schema and the vividness of the learning experiences that created the dominant schema. Experiences that were directly experienced would tend to be more vivid. Combining these, he developed the proposition that the individual experience of a small country with its alliance policy in a big war would determine its subsequent alliance policy. If a given alliance policy—neutrality or alignment—had led to mili-

tary defeat and occupation, it would be reversed. If not, it would be retained. He then tested whether the individual negative or positive experience of a country with its alliance policies—neutrality or alignment with
a great power—in the most recent world war predicted its alliance behavior after the war. Norway, for example, had a severely negative experience with neutrality in World War II and so moved away from neutrality after the war. Sweden, in contrast, was neutral in World War II, had
positive experiences, and so stayed neutral. Reiter compared this individual learning argument against a systemic learning argument. Perhaps
Sweden could have learned from the general experience of all small
countries in World War II that neutrality was risky. This kind of learning
would involve less emotion because it involved the study of other people's experiences in ways that might not be consistent with one's own
emotional history. If all available knowledge was used, a small nation
might learn that while it prospered in a war as a neutral, the general experience of all small neutrals indicated that neutrality was a bad policy
and ought to be abandoned. He found that individual learning correctly
predicted behavior in 111 out of 127 cases. In those cases where the general system lesson about alliances indicated behavior that was the opposite of individual experience, the predictions based on individual learning
were correct in 80 percent of the cases, whereas the general learning argument correctly predicted only 20 percent of the cases.[37]

Quantitative studies of national behavior do seem to support the hypothesis that massive social violence or trauma can generate shared emotional experiences and memories, which can then determine state behavior. Can this hypothesis be used to explain individual decisions? There is
certainly a large degree of variation in individual emotional experiences,
which may be very vivid, if less widely shared. Personal experiences may
also arouse people directly. In addition to quantitative studies, detailed
accounts of individual decisions may help establish whether conscious, serial calculations are responsible for decisions, or whether pattern recognition driven by individual emotional memories has affected the decision.

In tracing individual episodes of decision making, it would be easy to
slip into a search for something that looked like pattern recognition and
then use anything that looks like pattern recognition to "explain" decisions that look, after the fact, to have been "mistaken." The same problem dogs efforts to prove that "correct" decisions were "rational." As
stated in chapter 1, such accounts are plausible, but no more. To avoid
this problem, we should try to deduce from the model of decision making what the characteristics of one kind of decision-making process are,
as specifically as possible, without regard to their outcome in practice. In
the case of emotion-based pattern recognition, those characteristics are
reasonably clear.

First, when emotion-based pattern recognition occurs, the time required to make the decision should be short. Decisions should emerge in response to the first exposure to the problem, not after lengthy searches for data that could confirm or disconfirm alternative strategies. The logic of pattern recognition is that it has value because it enables people to react more quickly to complex situations by arousing the body for action. On the model of visual pattern recognition and multiple observations of real-world decisionmakers, there should be some sort of "pop-out" effect in which what is perceived and the very general character of what should be done appear together.

Second, the decision should be associated with emotional arousal. In the absence of physical monitoring, we must rely on subjective reporting. However, among people with responsibilities for war and peace, there is often a bias against admitting that emotions affected decisions. Self-reporting that emotion did play a role is not likely to be something consciously fabricated to create a positive impression.

Third, and finally, emotion-based pattern recognition driven by emotional memory should treat the connection between past events and current decisions as "obvious," and not requiring any effort to establish that the current situation fits the pattern formed by emotional experience in the past. Emotional memories are easily recalled and do not require that the new situation be a close fit. In cases where the objective data are ambiguous, it may not be clear whether emotion-based pattern recognition is or is not leading to a distorted picture of reality. If, however, the decision stands in the face of clear disconfirming data, this may be taken as an indication of the operation of strong pattern recognition shaped by emotional memory.

To sum up, this analysis leads to the following propositions that are, in principle, testable:

- If decisions are made on the basis of emotion-driven pattern recognition, the decision will be made quickly and early in the process, despite the complexity of the situation and the availability of contradictory analysis and data.
- The decisions will conform to past emotional experience in a straightforward way. Situations that evoke an emotional memory of a negative experience will lead the actor to select away from the policy that was associated with the negative emotional experience. Situations that evoke a positive experience will lead the actor to select toward the policy that was associated with the positive emotional experience.
- Those decisions will resist contradictory data.
- These decisions can be distinguished from those that are delayed and deferred in order to permit the accumulation of data and analysis, and which bear no strong relation to past emotional experiences.

Cases: FDR, HST, JFK, LBJ

Munich

One of the better-researched incidents involving this kind of direct emotional reaction to the nonverbal content of statements made by political
leaders is Barbara Farnham's reconstruction of the reaction of Franklin
Roosevelt and his cabinet to radio broadcasts made by Hitler and Neville
Chamberlain at the time of the Munich crisis. Prior to the immediate crisis period set off by the 22–23 September Godesberg conference during
which Hitler escalated his demands on Chamberlain, Roosevelt increasingly expected a European war. If that war occurred, he said, France and
Britain would suffer from German air attacks, would stay on the defensive on the ground, and would, on the whole, have a difficult but ultimately successful war. He also believed that the appeasement of Germany
could achieve a temporary, local peace but would stimulate the aggression
of dictators around the world. He opposed appeasement for that reason,
but he remained resolved that the United States should not become involved *diplomatically* in the affair. When Hitler proved to be unwilling to
settle the crisis at Godesberg, FDR's estimate of the likelihood of war very
reasonably went up further, but he remained opposed to American *diplomatic* intervention, as late as 23 September. By 25 September, he had
shifted his position slightly, and late on the night of the 25th he finished a
draft of a speech that appealed to all parties to try to avoid war, but which
stopped short of any hint of American mediation or diplomatic action,
such as the offer of American good offices to hold a conference to revise
the Versailles treaty in order to avoid war. Hitler responded to this appeal
by means of a public speech heard in the United States on the afternoon of
26 September. The following afternoon, 27 September, FDR and his cabinet resolved to help the British and French in all ways possible that did
not involve the United States in war. On the 27th, FDR began to exert
U.S. diplomatic pressure on Hitler to resolve the crisis on terms accept-
able to Great Britain and France, and he sent two messages to Hitler.
FDR's policy to avoid any diplomatic involvement of the United States
had been reversed. In the five-day period of 23–27 September, as far as
can be determined, no new information was received that caused FDR to
alter his subjective evaluation of the expected utility of the policy alternatives open to him. What did happen? By his own testimony and the testimony of others, the nonverbal content of Hitler's and Chamberlain's
radio speeches reversed FDR's attitude toward intervention. According to
Arthur Murray, two weeks after he made his decision, FDR told Murray
how he had had his cabinet listen to the broadcast of Chamberlain's
speech on Tuesday the 27th. "When it was finished I looked round the

table and there were tears in the eyes of at least four members of the Cabinet and I felt that way myself. I had listened to Hitler on the Monday, and so had most of my Cabinet. The contrast between the two just bit into us—the shouting and violence of Hitler, and the roars, through their teeth, of his audience of 'Krieg, krieg,' and then, the quiet, beautiful statement of Chamberlain's."[38] The cabinet immediately resolved to begin work to intervene in ways that would help Britain and France. Hitler's objective characteristics were familiar to the cabinet, as were the policy options and their costs. What changed was the emotional reaction. As was the case in clinical and laboratory studies, humans in this case appear to have made decisions about the approachability of other humans on the basis of information processed by the amygdala and that triggered emotional responses without the action of conscious cognition. Activation of the emotional response and the decision to oppose Hitler diplomatically were one event, and the decision does not appear to have been the product of conscious, serial calculation.

The argument in favor of emotion-based pattern recognition in this case is strengthened by the fact that conscious, serial calculations had been performed in the period before 27 September but had led to the decision not to act. In this case, perhaps the objective data was sufficiently ambiguous that a model of decision making based on conscious, serial calculations of the expected outcome of alternative policies would be indeterminate, and whatever the decision might have been, it could have been explained after the fact as "rational." But the sharp emotional response and the immediacy of the decision do appear to be quite clear.

Potsdam

In other cases, the impact of emotion may be the result of patterns of human appearance and behavior that we have, in earlier encounters, associated with positive emotional experiences. Deborah Larson intensively studied how Harry S. Truman made decisions about the Soviet Union in the months immediately after the defeat of Hitler. The Soviet Union had taken a number of actions in Poland and elsewhere over the objections of the United States. Truman did not have a great deal of experience in foreign affairs, and he had been famously willing in 1941 to let Germany and the Soviet Union bleed each other in war. Prior to his first encounter with Stalin, he had supported policies that gave the Soviet Union more freedom to control the government of Poland. There was a division in the West and in the United States about whether to be more or less accommodating to the Soviet Union. What is striking is how Truman reacted to Stalin when they first met. Truman recorded his impressions of Stalin in his diary entry 17 June 1945: "He is direct. We can get along.

... I can deal with him. He is honest—but smart as hell." After their Potsdam meeting in July 1945, Truman wrote: "Stalin is as near like Tom Pendergast as any man I know." Stalin was a man "who, if he said something one time would say the same thing the next time. . . . he could be depended upon." "I got the impression Stalin would stand by his agreements and also that he had a Politburo on his hands like the 80th Congress." This characterization of Stalin survived the events that led Truman to propose the Marshall Plan and the Truman Doctrine in 1947. In 1948 he stated, "I like old Joe. He is a decent fellow. But Joe is a prisoner of the Politburo. He can't do what he wants to. He makes agreements, and if he could he would keep them. But the people who run the government are very specific in saying that he can't keep them."[39]

The "Tom Pendergast" to whom Truman referred was of course Truman's political patron, the Missouri political boss who had made Truman's early political career, and from whom Truman had learned what he called "the code of the politician," which reduced to the proposition that politicians must keep their word to other politicians. From Pendergast Truman appears to have acquired a picture, a pattern, of what a trustworthy politician looked like, and how such a politician behaved. Associated with that sensory pattern were positive emotional experiences, which could be aroused by the activation of that pattern. Stalin fit that pattern. Under conditions in which the objective information was unclear as to whether or not the Soviet Union could be trusted, Truman was put face to face with a man who was the image of a shrewd but trustworthy boss, and the decision to trust Stalin and the recognition of the pattern were one action. Reading Truman's diary and his efforts to explain how Stalin could be trustworthy while the Soviet state was duplicitous is a curious experience: Truman argues that Stalin, the most absolute ruler of the time, was the prisoner of his Politburo. This appears somewhat odd to us. Evidence was easily available about the unlimited extent of Stalin's power over the Soviet state, and its rejection is consistent with the operation of pattern cognition driven by emotional memory.

The Cuban Missile Crisis

Two of the more closely studied episodes in American foreign policy decision making involve the 1962 Cuban missile crisis and the decisions concerning the American war in Vietnam made in 1964 and 1965. Because conversations in the White House were recorded on tape in this period, we have more detailed accounts of the informal decision-making process than are often available, accounts that provide information that can be lost or edited out of formal documents. The Cuban missile crisis was successfully resolved, while the Vietnam decisions led to policy failure. The Cuban missile crisis is often portrayed as an example of the careful evaluation of alternative options, and a conscious search for information to illuminate those options. Robert McNamara was a major player in both decisions, and he was committed to the search for alternative options and to rational evaluation of choices. One of the members of his staff said that McNamara "seeks alternatives like the Holy Grail."[40] But if, despite this emphasis on rational search and evaluation, emotion-based pattern recognition was involved, we should see decisions made very early in the process. The decision should be based on earlier emotional experiences, and not be modified in response to additional information. If conscious, serial processing of information to assess the value of alternative courses of action occurred, we should see decisions being driven by data and analyses that bear on the expected utility of differing courses of action. What do we observe?

The hypothetical issue of Soviet offensive missiles in Cuba was first considered by the president in August 1962. CIA Director John McCone first raised with John Kennedy the possibility of Soviet missile deployments to Cuba on 10 August 1962, before any hint of such activity had been picked up. On 21 August, still before any evidence of suspicious activity had been collected, McCone argued for early military action against missiles in Cuba. At the same meeting Robert Kennedy argued in favor of an air strike, but only if Castro could be maneuvered into attacking the American base at Guantanamo first. McGeorge Bundy argued that if the United States took action against Cuba, the Soviet Union would respond by putting pressure on Berlin, or Turkey, or Italy, where American ballistic missiles were located. A blockade of Cuba would drag on, the way the Soviet blockade of Berlin had. There seemed, in short, to be strong differences of opinion about whether military actions by the United States would have the desired results. The correct course of action should have appeared unclear. Nonetheless, John Kennedy appears to have decided at the next meeting on 23 August that the still hypothetical Soviet offensive missiles in Cuba would be intolerable, and that the United States would have to use some form of military force to remove them. Kennedy had made up his mind before the event, and certainly before the initiation of serious searches for and evaluation of alternative options began, since that process was undertaken only after the missiles were detected. As the historian Timothy Naftali put it:

Kennedy crossed a threshold during the course of the discussion [on August 23]. Although he still doubted that Moscow would put nuclear weapons on Cuba, he spoke as if he had made up his mind to use force against those missiles in the event Khrushchev tried. After McCone and McNamara explained the limits on what the United States could know about events in Cuba,

Kennedy asked the group to consider the limits on what the country should do to the Soviet missile sites on the island. Would an air strike be enough? Was an invasion necessary; or, conversely, could the missiles be destroyed by sabotage? On August 23, there seemed to be no doubt in Kennedy's mind that he could never accept Soviet nuclear missiles in Cuba.[41]

Evidence that ballistic missiles had been placed in Cuba led to the White House meetings of October. If the White House discussions were structured in the form of a decision tree, the first branch point might come with the question, should the Soviet missiles be allowed to stay in Cuba? The answer to that question would be determined by an evaluation of the costs of forcing the Soviets to remove the missiles, as well as the costs of allowing them to stay. One of the biggest costs of forcing the Soviets to remove the missiles would be those associated with a general nuclear war, discounted by the subjective probability of that event. One of the major costs of allowing the missiles to stay would be the political and military costs associated with acquiescing to the Soviet advance. If the answer was that the missiles had to go, the next question might be, should military force be used to remove them? A more refined evaluation of the costs and benefits of military and nonmilitary options would then follow. If the answer was that military force should be used, then different use-of-force options would constitute a tertiary decision point, with multiple branches.

What is obvious from the tapes is that no one advanced the option to allow the missiles to remain in Cuba, and that the option to get the Soviets out by nonmilitary means was quickly dismissed with almost no discussion. At the first White House meeting, Secretary of State Dean Rusk did suggest an appeal to the Organization of American States, or the use of the Canadian ambassador to Cuba to suggest to Castro that the Soviet missiles were not in Cuba's interest, followed, if necessary, by renewed efforts to support guerrillas in Cuba.[42] Rusk's proposal to try diplomatic efforts was immediately followed, not by a discussion of the pros and cons of diplomatic action, but by a discussion of whether to conduct limited or extensive air strikes against Cuba, followed by an invasion, and Rusk's ideas never reemerged. When the issue of nonmilitary options was raised again, Kennedy returned the discussion to the question of how to conduct air strikes. Fursenko and Naftali commented that at this point, "Kennedy was dodging efforts by his advisers to have him concentrate on a nonmilitary exit from the crisis."[43]

Whatever one thinks about the quality of the decisions finally taken, it is impossible not to acknowledge how quickly the turns at the first two branch points in the decision tree were taken, without any explicit discussion of the expected outcome of different courses of actions. Extensive discussions did follow about what form of military action might be best, but they seemed to have rested on a prior decision to force the withdrawal of the missiles by the use of force, a decision that had not been made on the basis of the evaluation of expected outcomes. In his review of the decision-making process, Marc Trachtenberg noted that there was a potential debate about the military importance, or lack of it, of the Soviet missiles in Cuba. When asked at a White House meeting how important the missiles were militarily to the United States, McNamara responded: "I asked the Chiefs [Joint Chiefs of Staff] that this afternoon, in effect. And they said, substantially. My own personal view is, not at all." The overall nuclear balance was very favorable to the United States and, McNamara argued, would remain so even with the missiles in Cuba. Forcing the Soviet Union to remove the missiles from Cuba, however, carried with it the chance of a nuclear war.

What would be the costs of such a war? McNamara and others believed that no one could guarantee that a few Soviet nuclear warheads would not explode on American targets. Was this the result of a calculation of the value of the possible outcomes of decisions discounted by their probability? As one historical review put it, the answer was "no." "Even though the doves did estimate the risks somewhat higher than did the hawks, their probability judgments do not appear to have played much of a role in their deliberations. How can this be? Why would the Secretary of Defense, for instance—a man renowned, then as now, for his enthusiasm for quantification and for calculating and playing the odds—toss probability logic out the window?"

The possibility of one disastrous outcome easily tipped their decisions against air strikes. The point is that the real military significance of the Soviet missiles and the dangers of air strikes were simply not probed. When asked afterwards what would have happened if there had been a war between the United States and the Soviet Union, Robert McNamara replied: "That is a very important question. Important mainly because I have no idea what the answer is. I'd thought about it and I had discussed it with the President. . . . Now, I know the SIOP called for a massive response. . . . No way we would have done that. But—and this goes to my main point—during the missile crisis we never even talked about it. . . . We should have, but we did not."[44]

Marc Trachtenberg, after reviewing the transcripts of the White House tapes, concluded that "there is no evidence that President Kennedy and his advisers counted missiles, bombers, and warheads, and decided on that basis to take a tough line. The veterans of the crisis have often denied that any calculation of that sort had been made, and there is no reason to dispute them on this point." Kennedy himself, at the first meeting, seemed to acknowledge that the missiles by themselves were not a problem. He listened to the debate about when and how to conduct air strikes and said, "Last month I said we weren't going to [tolerate the presence of offensive missiles in Cuba]. Last month I should have said . . . that we don't care. But when we said we're not going to and then they go ahead and do it, and then we do nothing, then. . . . I would think that our risks increase."[45] This suggests that Kennedy made public statements that locked him into the military course of action. A poor choice of words and domestic politics, not emotion, drove the decision-making process. Was Kennedy's decision driven by an implicit calculation of the domestic political costs of backing down? As a politician, it would be hard to survive two humiliations in Cuba in as many years. Yet personal political failure is not as bad as a nuclear war, so if Kennedy were trying to maximize his own political fortunes, some consideration of the costs and likelihood of bad outcomes associated with the use of military options versus the costs and likelihood of bad outcomes that followed from a policy of doing nothing or taking only diplomatic options still should have been conducted. Given the costs of nuclear war, even a small chance of such a war should have weighed heavily. They were not. But the most important point is that Kennedy privately favored military action in August, *before* his public statements of 4 September[46] that allegedly locked him on a course of action had been made.

Inevitably, there will be debate about what was in the minds of the decision makers. It is important to note what seems to be clear about the observable behavior. First, the decision that the missiles must go and that military force should be used was taken quite early in the process, perhaps as early as 23 August, certainly no later than the first White House meeting. There was no discussion of the option to accept the presence of the missiles as nonthreatening, nor any real discussion of nonmilitary options. There was no explicit discussion of the expected costs of a nuclear war associated with the use of American military force. This lack of discussion occurred despite the fact that the costs of nuclear war were obviously very large, that the secretary of state sincerely believed that the diplomatic option was reasonable, while the Secretary of Defense believed strongly that the missiles did not create a greater military problem for the United States. At a minimum, this was a situation in which the available data and analysis about expected outcomes of alternative options were very ambiguous. Yet the key decisionmaker was sure of what he wanted to do, though the military details of alternative military options were debated at length. A decision-making process based on explicit, serial calculations of the expected utility of alternative courses of action would not seem to have supported this certainty.

Would another model of decision making better explain the observable behavior? The argument is that emotion-based pattern recognition could do so. This form of cognition would recognize and characterize an event very quickly, even in the absence of unambiguous data. A person who had caused a negative emotional reaction in the decisionmaker in the past would be a stimulus that would tend to trigger the same emotional response in the target and a policy choice the opposite of what had earlier caused the negative experience. This emotional response would predispose the decisionmaker toward certain broad courses of action such as trust/distrust, cooperate/fight. After that, the serial evaluation of options would occur in order to specify a course of action consistent with the broad emotional response. This does seem to be what happened as Kennedy and Khrushchev interacted in the period beginning in 1961 and up through the Cuban missile crisis.

It has long been known that the Kennedy/Khrushchev summit meeting at Vienna went badly and left Kennedy upset. As Robert Kennedy later reported, "Vienna was very revealing: This was the first time the President had ever really come across somebody with whom he couldn't exchange ideas in a meaningful way and feel there was some point to it. . . . It was a shock to him."[47] There is little doubt that John Kennedy had a negative emotional reaction to the experience. It can be suggested that he acquired a set of emotional responses such that actions by Khrushchev quickly triggered a general predisposition on the part of Kennedy to dislike/mistrust/resist Khrushchev. If such an emotional response occurred, it would probably have been reinforced by Khrushchev's statement to a member of Kennedy's cabinet in September 1961 that "it's been a long time since you could spank us like a little boy—now we can swat your ass." This was followed by Khrushchev's comments to Robert Frost, reported back to Kennedy, that the United States was too weak and worn out to fight. The United States, Khrushchev said, was like an old man who wanted to have sex: "The desire is the same, it's the performance that's different."[48] That emotional predisposition would close off cooperative policy options and focus attention on active resistance, even if the data did not unambiguously support a decision to resist. Kennedy's first response to the evidence of the missiles in Cuba has been downplayed, but he is reported to have first reacted to the crisis by saying angrily, "He [Khrushchev] can't do that to *me*."[49] This would be generally consistent with the kind of emotional response that the emotion-based pattern-recognition model would predict.

An account that wished to avoid referring to the subjective emotional state of the president and set aside the possible impact of emotion on decision making would argue that Vienna was a learning experience in which Kennedy acquired information about how hard Khrushchev would fight to get what he wanted, as opposed to how interested Khrushchev was in reaching agreements. Hence, a decision to use force to remove the missiles need not have been driven by emotion. But this account does not explain the basic decision not to accept the missiles, even if getting them out ran the risk of nuclear war. It is unclear how an account that did not refer to the emotional memory that Kennedy acquired could explain the quick decision to go down a road that involved direct United States–Soviet Union military confrontation. The outcome of the crisis was satisfactory, and so the temptation is to assume that it was the product of clear thinking. The evidence for that interpretation, however, is shaky.

The American War in Vietnam

Very few people would still characterize the decision to use American military power in the Vietnam war as satisfactory, but that does not mean that the decision was made without a careful consideration of the options available and their expected outcomes. Richard Betts and Leslie Gelb have laid out the case that American leaders did not have overly optimistic expectations about what American military power could do and were properly mindful of the real possibility that the conflict in Vietnam might escalate to a war between the United States and China. The policies adopted by the administration of Lyndon Johnson were the best that were available, even if they turned out to have failed.[50] Larry Berman wrote that contemporary personal criticism of Lyndon Johnson—the alleged "Caligula syndrome" created by his overbearing personality and his willingness and ability to crush internal opposition to his policies—may have overstated the emotional elements of the decision to commit American ground forces to combat at the end of July 1965. The decision made that July, he argued,

> resulted from extensive deliberations among foreign policy advisors and between those advisors and the president. In his background briefing of the press, Secretary of Defense Robert McNamara emphasized that "not since the Cuban missile crisis had such care been taken in making a decision." . . . These White House deliberations reflected what is generally assumed to be one of the few times that the principal Vietnam advisors focused intensively on fundamental questions of policy and not solely on the technicalities of military strategy.

The decision, Berman writes, was a complex one, and not the result of a personal reaction by Lyndon Johnson to Ho Chi Minh.

That does not mean that the decisions about Vietnam were simply conscious, serial evaluations of alternative strategies. Even Berman concluded that although Lyndon Johnson was exposed to at least two voices opposed to the war in the period—George Ball and Clark Clifford—they were outnumbered and outranked. Some activities that were purportedly searches for information were in fact not real searches for data at all. The fact-finding missions conducted by McNamara to evaluate the decision to send ground combat troops were, in reality, efforts to build a consensus for a decision already taken. Some options were not evaluated at all. Most importantly, the options to leave South Vietnam were not studied in 1965.[51]

Works published after Berman have tended to confirm the proposition that data and analysis that supported options other than the gradual escalation of American military power in Vietnam either were not reviewed at all by Johnson or his senior advisors or were cursorily rejected. In the period February–April 1965, a considerable range of views developed in the American government. Hawks such as CIA Director McCone and Treasury Secretary C. Douglas Dillon urged rapid military escalation, bombing, and the rejection of negotiations. Doves such as Senator Mike Mansfield and Vice President Hubert Humphrey urged a greater emphasis on negotiation with no further American military deployments to Vietnam. After tracing the way in which such proposals worked their way through the decision-making process, Fred Greenstein concluded, "As far as can be determined from the historical records, the position McCone advanced, like those of Taylor, Humphrey, Mansfield, and Clifford, was not rejected after discussion; it was not discussed." Greenstein reported that staff-level analysis that opposed military escalation was not passed on to senior decisionmakers, and that the few papers by opponents of the military escalation were watered down from their original version before they reached the president. In this sense, analysis to evaluate the expected outcome of options was not conducted. Greenstein also reported the results of two war games conducted by the Joint Chiefs of Staff, Sigma I, conducted in 1963, and Sigma II, conducted in July–August 1965. Sigma I simulated the course of the war in Vietnam over a period of ten years. Senior figures such as McCone, General Maxwell Taylor, and George Ball played American and Vietnamese leaders. The game ended with 600,000 American troops deployed to Vietnam, American domestic politics in an uproar, and the Viet Cong in control of most of South Vietnam. Sigma II was more limited and involved middle-level bureaucrats as players. It simulated only thirteen months of real-world time, ending on the simulated Labor Day, 1966. At the end, the Viet Cong and Democratic Republic of Vietnam players felt they were winning, and that time was on their side. The Blue or American team had made no appreciable progress toward its goals. Both teams agreed that while the United States could stalemate the war militarily, in the long run, American and world public opinion would make the American position in South Vietnam untenable. On 5 August 1965, an effort was made to brief McGeorge Bundy and Chair of the Joint Chiefs of Staff General Earle Wheeler on the outcome of game, but they could only stay for less than half an hour of discussion because of their other duties.[52]

This research suggests that the decision-making process was not as closely linked to the formal evaluation of policy options and their expected outcomes as has been argued by Berman, Betts, and Gelb. Decisionmakers did not appear to receive or respond to new information about the expected outcomes of alternative policies. But perhaps the formal paper trail does not capture how it was that the decision makers actually debated their options. Lyndon Johnson, like John Kennedy, selectively taped conversations in the White House. These tapes and interviews with the advisors to Johnson allow a close look at the informal decision-making process. Information from archives has also been released. What can we now observe?

The most complete biography of Johnson points out just how early Johnson's commitment to the defeat of the communist forces in Vietnam emerged in the form of directives to his staff. On 24 November 1963, the weekend after the assassination of John Kennedy, Johnson met with his senior advisors on Vietnam. According to one participant, McGeorge Bundy, Johnson said, "I am not going to lose Vietnam. I am not going to be the President who saw Southeast Asia go the way China went. . . . I don't think Congress wants us to let the Communists take over South Vietnam." Bill Moyers recalled that after a meeting that same day with the ambassador to the Republic of Vietnam, Henry Cabot Lodge, Johnson chatted with Moyers.

> *LBJ*: If we don't do something, he [Lodge] says, it'll go under—any day. . . .
> They'll think with Kennedy dead we've lost heart. So they'll think we're
> yellow and don't mean what we say.
> Who? [Moyers asked.]
> *LBJ*: The Chinese. The fellas in the Kremlin. They'll be taking the measure of
> us. They'll be wondering just how far they can go.

Before McNamara visited Vietnam in December 1963, Johnson lectured him on the need to do everything possible for Vietnam, that the United States was not then doing all it could. When McNamara returned more pessimistic about the war because of the cycle of coups d'etat in Saigon, Johnson publicly increased his personal support for the current leader of South Vietnam.[53] On 27 May 1964, Johnson spent his day on the telephone talking to his advisors about Vietnam. He also called his mentor in the Senate, Richard Russell, and asked him about Vietnam.

> *LBJ*: How important is it to us?
> *Russell*: It isn't important a damn bit, with all these new missile systems.

LBJ: Well, I guess it's important to us—

Russell: From a psychological standpoint.

LBJ: I mean, yes, and from the standpoint that we're party to a treaty. And if we don't pay any attention to this treaty, why, I don't guess they think we pay attention to any of them.

Johnson then stated that he was convinced that if the communists in North Vietnam were brought to the point of collapse, the Chinese government would intervene militarily in the war. He then returned to the question of American policy.

LBJ: The whole question, as I see it, is it more dangerous for us to let things go as they're going now, deteriorating every day—

Russell: I don't think we can let it go, Mr. President, indefinitely.

LBJ: Than it would be for us to move in.

Russell: You can make a tremendous case for moving out, not as good a one for moving in, but. . . .

Johnson then interrupted with a discussion of Republican Party leaders and their positions on the war. He concluded by saying, "Well, they'd impeach a President, though, that would run out, wouldn't they?"[54] In this and subsequent conversations, Johnson also expressed his reluctance to send American troops into combat and mentioned how he thought of his military valet and the valet's family when he thought of the American Army being sent into combat. But he did also return to the need not to back down. On 11 June, he spoke again with Richard Russell. He mentioned that the analysis of the consequences of American withdrawal from Vietnam was being studied.

LBJ: I've got a study now being made by the experts [CIA tasked on 9 June] whether Malaysia will necessarily go and India'll go and how much it'll hurt our prestige if we just got out and let some conference fail or something. A fellow like A. W. Moursund [a Hill County, Texas, insurance man, and a long-time intimate of LBJ] said to me last night, "Goddamn, there's not anything that'll destroy you as quick as pulling out, pulling up stakes and running. America wants, by God, prestige and power." . . . I said, "Yeah, but I don't want to kill these folks." He said, "I don't give a damn. I didn't want to kill 'em in Korea, but if you don't stand up for America there's nothing that a fellow in Johnson City"—[LBJ interpolates] or Georgia or any other place—"they'll forgive you anything except being weak." . . .

Russell: . . . It'd take a half million men. They'd be bogged down in there for ten years. . . .

LBJ: We never did clear Korea up.

In the conversation, Russell is clearly trying to sway Johnson against a decision to take additional military action in Vietnam, but without openly opposing Johnson. Johnson finally concluded by saying that as president, he must speak to the American people. "I think I've got to say that I didn't get you in here, but we're in here by treaty and our national honor's at stake. And if this treaty's no good, none of 'em are any good. Therefore we're there. And being there, we've got to conduct ourselves like men. That's number one."[55]

Because the Vietnam war was a disaster, it is tempting to find "irrationality" in the decision-making process and possible personality flaws in Lyndon Johnson. But what is striking is that the process in the Cuban missile crisis, which was a success, and the process in the case of Vietnam have notable similarities. In both cases, a close examination clearly shows that the basic decision was made very early in the process, before it was necessary to decide, and quite clearly before all the relevant information had been received. In both cases, the decision was not changed, or even reconsidered, when important information or analysis was received that was not consistent with the decision. And, in both cases, it is possible to argue that the president acted to avoid domestic political punishment, but only if one is willing to assume that the president would try to stay in office by involving the country in a major war, accepting the possibility of thousands or millions of casualties, and did not care about the domestic political punishment associated with those costs. In the case of Johnson, the argument about his fear of domestic political punishment has to be weighed against the fact of his massive election victory in 1964. This clear fear of electoral punishment if Vietnam fell may itself have been the result of past emotional experience. Lyndon Johnson's race for the Democratic nomination for United States senator in 1948 was the event that made him a national figure. It was a close race, and both sides used all the means at their disposal. LBJ referred to his opponent as soft on communism, and his opponent responded in kind.[56] It might be the case that this gave Johnson an emotional perspective on the electoral costs of appearing soft on communism, but this cannot be proven. What does seem to be clear is that Johnson's decisions to use force, like those of JFK, could be argued to have displayed a conscious calculation of costs and benefits rationality only if the downside costs of the use of force were severely discounted or not considered at all. What is also clear is that in complex situations in which it was difficult to say with any certainty what the consequences of any decision would be, two presidents sized up a situation quickly as one in which they were being personally challenged. From that emotional recognition, both knew emotionally that in such a situation, they had to fight.

Conclusions

Kennedy and Johnson, like FDR and Truman, made both good and bad decisions, but the way they made those decisions simply does not correspond to a model in which a full range of information is received and used in a meaningful way to evaluate the expected outcomes of alternative policies. The rapidity of the decisions and the complexity of the situations combined with what we know of the capacity of the human mind consciously to process information strongly suggests that something in the minds of the presidents must have, in some way, radically simplified the factors to be considered, and narrowed the range of past experiences to be reviewed. There is good evidence that the human mind has a mechanism for making decisions quickly by means of its emotional reaction to patterns that recall past emotional experiences. This reaction can be functional but is not necessarily so. Human beings who cannot react and decide emotionally can easily become paralyzed with indecision in settings far less complex than those faced by the presidents we have examined. If a decision is to be made at all, and to be made with conviction sufficient to persuade others, an emotional response is necessary. But that emotional response is not a guarantee that a policy will be chosen that optimizes the returns to the actor. If decisionmakers could be shown quantitatively to be acting in their own interest, we might shrug and say that although we cannot say how they were making these decisions, they were acting "as if" they were rationally maximizing utility. But both large-N studies and case studies show that the actors we can study have not always acted "as if" they were maximizing utility. The hypothesis of decision making based on emotional pattern recognition is grounded on direct and indirect observation of the operation of the brain and does fit the observable characteristics of the decision-making process, as well as the mixed pattern of outcomes.

Is the hypothesis of emotion-based pattern recognition falsifiable? If it produces both good and bad outcomes, how could we prove it was not in operation? By specifying the characteristics of the decision-making process, we can propose both historical checks on the hypothesis and "thought experiments" that could confirm or disconfirm the hypothesis. The argument hinges on early, rapid decision making based on past emotional experience. The process yields a decision that avoids policies associated with bad emotional experiences, and the reverse. One can search for cases in which decisions did not have those characteristics, and then see if the decisions taken did or did not have the predicted characteristic. In a large-N study, one could try to encode the most recent past experiences large enough to create mass emotional experiences to test the hypothesis of the emotional force of past experience with regard to issues other than war termination or alliances. One could also try to encode decision-making processes along the dimension of deliberation versus celerity. A system of checks and balances, such as that found in the United States, would tend, on average, to make it difficult to make rapid decisions in a crisis. An autocratic system would, on average, tend toward more rapid decision making. A parliamentary system would fall somewhere in between.

Thought experiments are also possible. Emotional experiences, in this argument, are associated with the arousal of the ANS. The state of bodily arousal can be monitored. We could, in principle, wire up decisionmakers and monitor bodily reactions such as heart rate and test their blood or urine to measure endocrine system responses. We do this routinely with astronauts. Remote sensing technology has developed to the point where such monitoring could be done less intrusively. Studies could then be done of real-world decisionmakers to see how emotional responses did or did not correlate with decision-making time and conformity to past emotional experiences. While somewhat farfetched, thought experiments such as this might suggest less direct ways of monitoring emotional response, such as videotaping participants in real-world decision making. While not the kind of research that could be undertaken easily by graduate students, such thought experiments suggest how a research agenda executed by other kinds of analysts could be developed to explore the hypotheses raised in this book.

Chapter Three

Status, Testosterone, and Dominance

THE ASSERTION THAT human beings are naturally motivated to pursue status, and that this pursuit of status, honor, and prestige affects the behavior of states, is at least as old as Thucydides but remains a perennial source of debate. Everyday observation suggests that political leaders often talk and write about international politics in ways that appear to reveal a steady interest in these issues. In the study of international relations, it is the observation of European diplomatic historians that status issues, particularly local status issues, were central to questions of peace and war in the eighteenth and nineteenth centuries. The long peace in Europe in the nineteenth century occurred despite the fact that the distribution of material power was about the same as it had been in the war-prone eighteenth century. The peace was in part the result of the acceptance of a set of rules known collectively as the Concert of Europe system. As Paul Schroeder has written, there was one paramount rule to be observed in that system if big wars were to be avoided: "Above all, direct challenges and confrontations between individual great powers had to be avoided at almost any cost, mainly by referring the quarrel to the decision of the Concert. The first and great commandment of the Concert was, 'Thou shalt not threaten or humiliate another great power.'"[1]

Game theoreticians have demonstrated that the desire, not to do well, but to do better than a rival can impede the emergence of cooperative strategies, and statistical analyses have shown that discrepancies between the material national power and the diplomatic status accorded to a state increase the likelihood that it will be engaged in war.[2] One economist has shown that in business organizations, executives display a willingness to take jobs in small firms, and to accept lower salaries than they could receive in big firms, in return for a higher position. People are willing to pay money for local status, to be a bigger fish in a smaller pond. Robert Frank, in his book *Choosing the Right Pond*, discusses the reasons that people seek status, and the ways in which they elicit it. He writes that there is

> evidence suggesting that we come into the world equipped with a nervous system that worries about rank. Something inherent in our biological makeup motivates us to try to improve, or at least maintain, our standing against those with whom we compete for important positional resources. A critical feature

of this motivating mechanism, often too little emphasized, is that it is much more responsive to local than to global comparisons. Negative feelings are much more strongly evoked by adverse comparisons with our immediate associates than by those with people who are distant in place or time.[3]

On the other hand, if status is defined in terms of differences in access to available resources such as food, mates, or other material assets, behavior (as opposed to rhetoric) that is clearly driven by the pursuit of honor or status can be hard to identify and distinguish from behavior driven by the simple pursuit of greater amounts of material gains. If I pursue status to get more money, why not simply say that I am interested in more money? Why drag status into the argument? Consistent with this approach, Robert Powell has shown, in the abstract, that if conditions are such that money or power can be stored up, and if early success in a competition gives someone an edge relative to a rival that he or she can exploit to build up bigger and bigger leads thereafter, then people will have to concern themselves with getting small relative gains over rivals, not because they care about being ahead, but because, under these circumstances, getting the most possible stuff in the long term can be done only by getting ahead of a rival early in the game.[4] This does not prove that states do not engage in status-seeking behavior for the sake of status alone, but it suggests that some such behavior could also be explained without reference to a desire for status itself. Barry O'Neill also uses a formal approach to show how a concern for status could be the result of certain conditions even when players have perfect information about each other's preferences.[5]

What about forms of conflict that seem to be "obviously" about status? A duel with deadly weapons appears to be about status and status only. No money or power is gained in the duel, and lives may be lost. All that is established by the willingness to duel is that I am a man of honor, and better than men who will not duel. Social scientists who have studied dueling, however, have developed arguments that show that if the actual risk of death in a duel is small and the social rewards of being a "man of honor" are large, even dueling could be explained by the simple desire to maximize utility.[6] This perspective is partly undermined by the observed fact that in Wilhelmine Germany, duels were conducted with modern automatic pistols and multiple exchanges of fire, precisely to make the chances of death high. In that environment, men such as Alfred von Kiderlen-Wächter fought three duels and became secretary of state for foreign affairs for Germany.[7]

This chapter will take a somewhat different approach. Instead of looking at status only as a static relationship in which one person *has* a position of superiority or inferiority to another, this argument will focus on the rewards associated with the dynamic process of *attaining* higher status by means of interpersonal struggles in general. Perhaps status matters, not because of what we get after we win, but because we enjoy the *process* of beating people. To take a homely example, if I am driving and someone cuts in ahead of me, perhaps I enjoy passing and cutting sharply in front of him or her, not because it makes me better off or gets me where I want to go any sooner, and not because this kind of reckless driving is not costly (I may get a ticket, have an accident, or become a victim of road rage), but because I enjoy the act of putting my challenger back in his or her place.

Specifically, this chapter will focus on what is known about how and why people have different reactions to challengers, and why some people are more inclined to react to a challenge by punishing the challenger. In experimental psychology, nonhuman primate and human anthropology, this is called dominant behavior. Understanding the subjective rewards associated with the process of *achieving* a position of relative superiority, rather than looking only at the rewards associated with *having* a position of superiority, helps us make sense of status-related human behavior. The chapter will refer to a set of empirical studies to make the argument that, for reasons linked to human evolutionary history, some states might engage in dominance-seeking behavior even when it is not in their interest to do so. The steps in the argument will be as follows:

1. Within human populations, there are variations across individuals in the base levels of circulating testosterone in the bloodstream, and these differences in base rates are stable over periods of time measured in years. There is evidence that these differences in levels are affected by genetic inheritance.

2. Higher base levels of testosterone are found among high-status males engaged in successful social struggles for status, relative to high-status males not engaged in a struggle to achieve or maintain high status, in human and nonhuman primate populations. These struggles for social status are not the same as aggression but rather take the form of reacting to challenges by punishing the challenger. This has been termed dominant behavior. Higher testosterone both causes and is caused by dominant behavior.

3. People with different base levels of testosterone can be socially selected or are self-selected into different social groups.

4. There is evidence and argumentation that groups of high-testosterone individuals in unstable social hierarchies tend to act in ways that elevate their circulating testosterone levels, such that variations in average testosterone levels across members of high- and low-testosterone *groups* is greater than variations across *individuals* not selected into such groups. This is consistent with the observation that high-status males engaged in social struggle have elevated testosterone levels relative to high-status males in stable social hierarchies. Hence, members of high-testosterone groups that have not established a stable

status hierarchy are even more likely than isolated high-testosterone individuals to engage in dominant behavior.

5. Successful dominant behavior, physical or intellectual, results in increases in the testosterone levels of individuals, relative to their base levels of testosterone, and is associated with a positive shift in subjective state of mind. *There is an internal, subjective payoff associated with successful dominant behavior, independent of the external rewards or costs.* Following the model developed by the economist Tibor Scitovsky, which shows how a dynamic process that has positive internal payoffs may lead to excessive consumption, the argument will be made that the rewards associated with successful dominant behavior may lead to excessive dominant behavior.

6. Groups of people with high base levels of testosterone who live in an unstable status hierarchy will have a predisposition initially to engage in dominant behavior and, if they are successful, will tend to become engaged in self-reinforcing cycles of social competition, beyond the point that would be justified by external rewards, until such time as they meet with defeat. Hence, if selection mechanisms operate to create state elites that are composed of groups of high-testosterone individuals, if there are no internal institutional checks on their dominant behavior in international politics, and if the international environment is initially permissive, these states will tend to engage in the international pursuit of dominance in ways that would not be predicted by external incentives and a standard economic utility maximization model that assumes that war is a purely costly activity.

In plain language, some people, under specified conditions, are more likely to fight when challenged. Subjectively, they get satisfaction from subduing challengers, apart from the rewards that others give to them. They will emerge from one victory in a status competition even more likely to engage in another competition, rather than remain content with what they have gained. Such people will tend to be high-testosterone men who are members of groups of high-testosterone men existing in unstable status hierarchies.

Behavior and Testosterone

Are there differences in behavior associated with the average differences in levels of testosterone? One way to answer this question is to analyze evolutionary history and the process of sexual selection. Charles Darwin is associated with the idea of natural selection as the driver of biological evolution. Natural selection is usually understood as a process that will favor some species and some variations within species. Over long periods of time, those species will survive and reproduce in ways that displace others. The struggle is against nature—other species, the climate, the prevailing source of food, parasites. Natural selection shapes the evolution of all species, including humans. That much is generally acknowledged. But in the work by Darwin that spoke directly to the human condition, he did not focus on natural selection, but on sexual selection. The full title of that book is, of course, *The Descent of Man, and Selection in Relation to Sex*. Sexual selection, the competition within a species for mates and for reproductive success more generally, was, for Darwin, a powerful mechanism for shaping species that was distinguishable from natural selection in its operation and in the biological structures it shaped. Organisms did not only struggle against nature, or compete with other species for space in environmental niches, they also struggled against other members of their own species. In particular, the males of species competed for access to females, or, more specifically, to the genetic material produced by females, for the purpose of reproduction. Since sperm are smaller and more mobile than ova, sperm tended to seek ova rather than the other way around. Hence, there was, according to Darwin, a reproductive advantage for simple male organisms that were better able than other males of the same species to place their sperm close to the available ova.[8] Males that were able to get to females for mating before other males would have an advantage in the sexual competition with other males. This tended over time to select for males that were more mobile, and better able to physically displace other males. If it happened that the initial assumptions about sperm transportability and reproductive advantage were not valid, and that the females of some species were more mobile than the males, sexual selection would operate on the females. Empirically, Darwin observed, the male of species had been more affected.[9]

This competition among males would have other aspects. The males that could better exclude other males from the company of females or attract the attention of females would also have a reproductive advantage. There would be some cases in which natural selection and sexual selection would tend in the same direction. Darwin did not have an adequate explanation for why traits that emerged in the males through sexual selection would not also be transmitted to females, but he did note the importance of male sexual organs and secondary sexual characteristics. Clearly, only males inherited testicles, and so there was some reason to suspect that testicles and their products might be the vehicle by means of which the characteristics produced by sexual selection operated in males. If sexual selection gave males more muscle mass or gaudier displays, for example, it would be logical that those traits would not be passed on to females if they were associated with male sexual organs. Again, empirically he noted that there were differences in males and females in their secondary sexual characteristics, and he argued that those traits emerged from sexual selection and could reliably be distinguished from the product of natural selection, or, as he put it, "the struggle for life." These traits were those associated with social competition within species, "the weapons of offense and the means of defense possessed by the males for fighting with and driving away their rivals—their courage and pugnacity," and their ornamentation.[10] Across mammals, he noted that the operation of "The Law of Battle" seemed more important than the competition in male ornamentation found in birds, for example, and that the traits associated with social competition among male mammals did not emerge if the males were castrated before maturity. This, he thought, supported the argument that these traits useful in intraspecies male competition were closely linked to male reproductive activity and the activities of the testes. He then concluded that "Man is the rival of other men; he delights in competition, and this leads to ambition."[11]

Have Darwin's inferences about the biological origins of human male competitiveness, drawn from what he could observe, been confirmed? The current scientific consensus is that Darwin was correct in identifying sexual competition as a major force in nonhuman evolutionary history, though there is a semantic argument about the extent to which it is proper to refer to sexual selection as somehow not "natural" selection.[12] What of the role of the gonads, castration, and testosterone? In brief, a great deal has been done to analyze how testosterone functions to regulate animal behavior, but much remains unclear about testosterone and human behavior. Fetuses, male or female, exposed to testosterone during gestation, display more aggressive patterns of behavior after birth because the testosterone induces the production of testosterone-sensitive neural circuits that are activated after birth, even if males are castrated after birth. Testosterone produced in the gonads affects testosterone receptors widely scattered in the brain and in the central nervous system and regulates behavior by activating complexes associated with those receptors. Those complexes then produce proteins that affect the functions of other cells in the body. Testosterone also acts on other cells that do not have receptors and regulates their activity directly.[13] The issue of testosterone receptors is significant because the number of receptors in an organism may affect its response to the levels of a hormone if receptors have an intermediate role in regulating behavior. In other words, it is not only the level of testosterone that may affect behavior: the number of testosterone receptors may also matter. An organism with lower levels of testosterone but more receptors may behave the same way as an organism with higher levels of testosterone but lower numbers of receptors. To make the issue more complex, if levels of a hormone go up and stay up in a given organism, the number of receptors for that hormone may go down during its life span, in turn affecting how levels of a given hormone affect behavior.[14] Thus, testosterone may play an important role in regulating behavior, but absolute differences in the levels of testosterone in an animal, by themselves , may not predict behavior if animals have differing numbers of receptors, and so have differing levels of sensitivity to testosterone.

In terms of behavior, it has been well established that variations in testosterone levels in animals are reliably associated with variations in levels of aggressive behavior. A 1996 review of the literature on male hormones and their effect on behavior sums up what is called "a wealth of data" on male hormones and lower animal behavior by stating that "the most compelling argument can be made for a role of androgens in sexual behavior, aggression, and, to some extent, social rank."[15]

What of the behavior of higher animals, such as nonhuman primates? Here, again, the relationship between testosterone and aggression has repeatedly been observed. Cynomolgous monkeys (macaques) have been chosen as subjects in studies of testosterone and aggression because they have highly ritualized patterns of aggression and conflict that make it easy clearly to identify when aggression is occurring. When male macaques were injected with weight-adjusted doses of testosterone proprionate, there was a clear increase in contact and noncontact aggression, and less affiliative behavior (e.g., grooming of other animals), relative to pre-injection behavior and to a control group that did not receive any testosterone injections. The average results, however, masked interesting variations. The social status of the male macaques was assessed before the injections began. Low-ranking macaques displayed more aggressive behavior after the injections, but males who had established themselves as high in status before the injections displayed increases in their aggressive behavior three time the size of the increases of the subordinate males. The meek became more aggressive, but the high-status males increased their aggressiveness even more, increasing the gap between the two. Interestingly, postinjection behavior also increased the average amount of submissive behavior. In response to the increases in aggressive behavior, all the macaques responded by engaging in more submissive behavior. The subordinate macaques, however, displayed increases in submissive behavior eight time the increases displayed by the high-status males.[16] Again, more testosterone magnified the differences between the two groups.

In another study, testosterone levels by themselves were found not to be good predictors of macaque social status. Body weight was the best predictor of which males would emerge as high-status males.[17] But increases in testosterone did appear to reinforce existing status hierarchies. In yet another study, testosterone levels in macaques did not predict status in pairs of macaques, but such levels rose in macaques after they had engaged in successful social conflicts with other macaques. Testosterone increases, in this case, were the result, not the predictor, of successful status competition.[18]

The controversy, now as in Darwin's time, concerns the extent to which arguments about nonhuman evolutionary dynamics can be used to explain human behavior. The same study that noted the clear relation of testosterone to aggression in animals also noted that "in contrast to the wealth of data suggesting the critical role of androgens in a variety of behaviors in lower animals, relatively little is known about the behavioral effects of androgens in humans."[19] Some of the more prolific students of testosterone and human behavior, Alan Booth and Allan Mazur, have performed many experiments over a decade, and have repeatedly observed correlations between testosterone surges following successful social competition, that are consistent with the observation of the testosterone surges in analogous circumstances in macaques noted above. Booth and Mazur also have observed correlations between base levels of testosterone and dominance-related behavior. They argue that while testosterone variations explain only a small part of the variation in some behaviors, this may be the result of the fact that those behaviors are low-frequency events and that testosterone plays a more complex role in affecting behavior than earlier thought. Other scientists reviewing the body of literature generated by Booth and Mazur claim that there is little or no relationship between adult testosterone levels in humans and dominance-related behavior.[20] The implication of these contrary analyses is that variations in dominance or aggressive behavior are largely social or cultural in origin. What are we to make of this?

One way to begin is by noting that men and women have clearly different levels of testosterone and do display differing levels of competitive behavior. Men and women also clearly live in societies that shape the way in which they behave in ways that may be independent of biological differences. Careful and replicated observations of human behavior, across a number of varying cultural settings, are available that suggest that human males engage in open and direct social competition with each other more often than do human females. The argument that this variation in behavior is the result of social conventions is weakened by the fact that social conventions vary considerably across space and time and from culture to culture, but the sexual differences in competitive behavior remain constant.

The Kiryat Yedidim kibbutz was founded in what was then British-controlled Palestine in 1920, with an explicit agenda of liberating women from household work so that they could become the full social equals of men. Women and men were given the same jobs on the kibbutz.

From birth, boys and girls were raised together in the isolated kibbutz environment, and played, ate, slept, showered, and toilet-trained together. They were given the same toys to play with. All play was structured by the teachers to be gender-neutral. Observed in 1951, the children still displayed sex-differentiated behavior, with boys gravitating toward play that required strength and strenuous activity. Girls played with toys less and engaged in fantasy role-playing more. Re-examined again by the same researcher in 1969, the children, who for two generations had been raised in a gender-neutral environment that deliberately empowered women, had grown into adults who had resegregated themselves into sex-defined labor categories, with 88 percent of the women working in child-care, education, and services, and men working in agriculture. Women had not entered into governance positions in significant numbers. Only 2 percent of the service governance committees were headed by women, for example. About two-thirds of the women did not participate in any governance-related activity at all.[21] The same findings were reported by an independent study of gender behavior in other kibbutzes.[22]

Groups of preschool boys and groups of preschool girls were observed in urban Montreal, rural Mexico, and Stanford, California. The findings were consistent. As reported by Eleanor Maccoby: "From this early age into adulthood, a robust sex difference in the rates of direct (overt) aggression is reliably seen." This difference in levels of aggression was not displayed by isolated boys toward adults, or by isolated boys toward girls, or by girls toward boys. The difference was found when boy-boy group behavior was compared with girl-girl group behavior. "Thus, fighting is a characteristic of male-male play—better seen as a property of male dyads or groups than of individuals. Part of the male aggressiveness pattern is a greater willingness to be aroused to anger by displays of anger in others." Maccoby concluded: "One of the things boys appear to be doing in their rough-and-tumble encounters is establishing a dominance hierarchy."[23]

Was this linked to testosterone? The differences in testosterone levels in pre-adolescent boys and girls is small, but boy fetuses develop testes after the first trimester, and testosterone levels in prenatal fetuses show considerable variation, with boys having much higher levels. Prenatal exposure to testosterone activates the development of testosterone-sensitive neural networks. Since testosterone is also produced in the adrenal glands, girl fetuses also produce testosterone. In a small number of cases, these adrenal glands produce larger than average amounts of testosterone, and in childhood, the girls whose prenatal levels of testosterone were close to average boy levels also displayed a propensity for rough-and-tumble play.[24]

A naturally occurring genetic enzyme deficiency in an isolated population of villages in the Dominican Republic yielded large numbers of boys
who were born with female genitalia, yet who had normal levels of
testosterone both before and after birth. In eighteen cases that were studied, such boys were raised as girls and kept close to their mothers doing
housework. At puberty, however, with the onset of adult androgen production, seventeen of the eighteen boys reversed their self-identification
along many dimensions, and sixteen displayed male behavior along all
dimensions, including aggressiveness.[25]

Across all societies about which we have data, men commit far more
violent crime than do women. Statistics of homicide committed against
unrelated individuals of the same sex show that male rates were some
eight hundred times higher than female rates in Chicago in the 1970s and
1980s, and thirty to fifty times higher in England and Canada. The most
common occasion for these homicides is what is referred to as the "trivial altercation"—slight real or imagined affronts to the status of males.
Further statistical analysis linked this human behavior to broader patterns of mammalian reproductive patterns. Studies of primates and other
large mammals showed that variations in the number of females that
male mammals impregnated varied with male-female body-length ratios.
When males and females were the same size, monogamous relations were
the rule. The bigger the males were relative to females, the more frequent
polygynous behavior (one male with many female mates) became, and
the more frequent male-male conflict over females became. Evolutionary
arguments have been advanced to explain these observable facts. When
males sired many children by many females, they played a smaller role in
childrearing. Risk-acceptant behavior and conflict with other males for
access to females was a more effective male strategy to ensure reproductive success than risk-avoidant behavior. When males had fewer children,
they had an evolutionary stake in avoiding conflict so that they could
contribute to the survival of their fewer children. Whatever the evolutionary case may be, it is possible to assess the correlates of human body-
size ratios. "It is clear where the human animal fits into this comparative
scheme. The difference in male and female size . . . suggests that we
evolved under conditions of slight effective polygyny: the most prolific
fathers had more children than the most prolific mothers."[26] This is associated with the large differences in risk-acceptant behavior found in
human males relative to human females, and the shorter life expectancy
for males associated with risk taking.

Finally, simulations of international relations behavior inadvertently
discovered that male-male dyads, given roles in fictitious interstate dis-
putes, were far more likely to engage in simulated arms-racing behavior
than female-female dyads.[27]

Variations in Behavior and Base Testosterone Levels among Males

Males and females differ in their levels of testosterone and their behavior, but there are also smaller differences within male and female populations with regard to testosterone. Efforts to understand the relationship of these more subtle differences within genders across individuals, as opposed to groups, in testosterone levels and behavior have tended to focus on males. A host of problems have complicated that study. Studies of variations in basal testosterone levels and behavior must be structured to take into account the natural daily variations in male testosterone production.[28] In the morning, in particular, testosterone levels are high and fluctuate quickly. Testosterone levels are affected by eating and fasting, body weight, and age, and all of these are difficult to control for in many human and nonhuman populations.[29]

Studies of testosterone and status in baboon populations in the wild, for example, carefully sampled males at the same time every day and found that there was no clear association between basal testosterone levels and status in baboon troops that had stable social hierarchies. In one troop that did not have a stable status hierarchy, however, the high-status males were always dealing with challenges and did have elevated basal testosterone levels. Interestingly, in all troops, high-status baboons reacted to stressors in the environment with transient increases in testosterone levels, while low-status males reacted to stressors with transient decreases in testosterone.[30] Similar observations have also been made of macaque monkeys in captivity. Variations in the testosterone levels of macaques kept in isolation did not predict what status level they would achieve when placed into a group.[31] No correlation was found between status and basal testosterone levels in macaque dyads in general, but the higher-status monkey in macaque monkey dyads marked by "contested domination" or "dominance reversals" did display elevated testosterone levels. The authors concluded that "higher testosterone concentration corresponded to social dominance in subjects dominant as the result of a contest, rather than a consequence of high relative rank."[32] *Achieving* dominance, as opposed to *having* high status, elevated testosterone.

Again, what about variations in testosterone in human males? Small-scale studies hinted at the relationship, not between status and testosterone, but between activities associated with social contestation and testosterone. One group of five medical doctors on a boat had their blood chemistry monitored daily. Their behavior was assessed covertly by three women doctors on the boat. A correlation between testosterone and dominance/aggression rank was noted.[33] This study, however, did not distinguish between achieved social status and levels of status-seeking activity. Other small studies did examine the possible connection between testosterone and social contestation. Trial lawyers are not particularly high status relative to other lawyers, but they do engage in much more combative, high-stakes social contestation than nontrial lawyers. One small sample found that male trial lawyers tended to have higher testosterone levels than male nontrial lawyers, and radically higher levels compared with female lawyers.[34]

Large-scale studies that included assays of basal testosterone levels were performed by the United States Armed Forces. In studies that were conducted to ascertain the possible effects of exposure to Agent Orange in the Vietnam War, 4,500 army veterans and a control group of nonveterans received medical examinations. An air force study sampled 1,800 respondents, along with a control group. The air force survey tracked the respondents over time. The examinations included tests to ascertain testosterone levels. The study showed that an individual's basal testosterone levels tended to be stable over a period of five to six years, controlling for age and time of day, and genetically based, though variations in testosterone levels were also associated with environmental factors. The average age of the men surveyed in the army survey was thirty-eight years. The range in the variation in testosterone levels was about 15 percent, with the lowest score being 625 nanograms per deciliter and the highest 725.[35]

When the data was examined more closely, it revealed heterogeneity in testosterone levels associated with marital status. In both the army and air force studies, for example, divorced men had testosterone levels about 10 percent higher than stably married men. The years surrounding the year of divorce showed elevations in testosterone production, relative to other periods of time.[36] This also suggests that people in contested social settings had elevated testosterone levels. Again, socioeconomic status and testosterone levels did not correlate, except negatively. The army survey asked respondents to identify their profession by standard census categories, and testosterone levels negatively correlated with economic status: men with higher testosterone tended to hold lower-status jobs, although the effect was modest. Other studies with smaller samples showed that football players and actors had higher testosterone levels than priests. Still another study, in contrast, showed that higher levels of testosterone in women were positively associated with higher occupational achievement. Women lawyers, for example, had higher testosterone levels than nurses or teachers.[37]

The genetic factors affecting basal levels of testosterone circulating in the blood are complex and include testosterone production, but also testosterone clearance from the blood, which prevents a steady buildup of circulating testosterone. In addition, there are factors that affect the levels of free, as opposed to bound, testosterone in the blood. Early studies suggested that 0.8 of the variation in testosterone production was heritable, but only 0.04 of the clearance rate was, so that only 0.3 of the variation in overall circulating levels of testosterone was heritable. The best study of 160 twin pairs, both mono- and dizygotic, and their parents showed that among adolescent boys and their fathers, 66 percent of the variation in testosterone was heritable, though fathers and sons had very different levels of testosterone at any given moment in time due to life-cycle factors. The heritability of testosterone levels from mother to daughter was weaker.[38]

In short, while there are small differences in the levels of testosterone found in human male populations, they are not clearly associated with broad categories of social status. The available data does suggest that variations in testosterone levels across the female-male divide and among men may be associated with levels of ongoing social contestation.

All this is suggestive, but far from conclusive. If testosterone is not directly linked with status, is it linked to other behavior that might indirectly be connected to status? For example, might it be the cause of increased aggressiveness, which could, in some social settings, yield higher status, but in other settings be linked to low status? At first, researchers attempted to find links between testosterone and criminal violence, but no clear relationship was found there. Biologists who studied criminal aggression, for example, were careful to note that levels of testosterone varied widely in the noncriminal male population, without producing variations in the display of violent crime. They also noted that "testosterone is usually connected with verbal aggression, masculinity and dominant tendencies (leadership). . . . So having high levels of testosterone can be a good thing. Still, we have found very high levels of CSF [cerebrospinal fluid] free testosterone among habitually violent antisocial young adults."[39] So testosterone was not easily linked to aggression, perhaps because the display of aggression could be affected by other factors, such as the availability of socially approved outlets for behavior that might, in less favorable settings, turn into aggression. The availability of those outlets could vary widely by social status and social setting.

This led researchers to shift the focus from the study of testosterone and aggression to testosterone and dominant behavior. What is dominant behavior? Alan Mazur distinguished dominant behavior from aggression. Dominant behavior seeks to "enhance one's status over other people. Sometimes dominant behavior is aggressive, its apparent intent to inflict harm on another person, but often dominance is expressed nonaggressively." Mazur noted that past studies had failed to find clear links between high levels of testosterone and aggressive behavior in prison populations, but they had found that dominant but nonaggressive males in prison did have high levels of testosterone.[40] Dominant behavior

is often manifested when there is a challenge or provocation that threat-
ens the status of the subject. The idea that testosterone levels were linked
not to status or aggression, but to levels of response to challenges, is consistent with the observations of baboons and macaques noted above,
which highlighted the association of elevated testosterone levels and responses, not to status, but to *status challenges*. It is also consistent with
Maccoby's observation, noted above, that boys were more likely to be
aroused to anger by displays of anger than were girls.

Are variations in dominant behavior linked to variations in testosterone levels? Nature gives us a natural experiment in testosterone variations and behavior in the form of male puberty. There are restrictions on
what one can do to artificially increase testosterone in males. One way to
accomplish the same thing naturally is to observe boys before and after
puberty, which produces a large natural testosterone surge. A Swedish
study studied fifty-eight boys before and after puberty, in grade six, before puberty, and grade nine, after puberty. Factors other than testosterone levels that might affect behavior, such as child-rearing practices
and personality factors, were assayed by means of interviews and self-
reporting, so that they could be controlled for. Controlling for these factors, there was some correlation between testosterone levels and simple
aggressive behavior, defined as engaging in fights or admiring students
who were fighters. Stronger, however, was the link between testosterone
levels and fighting *in response to provocations*, including perceived un-
fair treatment. Specifically, there was a weak correlation between low
frustration tolerance and aggression in grade six, and a strong correlation in grade nine, after puberty had led to an increase in testosterone
levels. In summary, the "results suggest that a high level of testosterone
in puberty made boys more impatient and irritable, which in turn increased their readiness to engage in aggressive behavior of the unpro-
voked and destructive kind."[41]

While interesting, this kind of study did not control for other factors.
Increases in testosterone at puberty also increase muscle mass. Greater
strength may give young men more ability to engage in physical competition, even if their personalities are not affected by testosterone. Adults
have very different social roles than do adolescent boys, and so variations in testosterone that are important in teenagers might not be important in adult populations. The study of testosterone and human behavior came down to the question of how to control more effectively for
the other factors affecting testosterone and affecting behavior. One
metasurvey of initial studies on testosterone and behavior by John
Archer showed that there was at best a weak relation between variations in male testosterone levels and crime or with self-reports about aggressive behavior.[42] This survey of earlier studies, however, was marred

by the absence of controls in earlier studies. These included environmental factors that affected testosterone levels. The problem of controlling for these factors was aggravated by methodological difficulties.
When testosterone could be measured only by taking blood samples,
testosterone levels were measured when subjects could have their blood
drawn, and were willing to have their blood drawn, not at the time
when they were engaged in aggressive behavior. Early testosterone sur-
veys were suspect, for example, because they assayed testosterone levels
of violent criminals in prison, awaiting trial. Their testosterone levels
were lower relative to available samples drawn from the general population. However, there was reason to suppose that environmental factors, such as being arrested and put in prison, would lead to depressed
testosterone production. Men examined in prison might have lower levels of testosterone, but at the time they were at liberty and faced with
the opportunity for aggression, they may have had very high levels of
testosterone. Subsequent work, aided by the advent of saliva tests for
testosterone levels that were easier to administer than blood tests, allowed researchers to assay testosterone closer to the points in time when
men committed aggressive acts, or not.

Ideally, one would want to control for all of the other factors that affected dominant behavior, then vary testosterone levels, and then study
the impact on dominant behavior of variations in testosterone. One way
that gets close to that ideal is to track variations in testosterone levels in
adult male individuals over shorter periods of time. Studying variations
in testosterone in one male over short periods of time would hold constant the effect of physical strength, as well as that of past personal experiences, social status, and so forth. Any measured variations in testosterone levels could then more reliably be associated with variations in
behavior. Saliva tests made it possible to do multiple tests of testosterone
across short periods of time. Using this method, the testosterone of
twenty-eight judo fighters in a tournament was assayed, before and after
each fighter engaged in his match. All matches took place within three
hours of each other. The fights were videotaped and later shown to observers who were given a set of rules that allowed them to code the
behavior of the fighters in terms of number of threats made, attacks conducted, and the duration of "fighting" defined as struggling without
achieving an advantage, as well as the frequency of "dominance," defined as gaining an advantage in the fight. There were strong correlations
(0.4–0.5) between prematch testosterone levels and the number of
threats and attacks made, and the length of time that fighters persisted in
fighting. The correlation between these forms of behavior and postmatch
testosterone levels was significant, but not as strong. The researchers
concluded that their findings did not show that elevated testosterone by

itself produced aggression, but that, in competitive settings, it predisposed individuals toward aggressive behavior.[43]

The rise in the use of synthetic testosterone by weight trainers and athletes to build muscle mass opened the way for another kind of carefully controlled study. Steroid use initially led to anecdotal reports of aggressive behavior—so-called roid rage. However, the people who chose to use steroids might already have been predisposed to risk taking and aggressive behavior. They might have been taking other drugs. Hence, the anecdotal reports were not evidence that synthetic male hormones by themselves produced changes in behavior. Concern about the use of steroids, however, led to laboratory studies. These studies are as close as one is likely to get to the ideal test of the impact of testosterone on behavior, with all other variables held constant. In a study published in 1995, eight healthy men were given increasing doses of synthetic testosterone, interspersed with doses of placebos. The amounts of testosterone administered were much lower than weight trainers had reported using in unsupervised settings. Urine tests were administered to ensure that the men did not take any other drugs while not in the lab. Behavior was tested by giving the subjects a computer game to play. The subjects were told that their computers were linked to another human player. The test, they were told, was a measure of reaction times. In fact, the players were playing against a computer program, and what was being tested was their willingness to punish an adversary in response to provocations. The players were given two buttons: the "A" button, if pushed, gave the player a monetary reward; the "B" button took money away from the (fictitious) opponent without giving the human player any additional monetary reward. The computer program was set up so that the fictitious opponent occasionally took points away from the human player. This constituted the provocation. The number of times the "B" button was pushed was counted at the beginning of the experiment to establish a baseline. Then, testosterone was administered. The frequency of "B" button pushes went up, in the aggregate, from 89 to 203 button pushes, but this masked some sharp individual variations. One individual increased his "B" button pushes 600 percent. The smallest increase was 50 percent.[44]

In a study published in 2000, fifty-six men varying in age from twenty to fifty, some of whom were weight lifters, some of whom were not, were given constant doses of testosterone over a period of six weeks. A control group was given placebos. Behavior was tested by means of the same computer program, but the subjects also were given personality tests and kept diaries, as did their significant others. The subjects who received testosterone doses displayed increases in observed and reported manic personality traits, and aggressiveness, as measured by the computer program. But the effects were highly variable, as was the case in the earlier study. Some men displayed small increases in dominant behavior. On the other hand, one man had to be removed from the study because his behavior in reaction to injected testosterone was so severe as to cause alarm.[45]

These studies do seem to suggest that in natural and laboratory settings, increases in the levels of circulating testosterone do increase the predisposition toward the display of dominant behavior. This, of course, does not mean that testosterone by itself causes increases in dominant behavior or aggression. Conditions in the environment must also be conducive to the increased display of these forms of behavior. Individuals reacted in different ways to increases in testosterone levels. Internal conditions also matter, since other changes in body chemistry can affect levels of aggression. Low levels of serotonin and high levels of norepinephrine have been linked to aggressive behavior in mice and are associated with depression and low social status.[46] Still, on average and other things equal, increases in testosterone levels in individuals do seem to be linked with increases in dominant behavior.

Testosterone and Men in Groups

When and why should we expect men with higher levels of testosterone to emerge in positions of political leadership, where their characteristics might be of some interest to students of decision making in international relations? The larger studies of military veterans, after all, suggested that higher basal levels of testosterone correlated with lower socioeconomic levels, and that trial lawyers, whose social status was lower than that of other lawyers, had higher testosterone levels. If higher levels of testosterone produce more dominant behavior, that does not mean that society will reward people with such behavior. In addition, basal levels of testosterone are not the same as testosterone levels of individuals at a given moment in time. The laboratory studies of men playing against computers and the studies of judo fighters tend to focus on men as individuals in one-on-one settings. Human beings usually function in complex social settings, not one-on-one. The ways in which people behave in response to testosterone levels could be reinforced by or attenuated by social influences. What can we say about the way in which testosterone levels, social setting, and behavior interact?

There are many ways in which one could go about answering this question. One way is to ask under what circumstances would social settings reinforce the tendency of elevated testosterone levels to produce dominant behavior, defined as punishing challengers. Logically, if individuals with higher than average levels of testosterone congregated, by choice or because of external pressures, the implication would be that men with individual predispositions to engage in dominant behavior, when placed among other high-testosterone men, would perceive the behavior of their companions as challenges. This would lead to more dominant behavior in response, which would then trigger more responses, and so on. This cycle of challenge and response would tend to keep testosterone levels high, and levels of dominant behavior high. Even without an initial population of high-testosterone males, if set in motion, this cycle of interaction could drive up levels of dominant behavior and keep them high.

What might initially produce a congregation of high-testosterone males? One researcher hypothesized that differences in testosterone levels might lead men with high levels of testosterone to collect in some occupations: "Because testosterone is an archaic hormone, present in many animals and even plants, there is no reason to expect it to be closely related to modern human occupations. However, behavioral and cognitive correlates of testosterone might make a person better suited to one occupation or another. In particular, anti-social and violent tendencies could lead to behavior and occupational levels that are more appropriate for some occupations than others."[47]

In the survey of Vietnam vets, a weak correlation was found between higher levels of testosterone and blue-collar, low-status jobs, jobs that men prone to antisocial behavior might gravitate toward or be forced to take. But some jobs might give advantages to people who were prone to engage in dominant behavior. Higher levels of testosterone also were associated with persistence in a task, as was the case with the judo fighters. Trial lawyers are regularly engaged in face-to-face struggles with hostile lawyers and must often manage clients who are criminals. One interview with a physically large trial lawyer suggested that this made testosterone an asset for trial lawyers. In court, appearing before the bench with an opposing trial lawyer, the lawyer said he "will stand close—shoulder to shoulder—so he feels my physical presence in the courtroom, feels my whole being . . . [because] . . . there is a subconscious knowledge between animals, including human animals, as to who is superior and who can win." Less subjectively, saliva tests were administered to ninety-two lawyers, male and female, trial lawyers and nontrial lawyers. Within each sex, the trial lawyers had testosterone levels that were, on average, 30 percent higher than those of nontrial lawyers, controlled for time of day. Note that this difference is much larger than blue-collar/white-collar differences that had been found in the study of Vietnam veterans. The largest difference in testosterone levels was between male trial lawyers and female nontrial lawyers, with the male trial lawyers having testosterone levels up to nine times as high as those of the women.[48]

Self-selection into social groups might produce local concentrations of high-testosterone men. College fraternities are organized to attract homogeneous groups of men. Three studies were conducted of college fraternities to determine whether fraternities that had been identified with the display of "rambunctious" behavior were populated with men with higher testosterone. Twelve fraternities at two universities, with a total of 240 subjects, were studied. Fraternities were selected by means of interviews with university officials and published descriptions of fraternities and were divided into "well-behaved" versus "rambunctious" fraternities. The well-behaved fraternities at one university had, on average, testosterone levels that were 15 percent lower than the rambunctious fraternities (14.3 ng/dl vs. 12.3). The rambunctious fraternities had lower grades, more parties, fewer academic awards, and fewer community projects. Two of the rambunctious fraternities were banned from campus while the test was underway. At the other university, the well-behaved fraternities had average testosterone levels about 30 percent lower than the rambunctious fraternities (10.3 vs. 14.0). The researcher's notes concerning the highest-testosterone fraternity are interesting. The notes read: "the highest [testosterone] fraternity was rough to a degree beyond rambunctiousness." The fraternity leader responded to the researcher's request that he to submit to saliva testing in return for $50 by asking his cohorts, "Anyone want to spit for a keg?" "I felt as if I had been thrown to the lions. Very good looking, pumped up. No manners. They'd walk around without shirts, belching. 'Macho meatheads' is very fitting."

The field notes describing the low-testosterone fraternity are interesting in comparison: "They talked a lot about computers and calculus. Very mild-mannered. They were nice. . . . Discussed their difficulty finding girls." "These guys were nice and cooperative. Their house was well kept."[49]

In the case of both the trial lawyers and the fraternities, groups of high-testosterone men displayed levels of testosterone that were more elevated relative to other groups of men than the variations found among individual Vietnam veterans, who constituted a large and dispersed sample of men not in day-to-day social contact with each other. There is some support for the hypothesis that groups of high-testosterone men in habitual contact with each other may drive their testosterone levels higher and keep them there, maintaining a predisposition to engage in dominant behavior.

Governments are not frat houses. But some societies do embody values that reward strong responses to perceived challenges. This means not only that men with a higher predisposition to react strongly to challenges will be rewarded, but also that, as these men interact with each other, a cycle of reinforcing behavior would emerge that could explain what has

been referred to as local "cultures of honor" that are marked by high levels of aggression that are provoked and sustained by perceived affronts
among habitually interacting males. The differences in behavior of men
coming from the northern and southwestern areas of the United States
has been explained in terms of the presence or absence of a culture of
honor, and the variations in culture have been speculatively explained on
the basis of initial differences in the major economic activities. Cattle
herding, the predation associated with it, and the need always to defend
against predation, the argument goes, created a culture in which challenges had to be taken seriously lest the perception of weakness emerge.[50]
Once established, the culture might survive its initial economic origins
because of institutions that inculcated and reinforced these patterns of
behavior. The biological argument suggests that, in addition to those cultural factors, the ways in which members of such cultures would tend to
interact with each other would produce elevated testosterone levels that
would also create a self-sustaining cycle, producing individuals who are
prone to punish challengers.

Testosterone and the Rewards of Dominant Behavior

One of the clearest, most often repeated experimental finding in the field
of testosterone-related behavioral research is that successful engagement
in social competition, when the victory is perceived as a deserved victory
and not the result of chance, is accompanied by elevated testosterone
levels and a subjective state of well-being. In a 1990 review, Theodore
Kemper cited seven independent studies that had found average elevated
levels of testosterone in males who had been successful in a social competition.[51] Many of these competitions involved physical exertion: judo,
tennis and hockey players in a match, military recruits in basic training.[52]

However, much social competition does not involve physical exertion
or openly sexual competition, and testosterone-related behavior in the
studies of physical competition might not be representative of the behavior found in other areas of competition. To investigate the possibility that
victory in nonphysical competitions might increase testosterone, competitions were arranged in laboratory settings with subjects and computers
that involved no physical exertion. One experiment included forty males,
eighteen to forty years old, in a computer-driven, reaction-time competition. "Winners" and "losers" were randomly assigned by adjusting the
feedback given to the players regarding their task performance. That is,
there was no obvious way for the subjects to tell what reaction-time responses were "naturally" superior, and so the experimenter could vary
what was judged as praiseworthy. Testosterone and cortisol levels were

monitored throughout competition. Winners, on average, displayed elevated levels of testosterone. Players who were arbitrarily assigned to the category "close winners" had even higher levels of testosterone in the immediate postcompetition period.[53] Another study examined the behavior of nine chess players in a regional chess tournament. The players were closely matched by their chess rankings. The victors displayed elevated testosterone levels, and the losers displayed depressed testosterone levels, all relative to their baseline testosterone levels. In addition, the testosterone levels of the winners surged the morning of the match, relative to the levels displayed the night before, while the losers displayed testosterone crashes the morning of the match.[54]

More detailed reviews of the findings revealed interesting specifics obscured by the average results. If winners in a competition felt that they had won because of their own good performance, or if winners *or losers* felt that they had performed better than they usually did, they experienced testosterone increases and elevated subjective moods. In experiments in which subjects were given rewards as the result, they were told, of a lottery, they did *not* experience testosterone increases. The relationship between elevated mood, the sense of a victory that was earned, and testosterone increases was striking and helped to explain the seemingly anomalous cases in which individual victors displayed depressed postmatch testosterone levels.[55]

These findings have led the researchers to hypothesize that there is a biosocial feedback loop, in which successful social competition leads to elevated testosterone levels, which primes the subject for more competition, and perhaps also for increases in sexual overtures. Losers, in the course of evolutionary history, would have had an interest in withdrawal from competitions that they were likely to lose and in which they could be seriously injured. Depressed testosterone levels would make them less predisposed for competition and would help them survive. As one study put it, "this scheme implies that testosterone serves as a non-conscious biological reinforcer, while mood serves as the consciously perceived 'explanation.'"[56] Another study suggested that there was a biological mechanism in which successful dominant behavior reinforces itself: "Thus, as an individual's testosterone level rises, he or she is assumed to become activated and increasingly willing to compete in contests for higher status. Reciprocally, the experience of winning such contests . . . is assumed to produce a rise in testosterone, or to maintain an already elevated level, sustaining the winner's readiness to enter subsequent contests. A loss of status produces a drop in testosterone."[57]

If it exists, this mechanism would have encouraged dominant behavior by creating an independent system that gave psychic rewards to successful individuals *in addition to the material reward* that they gained, and a separate set of nonconscious pressures to compete again, in addition to whatever conscious motives they had. The activity of winning status competitions, in short, would have its own rewards and compulsions. It is not only the external payoffs that mattered in determining behavior, but also the dynamic process of changing status upward.

The Testosterone and Overconsumption of Dominance

One economist concerned with what he considered to be overconsumption of material goods has developed a model of human behavior in which behavior is driven not only by the satisfaction associated with a given level of consumption, but also by upward shifts in well-being that provide an independent, subjective reinforcement of human behavior associated with the shift. Tibor Scitovsky asked what would happen if human beings experienced comfort—which he defined as the result of having an optimal level of some good, such as food—but also pleasure—which he defined as the sensation of moving toward the optimum state, either from below, as in the pleasure of eating while hungry, or from above, as when one has too much of a good thing, such as idleness. This modest, commonsense alteration of economic models of consumer behavior had major theoretical implications. Economists assume we want many scarce things, and that we want them less as we get more of them. We seek and consume the thing we want most, but when the cost of getting that thing is equal to its diminishing value to us, we stop seeking it and start seeking the thing we want next most, and so on. That is, there are limits to how much we indulge one particular desire. But what if seeking and getting the desired object is pleasurable in itself? Then we pursue the object beyond the optimum.

> If no pleasure accompanied eating, that is, if eating merely served to reduce hunger, we would expect the organism to stop eating and to start attending to its new, now highest priority need before it has eaten its fill and completely satisfied its hunger. But the opposite is true, because the process of satisfying a need is pleasurable in itself, and strengthens the force of whatever activity it is currently engaged in, causing the organism to continue whatever it is doing, often to the point of full satiation and beyond.

This overconsumption makes no sense from the standpoint of the model of rational economic behavior, Scitovsky notes, "but rational behavior as pictured by the economist and actual behavior as it is observed and explained in terms of the psychologist's motivating forces are not at all the same thing."[58] Scitovsky developed his model to explain what he saw as the overconsumption of material goods beyond the point where it gave consumers any satisfaction, hence the title of his book, *The Joyless Economy*, but he noted that it could also explain the insatiable desire for social status.[59]

Scitovsky first published his model as a hypothetical explanation of certain economic phenomena in 1976, before the work on testosterone and status competition to which we have referred had been done. The work on testosterone and successful status competition does seem to suggest that the mechanism that Scitovsky hypothesized has physical existence and is observable in human beings with regard to successful dominant behavior. Certain individuals appear to begin adult life with a greater predisposition to engage in dominant behavior. To the extent that they engage in successful social competition, they receive subjective positive feedback from engaging in dominant behavior that is above and beyond the external benefits that are associated with high status. The implication is that such individuals, and, more strongly, groups of high-testosterone men, will engage in dominant behavior and, if successful, will engage in dominant behavior past the point where it would be rational to do so from the standpoint of standard economic models.

Testosterone and Governments

All of the arguments about the relationship between testosterone and dominance in groups of males might be true but might be irrelevant to the study of international relations. Does any of this have relevance for the real world, and, in particular, the real world of international relations? Without direct assays of testosterone levels of rulers, can we say anything meaningful? Certainly, people engaged in the nonscientific study of politics have asserted that there will be political figures whose behavior is driven by an unlimited desire for social status, distinction, and honor, apart from whatever gain it might bring to their society. Abraham Lincoln described such an individual in his 1838 speech to the Young Men's Lyceum:

> It is to deny, what the history of the world tells us is true, to suppose that men of ambition and talents will not continue to spring up among us. And when they do, they will as naturally seek the gratification of their ruling passion, as others have: *so* done before them. The question is, can that gratification be found in supporting and maintaining an edifice that has been erected by others. Most certainly it cannot. Many great and good men sufficiently qualified for any task they should undertake, may ever be found, whose ambition would aspire to nothing beyond a seat in Congress, a gubernatorial or a presidential chair; *but such belong not to the family of the lion or the tribe of the eagle.*

What! Think you these places would satisfy an Alexander, a Caesar, or a Napoleon? Never! Towering genius disdains a beaten path. . . . It thirsts and burns for distinction; and if possible, it will have it, whether at the expense of emancipating slaves or enslaving freemen.[60]

Bismarck led Prussia to the domination of Germany through successive wars. Of domestic challengers to his political position, he said, "I am going my way; whoever goes with me is my friend, who goes against me is my enemy—to the point of annihilation." On another occasion, he said, "When I have an enemy in my power, I must destroy him." He referred to his "inability to stand superiors," his own "natural appetite for combat," and, to his fiancée, he confessed that "sometimes I feel like smashing windowpanes, glasses, bottles."[61] Peter Gay, who assembled this portrait of Bismarck, argued that there was a general European culture that both created and promoted men with high levels of aggressiveness.

There are many puzzles in international relations. One is whether the decision by Winston Churchill to continue the war against Nazi Germany in the period between June 1940 and July 1941 can be explained by the rational search for security. One intensive effort tried to recapture all of the information available to Churchill in that period that was relevant to the expected outcome of different strategies. The conclusion was that the best evidence suggested that continued war would lead to British defeat.[62] If this is true, there are many ways in which one could then try to explain Churchill's decision, but it may be helpful to take him at his own word. Recalling his thought early in the morning on the day he was made prime minister, soon after the British defeat in Norway and facing the German attack in France, Churchill wrote: "I cannot conceal from the reader of this truthful account that as I went to bed at about 3 a.m. I was conscious of a profound sense of relief. At last I had authority to give directions over the whole scene. I felt as if I were walking with Destiny, and that all my past life had been but preparation for this hour and this trial. . . . Therefore, although impatient for the morning, I slept soundly and had no need for cheering dreams. Facts are better than dreams."[63] Churchill, if he was telling the truth, was enjoying both his high status and the struggle for dominance. He seems clearly to have preferred retaining status and the prospect of dominance more than he valued his own life under conditions of low status.

Lincoln, Bismarck, and Churchill were exceptional individuals, and one aspect of their psychology might have been that they had high base levels of testosterone and responded strongly to their own internal variations in testosterone. We might guess the same thing was true for men like Napoleon and Douglas MacArthur from their actions and words.

But we cannot assay the testosterone levels of the dead. What can we say more generally that can be tested? In particular, since studies have shown that in the general U.S. population, high basal testosterone levels are associated with low socioeconomic status, why should we not assume that political elites will not tend to be dominated by men who behave like rowdy fraternity brothers? Even if political elites were full of high-testosterone men, there are political institutions designed to constrain individual behavior, often because the framers of political institutions were fully aware of the nonrational elements of human decision making. In a survey of many primitive societies, one author found that mechanisms for limiting the power of assertive individuals had been constructed in all of them. There will always be individuals who will engage in dominant behavior, but other people do not like to be dominated, so social mechanisms regularly appear to sanction those who too offensively engage in dominant behavior.[64]

The proper response is that some social and political institutions may constrain or weaken certain individual impulses, but others may reinforce them. In the case of testosterone and dominance behavior, are there societies and political institutions that we would expect to select for and reinforce the behavior of high-testosterone males? The answer, in theory and empirically, is that there are and have been societies and political structures that do just that.

Montesquieu noted that in aristocracies, while it is easy for the nobility to enforce laws to restrain the will of the people, "it is difficult [for the aristocrats] to restrain themselves." Thus, the nobility had to be animated by the principle of honor, and defending their honor, which would lead them into combative ways of life and into military service, and would teach them to place no value on preserving their own lives in conflicts, and to place supreme value on behaving in the manner prescribed by their rank in society.[65] In modern societies, we would expect that states governed by military or militarized elites would select for individuals who sought social distinction and did not avoid social conflict, and would reinforce those tendencies. What one can observe of nineteenth-century imperial Germany certainly suggests that the German political elite behaved in the way prescribed by Montesquieu. The culture of dueling was a mechanism for insuring that the men who controlled German foreign policy had a certain well-defined character, and a predisposition to react vigorously to challenges to status. Bismarck was not an accidental anomaly, but a representative, if overdeveloped, product of that culture.

Is this in any way linked to testosterone levels? Researchers attempting to understand regional differences in violence in the United States identified a "culture of honor" in the southern states. Southern males, subjected to insults in realistic simulations, reacted with anger far more often than northern males to the same simulated social situations. Northern males in the experiment reacted with humor to the insult 65 percent of the time. Southern males reacted with humor only 15 percent of the time.[66] When the circulating testosterone levels of the subjects were measured, southern males displayed surges in testosterone that were four times the level of southern males who were not insulted, and twice the levels of northern males who were insulted.[67]

Small groups of men, all of whom have achieved power and status, interacting with each other on a day-to-day basis in an unstable dominance hierarchy, might challenge each other, and so create the cycle of challenge and response that kept testosterone levels high in troops of baboons and college fraternities. However, some oligarchic systems have developed powerful institutional mechanisms for limiting intra-elite dominant behavior, as in the case of the modern parliamentary and the early modern party system in Great Britain, for example, which is said to have valued "sound" and loyal party members who knew their place and waited for advancement. However, in the presence of low levels of political institutionalization that constrained such elites from displaying dominant behavior, we would expect to see oligarchies display higher levels of dominant behavior internationally, relative to political systems that had strong checks on elite behavior and a political ethos that punished obvious dominant behavior.

If this is the case, a population of states run by groups of men who are prone to react to perceived challenges by punishing the challenger should see more conflict. Such systems will be prone to war as the result of "noise" in the system, garbled or ambiguous information that is perceived as a challenge and that elicits punishing behavior, leading to an escalatory process ending in war. To some extent, the absence of such governments should also predict a lower incidence of war. That is, the addition of status considerations may help events such as the outbreak of war in 1914, and explain parts of the democratic peace. Democracies will tend less to engage in dominant behavior internationally. In democratic dyads, there will tend not to be status competitions that exacerbate material disagreements. The reverse would be true in dyads involving oligarchies with low levels of political institutionalization.

Nations that initiate wars as the result of the dominant behavior of the ruling elites might tend to lose wars more often than those countries that make decisions reflecting calculations about expected outcomes. In a very rough way, we might expect democracies, therefore, to do better than oligarchies and tyrannies. The best existing statistical analyses of war initiation and victory are consistent with this hypothesis. Democracies do very well in the period 1816–1985, winning fourteen and losing only one of the wars they initiate, while anochracies win twenty-one and lose fifteen, and autocracies win twenty-one and lose fourteen. War initiators choose to go to war, and democracies seem to choose more carefully. Though this has been explained in terms of the care with which democracies treat the lives of their citizens, it might also be explained by the excessive interest of other types of regimes in status.[68] The conclusion that democracies tend to win the wars they initiate, however, is obviously fragile, given the small number of wars initiated by democracies in the data set. Small shifts in the way in which "war initiation" is coded, for example, could erase the advantage that democracies appear to have. However, oligarchies also appear to have problems terminating wars.[69] Again, this may be the result of log-rolling behavior, but it might also be related to predispositions to dominant behavior.

The statistical test most consistent with the hypothesis developed in this book would not only code regime type in terms of the distribution of power within the state among one, few, or many, but would also code for factors in the decision-making processes affecting war, which would include, but not be limited to, checks upon the power of the executive branch and the military, and the presence or absence of political discourse that favors egalitarian or status-neutral norms. The states that scored high on factors that favored the unrestrained exercise of dominant behavior and status-conscious language should tend to pursue more aggressive military activity or coercive diplomacy following a successful engagement in war or coercive diplomacy.

Since testosterone levels in males decline steadily with age after puberty, the age of rulers unconstrained by internal checks ought to be negatively correlated with dominant behavior and the tendency to engage in more aggressive war or coercive diplomacy following initial successes in war or coercive diplomacy.

Finally, the argument linking testosterone to "overconsumption" of dominant behavior may help us understand a puzzle created by Jonathan Mercer's work on reputation. Mercer suggested that there were reasons rooted in social psychological analysis that made it difficult for states to develop a reputation for yielding in international relations.[70] State leaders look at other state leaders and attribute to them a disposition to act in ways that cause them to resist challenges. Even if a state backs down in one crisis, it will not develop a reputation for yielding in general. In the next crisis, states will expect the state that yielded last time to stand firm. This extremely counterintuitive finding is supported by some empirical data. Hence the puzzle. Why do people worry about the consequence of yielding, if reputations for yielding do not develop? The reason for this may have nothing to do with reputations. If people are aware in a general way that men who win in a social interaction experience a subjective

elevation of mood and become more likely to engage in subsequent challenges, they will worry about yielding. The problem is not what the winner will think of the state that gives in. The state that gives in may simply
be primed by basic biological impulses to engage in further challenges.
This, in fact, is the folk wisdom that Harry Truman gave voice to when
he said in 1950 that aggression must be resisted or it will be encouraged.

Chapter Four

Stress, Distress, and War Termination

EXPLAINING how and why wars end is at least as difficult as explaining how and why they start. If anything, explaining the beginning of wars may be easier. It is at least possible that decisions to start wars resemble other peacetime decisions. It may be the case that wars are undertaken after economic calculations. In peacetime, leaders might be able calmly to consider all the available information, and decide whether to enter or avoid international confrontations, knowing that those confrontations have some risk of war. Unlike the decision to go to war, however, the decision to end a war, by definition, takes place under conditions that are different from peacetime, and which may well make calm, economic calculations difficult. For a war to end, a war must be going on. Men and women, civilians and soldiers will have been killed, and more will be dying as leaders deliberate. The best prewar plans are likely to have gone wrong, especially for the losing side. The fog of war may make it harder than in peacetime accurately to gauge what is going on within the enemy's camp. Months, maybe years of suffering, will have changed the men and women who make decisions, perhaps making them harder, perhaps more easily discouraged. It is in this context that decisions to end wars take place, and it is this context that makes it intuitively plausible that the economic model of decision making may not be the only decision-making process in operation at the end of wars.

A limited debate has taken place about how wars end. All can agree that most wars end before the physical capacity of the loser to resist is completely destroyed. Nations almost never fight until the last soldier is killed, and so wars usually end when one side capitulates after negotiations of one kind or another. Beyond that, there is not much agreement about what has been observed. There are disagreements about when and how capitulation occurs. These disagreements result, in part, from debates about the extent to which actors make decisions about war termination in the same way that economists assume that people make economic choices. The idea that soldiers under fire make decisions about whether to continue fighting the same way that shoppers do may not be correct. Even the idea that the leaders of states, observing their country going down to defeat in war, make decisions in the same way that they make decisions about highway construction programs in peacetime, for example, seems odd. This chapter will argue that soldiers losing battles and wars, under specified conditions, will not make decisions in the way that economists suggest. It will also argue that leaders approach the subject of war termination in ways that are affected by this noneconomic behavior of the soldiers. It may also be the case that leaders who are losing wars themselves may behave in ways similar to the behavior of soldiers losing a battle. The form of decision making that operates on the losing side of battles and wars, it will be argued, is linked to something that happens to the loser, who will be defined as the side that perceives it cannot control events during the war. The loser may in fact be gaining or losing in power relative to the adversary, but knowledge of the relative balance of power will be obscure. While losers cannot be sure what they see when they look outward at the enemy, when they look inward, they know that they are not achieving what they seek on the battlefield. They cannot control events, in terms of their own objectives, by means of their actions. It is the winners who can do those things. The perspective of the losers changes because of this loss of control, and it affects the way in which they look at the world, themselves, and their options.

Specifically:

1. Uncontrollable levels of stimulation, or stressors, in the environment induce a condition in which the subject feels helpless, a condition that has been given the name "distress." Distress induces a condition very similar, and perhaps identical, to the psychological and physiological state of depression. Depression is defined symptomatically in terms of pessimism about the outcome of one's actions, lack of energy to perform tasks, and, in the extreme case, a collapse into near complete inaction. Physiologically, it is correlated with levels of cortisol in the bloodstream that are high and that remain high.

2. The loser on a battlefield, as well as civilians who are the target of enemy military action, are exposed to stressors that they cannot control. The will to fight of these rank-and-file soldiers and nonelite civilians is broken because of distress-induced depression. These distressed people are reacting to their inability to control their environment. They are not reacting to the perception that they are suffering more than the enemy, or that the relative balance of power has shifted—only to the fact that they are helpless and depressed.

3. Soldiers and civilians who are in the presence of or who are aware of distressed losers will be affected by the signals they send out. Information cascades can form when large numbers of individuals make decisions sequentially and decide what to do at least in part on the basis of what they see other people doing, even if their own private information would lead them to act contrary to the group. These information cascades are easily created, but also easily reversed, suggesting that the moral influence of officers on the battlefield, or wartime political leaders more generally, in steadying troops and civilians may

have an informational basis. When such leaders are not present, the individual behavior of distressed soldiers and civilians can easily become mass behavior. There is evidence that leaders who remain capable of constructive action while others are distressed have higher than average levels of neuropeptide-Y, a natural opiate.

4. The mass behavior of soldiers and civilians affects the decisions of elites to terminate wars. When large groups of soldiers and civilians are unwilling to fight, the war becomes more difficult for the ruling elites to sustain.

5. Distress and depression may also affect elites directly, but the ability of elites to manage and control their immediate environment and to cope with stress may be less affected by the events of the war, and so they are likely to be affected less by this phenomenon. Because other factors, in addition to the distress-induced depression of soldiers and civilians, affect elite decisions, the factor of distress-induced depression identifies a key part, but only a part, of the war termination puzzle.

Opposing Views of War Termination

The idea that wars could end either as the result of a calculated decision or because of some internal, subjective collapse in the mental state of the nation losing the war is, of course, not new. Clausewitz referred to both kinds of behavior. He observed that wars *ought* to be ended through negotiations, as the expected value of the political objects of the war were exceeded by the expected costs of the war.

> We see then that if one side cannot completely disarm the other, the desire for peace on either side will rise and fall with the probability of further successes and the amount of effort these would require. If such incentives were of equal strength on both sides, the two would resolve their political disputes by meeting half way. If the incentive grows on one side, it should diminish on the other. Peace will result so long as their sum total is sufficient—though the side that feels the lesser urge for peace will naturally get the better bargain.[1]

There is, of course, the question of whether and when the objectives of the belligerents would come to overlap during the war. This would not happen simply as the linear result of the experiences of battle, because, as Clausewitz wrote, the incentives to settle the war do not necessarily move both belligerents toward each other: as one side starts to lose a war, the other side may see itself starting to win. The losing side becomes more willing to seek peace, but the victor could become more demanding. As a result, agreement on peace terms could become hard to find, and wars could drag on.

In this, Clausewitz anticipated modern rationalist studies of war termination such as the book by Hein Goemans, *War and Punishment*. Goemans establishes what he calls a "rationalist baseline explanation." What happens in war, he argues, along with Geoffrey Blainey and James Fearon, is that belligerents gain more accurate information about relative capabilities from battle. In peacetime, states will have incentives to exaggerate or minimize their apparent strength to each other, and to conceal weaknesses. In battle, these exaggerations and efforts to conceal are torn away: *"war provides information."* This new information enables the belligerents to judge their relative capabilities more accurately than they could in peacetime and allows them better to assess the odds that they can obtain their goal by fighting. Goemans asserts that "after even a few days fighting decision-makers are better able to anticipate the consequences of continued war. Moreover, it is easy to evaluate the choice for peace because peace can always be had on the opponent's terms." This new information will be most important when it is unexpected, when it disproves peacetime assumptions. Victory on the battlefield, if not expected, showed that the winner was more powerful than he thought, and the opposite for the loser.[2] How quickly and when this learning takes place is not clear from Goemans' presentation. At one point, it is suggested that "even a few days" is sufficient. Elsewhere, it is argued that "some time," or "sustained" or "continuous" warfare is necessary. Goemans also points out, correctly, that since war is dynamic, new hidden or "private" information may be continuously created in wars and so cannot be revealed by prior activity in wars. It is also true, of course, that losing battles sometimes reduces the collective will of the loser to fight, but sometimes does not. The dynamic character of war raises the question about why we should expect that learning in war, even if accurate about the *current intrawar* balance of power, is necessarily predictive of *the future intrawar* balance of power, which is, of course, what should affect decisions about future actions, such as continuing war. Nonetheless, Goemans insists, the logic will prevail: secret or private information will become public.[3]

Goemans also notes, like Clausewitz, that wars conducted by rational actors might not produce agreement between the loser and winner on the terms of peace because the party winning the war could be increasing his estimate of what he could gain by continuing the war, precisely because he was winning. Only if the losing side experiences a more than symmetrical decrease in willingness to wage war would the war end.[4]

Like Goemans, Clausewitz argued that leaders should make rational calculations about war termination, but unlike Goemans, he disagreed with the proposition that battle yields accurate information about relative capabilities. In war, he claimed, any reliable information about the enemy's current condition, much less the nature of the enemy's capabilities in the future, is near to impossible to obtain. He regarded as fantastic the idea that the conduct of war made the parties to the war more knowledgeable about their relative capabilities, in ways that might help them decide on an agreement to end the war. War obscured more than it illuminated. As events in war unfolded, "We now know more, but this makes us more, not less, uncertain. The latest reports do not arrive all at once; they merely trickle in."[5] Even if information were available, men in battle are often not subjectively capable of understanding it clearly. "In the dreadful presence of suffering and danger, emotion can easily overwhelm intellectual conviction, and in this psychological fog it is so hard to form clear and complete insights that changes of view become more understandable and excusable. Action can never be based on anything firmer than instinct, a sensing of the truth."[6]

Clausewitz said that men *ought* to make rational decisions in war, and in the chapter on "Genius in War," he specified the personality of the men who might be more likely to make rational choices under terrible conditions. Such men were steady and slow to arouse, and his general description calls to mind the image of such generals as Ulysses S. Grant, calmly writing dispatches while men around him were being shot. But Clausewitz also discussed the manner in which wars often *did* end, as opposed to the way they ought to end. He focused precisely on the factors that might produce a sharp reduction in the willingness of the loser to go on fighting. How this happened was not determined simply by material outcomes. Wars might end because the enemy's army was disarmed or the country occupied, but they might not. "Yet both these things may be done and the war, that is, the animosity and reciprocal effects of hostile elements, cannot be considered to have ended so long as the enemy's *will* has not been broken; in other words, so long as the enemy government and its allies have not been driven to ask for peace, or the population made to submit."[7] We are thus left with the question of what occurs in war that might bring about this ill-defined but all-important "breaking of the will" of the enemy.

Physical exertion is one factor, according to Clausewitz. "If no one had the right to give his views on military operations except when he is frozen, or faint from heat and thirst, or depressed from privation and fatigue, objective and accurate views would be even rarer than they are. But they would at least be subjectively valid, for the speaker's experience would precisely determine his judgment."[8]

More important, however, are the psychological conditions associated with losing a battle. The commander's state of mind, justified or not, affects the mood of those around him. In any battle, a losing commander will notice, not the relative balance of power, but his own loss of soldiers, his own retreat, his own need to abandon exhausted men, wounded, among whom are often the bravest.

> The feeling of having been defeated, which on the field of battle had struck only the senior officers, now runs through the ranks down to the very privates. . . .
>
> Worse still is the growing loss of confidence in the high command, which is held more or less responsible by every subordinate for his own wasted efforts. What is worse, the sense of having been defeated is not a mere nightmare that may pass; it has become a palpable fact that the enemy is stronger. . . . One may have been aware of it all along, but for the lack of more solid alternatives this awareness was countered by one's trust in chance, good luck, Providence and in one's own audacity and courage. All this now has turned out to have been insufficient, and one is harshly and inexorably confronted by the terrible truth. All these impressions are still far removed from panic."

These emotional shifts are not the same as objective appraisals of the relative balance of power, but they are "certain to appear; they produce an effect on which one may infallibly depend." This effect will continue until a change in "external factors produces a new turn of events." Beyond the battlefield,

> the effect of all this [defeat in battle] outside the army—on the people and on the government—is a sudden collapse of the most anxious expectations, and a complete crushing of self-confidence. This leaves a vacuum that is filled by a corrosively expanding fear which completes the paralysis. . . . This effect may differ from case to case, but it always exists to some degree. In place of an immediate and determined effort by everyone to hold off further misfortune, there is a general fear that any effort will be useless. Men will hesitate where they should act, or will even dejectedly resign themselves and leave everything to fate. . . . Our argument is that the effects of victory that we have described will always be present. . . . These effects are indeed quite inevitable, being based on the nature of the case.

Clausewitz concludes, chillingly, not by observing that men are rational in time of war, but something like the reverse: "All war presupposes human weakness, and seeks to exploit it."[9]

Military commanders in war have implicitly tended to have more sympathy for Clausewitz's view of war termination. General William T. Sherman wrote to his brother in March 1864 that there was no end to the war in sight despite the, to him, overwhelming material losses inflicted on the Confederacy, because the enemy's will to fight had not been broken: "No amount of poverty or adversity seems to shake their faith: niggers gone, wealth and luxury gone, money worthless, starvation in view within a period of two or three years, causes enough to make the bravest tremble. Yet I see no sign of let up—some few deserters, plenty tired of war, but the masses determined to fight it out."[10] His campaign, famously, was intended to change this state of mind in the South, and to break the will of the enemy.

Rear Admiral James B. Stockdale was a prisoner of war in North Vietnam and commented on what he perceived, correctly or incorrectly, to have been the impact of the sustained B-52 bombing of Hanoi in December 1972 as he observed it from his prison cell: "Night after night, the planes kept coming in. . . . The *shock* was there—the *commitment* was there—and the *enemy's will was broken.* You could see it in every Vietnamese face. They knew they lived through last night, but they also knew that if our forces moved their bomb line over a few thousand yards they wouldn't live through tonight."[11]

What should we make of this virtual debate across the centuries? Is war ended by means of rational choice motivated by the improved information about relative capabilities that war provides? Or does the subjective state of the loser change? What does it mean when we say the "enemy's will was broken?" If the enemy's will has been broken, what has happened? The bulk of the evidence, first, suggests that information about relative capabilities is extremely ambiguous in time of war and can hardly be expected to bring about a confident recalculation of the expected utility of continued fighting. Second, medical studies of fatigue, stress, and distress now allow us to state with some certainty that the sustained presence of stressors in the environment, combined with an inability of the person subjected to the stressors to take effective action, lead, at the level of the individual, to a condition that has been termed distress, which is cognitively, behaviorally, and biochemically similar to, if not indistinguishable from, the disease known as major depression. In that state, people become pessimistic about the outcome of endeavors, lose energy to perform even routine tasks, and, in the most severe cases, become physically inactive. The conditions that induce distress are the conditions that soldiers face in battles and campaigns that they are losing. If soldiers and civilians take their cues from the behavior of these distressed soldiers, the behavior of large numbers of people not directly affected by battlefield defeat will change, and the changed behavior of these people will, in turn, affect others, in what has been termed an "informational cascade." The behavior of people directly and indirectly suffering from distress is consistent with the breaking of the will of the enemy to fight described by Clausewitz and the observed behavior of troops that have given up on the battlefield. Distress and depression, together with calculations, are factors that are relevant to war termination.

War and Information

The idea that engaging the enemy in war provides one with better information about the relative balance of military capabilities is as plausible
as its opposite, that in war, the chaos of battle and the active, violent efforts of the enemy will obscure the relative balance of power. In recent
times, Geoffrey Blainey, and then, more formally, James Fearon, have
popularized the notion that states make war when they lack information
about the relative balance of material power, and resolve, or willingness
to continue fighting, and they end wars when they obtain information
that gives them a more accurate understanding of the costs of continuing
the war.[12] It is no doubt true that, in peacetime, states may over- or un-
derstate their real capabilities for strategic purposes and use military secrecy to deny information about their real capabilities to the adversary. It
is also true that in war, military power is used in battle, and that battle
outcomes indicate how effective the portion of the military organization
engaged in the battle is, relative to its enemy, at the time of the battle. Finally, it is true that when a war is over, both states know, at least for a
moment, which state had greater power and resolve.

All of the above may be true and still be irrelevant to the question of
war termination. Does engaging the enemy in battle provide accurate
predictive information about the enemy's ability and willingness to continue the war in the future? That is what must be known in order to calculate the anticipated costs of continuing the war. Once the war is over,
of course, one knows what price the enemy was willing to pay and what
the limits of the enemy's capabilities were, but that information is not
available to leaders before the enemy surrenders, and so cannot be part
of the decision-making process.

Do the first battles of a war remove the blinders of peacetime with regard to the enemy? In a close study of the information and intelligence
available to Winston Churchill and the British government in the spring
and summer of 1940, David Reynolds reviewed what predictive lessons
the British drew from the battles in Norway and the Battle of France. His
carefully documented conclusion was that every prediction the British
government made about German behavior was wrong. In May, for example, the British predicted that the bombing of Germany would turn
the war around in three months. Reynolds crisply summarized what the
British learned from the first year of the war: "British expectations about
Germany and about the USA were almost entirely erroneous."[13]

In a more extensive study, Charles Heller and William Stoft reviewed
all of the first battles in the wars fought by the United States up to 1965.
What were the lessons of World War I? The first major battle fought by

American troops in World War I (Cantigny, 28–31 May 1918) showed that American troops were less than adequately trained, could launch an offensive operation, but were unable to make any gains against the Germans. The battles immediately following were defensive battles in which the Americans took catastrophic losses, and in which it was "proved once again that infantry on the Western Front could not fight—they could only die—without massive accurate . . . artillery support." The rapid victories of the American troops against the Germans later in 1918 were not obviously suggested by their first battles. Nor were the first battles in World War II good predictors of the future military balance of power. In World War II, the American Army's initial performance in the Philippine Islands in 1942–1943 at Buna were "too costly for the gains achieved." The defeat of the American Army at the battle of Kasserine Pass in 1943 and the destruction of Task Force Smith in Korea in 1950 are well known. The first encounter of the 1st Cavalry Division (Airmobile) with the North Vietnamese Army destroyed two out of the three North Vietnamese regiments engaged and killed as many as three thousand of them, an impressive victory, but hardly indicative of the outcome of future battles.

What could one conclude from these first encounters with the enemy? Should leaders have inferred from the initial American defeats in World Wars I and II that the United States would lose the war? Should we have inferred from the initial American victories in Vietnam that we would win that war? Obviously not. The initial battles revealed very little about the ultimate costs or outcomes of subsequent battles in the same war. The reason is fairly straightforward. The American army *changed* in response to first battles. So did the enemy army, most dramatically with the North Vietnamese Army, which decided it would no longer stand and fight the Americans. For that reason, the authors of the study concluded that first battles were "peculiar," and not representative of the emerging balance of power.[14]

If initial battles could be misleading, what about extended operations? Perhaps enduring, accurate information about the relative balance of power and resolve might emerge from a series of battles, a campaign. Since this issue could be of major importance for war termination, Fred Ikle examined this question in his book, *Every War Must End*, in the chapter entitled "The Fog of Military Estimates." As the title indicated, he found little that would suggest that civilian leaders came to more accurate understandings of the capabilities of the enemy and the enemy's willingness to fight during extended campaigns. The belief that bombing German cities would produce a collapse of German civilian morale persisted well into 1944. Mussolini argued to his entourage in March 1943 that the naval losses that Italy had suffered up to that point in the Mediterranean were not a good indicator of what would happen in the rest of the war. The conclusion of the American Army in August 1952 was that the Communist forces would never give up in Korea, and so the war had to be ended by expanding it to destroy the enemy's war-making capacity. The problem is that sustained fighting in the past sometimes spurred the enemy to fight on, but sometimes it led him to give up. Sometimes the enemy extracted more resources from society after losing a campaign and used them more appropriately for military purposes. Sometimes not. One could seldom know beforehand with any assurance which it would be.[15]

Studies of military innovation have argued that innovation would occur in time of war because information about how the enemy fought would be available in ways that it was not in peacetime, and that new information could lead to the development of more appropriate modes of fighting. Related to this was the question of whether military innovation was necessary in time of war. The answer depended on an evaluation of how well or poorly existing military operations were doing. In *Winning the Next War*, I looked in depth at what states knew about the effectiveness of ongoing military operations in wartime. The data revealed how little was known about the effect of one's own operations on the enemy. In World War I, for example, the objective of trench warfare after 1914 was to inflict higher casualties on the enemy than the enemy could inflict on you. In the case of the British evaluation of German casualties, it is demonstrable that the answer was not known. Charles Callwell was the director of military operations at the War Office, reporting to Lord Kitchener. In December 1914, Lord Kitchener asked Callwell to estimate the time at which the Germans would run out of men of military age due to the casualties they were suffering. Callwell's response to this request, in a private letter, was revealing: "K has told me to prove that the Germans will run out of men within the next few months—and I have. I could just as easily have proved that they were good for another two years. One must be a mug indeed if one cannot prove anything with figures as counters." Writing after the war, Callwell explained his problem further: "The question seemed to base itself on what premises you thought fit to start from. You could no doubt calculate with some certainty upon the total number of Teuton males of fighting age being somewhere about fifteen million in August 1914, upon 700,000, or so, youths annually reaching the age of eighteen and upon Germany being obliged to have under arms continually some five million soldiers. After that you were handling indeterminate factors."

How many men did the Germans have? How many were being killed? The only available data was "based on suspicious enemy statistics, and the perplexities involved in the number of wounded—who would, and who would not be able to return to the ranks.[16] Since wartime encounters with the Germans did not provide the data that would enable the British to make nonarbitrary judgments about the ability of the German empire to continue war, estimates of how much longer it would be before the Germans gave up were generated that ranged from six months to three years. The estimates tended to support the strategy that was already being advocated by the author of the estimate.

The United States Army Air Force in World War II had fierce debates, internally and with the Royal Air Force, about how to conduct the strategic bombing of Germany. The answer to that question depended on how one evaluated the ongoing bombing campaigns. One central question was how much damage one could do to the Germans by bombing their oil refineries and storage areas. The British Bomber Command did bomb German oil refineries in the Ruhr area in the period October–December 1940. The question was then posed, had the bombing reduced the ability of the German military to fight? To this question British intelligence replied simply that it had no idea, because it had no idea what the total amount of oil stored in Germany was, it had no idea what German rates of oil consumption were, or what the production of the synthetic oil plants might be. How much stored oil did the Germans start the war with? The Americans said five million tons, the British said three million, so they split the difference and said four million. Mathematical models could be and were built that tried to simulate the operations of a synthetic oil plan, and these models then had components shut down by simulated bombing. An estimate was produced of the reduction of oil production. Was the model valid? Its creators candidly stated that since no intelligence was available to validate the model, no one knew.[17] All of this was relevant to the question of whether Allied leaders could assess the capacity of the Nazi empire for continued fighting.

All of the guesswork concerning the German oil stocks was science compared with the estimates of Japanese oil stockpiles and the impact of the American submarine and air war against Japanese oil stockpiles. American and British economic interaction with Japan in the 1930s was very limited. The last firm figures that American wartime intelligence had about the Japanese oil industry dated from 1929. How much oil was Japan producing in conquered areas of the Dutch East Indies? No one knew. How many Japanese oil tankers had been sunk by American submarines? Answering this question involved a careful tabulation of confirmed, observed kills that eliminated double counting, and the use of intercepted Japanese coded radio messages about their losses. This time-consuming tabulation was not completed until after the war was over. In a way, it did not matter, because American intelligence did not know how fast Japanese shipyards were building new oil tankers to replace the ones that had been lost. It is not surprising to learn, therefore, that postwar inspection of Japanese oil stocks revealed that the United States had overestimated Japanese reserves of aviation gasoline, for example, by a factor of two. This was not a trivial error, since it affected how long and how fiercely American leaders thought that the Japanese would be able to fight to resist an American invasion of the Japanese Home Islands.[18]

The idea that engagement with the enemy provides wartime leaders with accurate, predictive information about the relative capacity of the two belligerents for continued warfare needs to be modified. The idea that wars end when calculations based on wartime data reveal that the anticipated costs of continued war exceed the expected benefits is too simple. Yet wars do end. People do decide to stop fighting. What happens if not simply calculation based on data? Ikle did not know, but he suggested that what might be at work had little to do with rational calculation. "To bring the fighting to an end, one nation or the other almost always has to revise its war aim. This revision is stimulated by a reevaluation of the military prospects, but not in so direct nor in so logical a fashion as a rational approach to national policy would dictate."[19] Something happens inside people to change how they think. What might that change be?

Combat and the Physiology of Stress

Instead of beginning the study of war termination by assuming that men at war act like economic utility maximizers in peacetime, it is possible to begin, as Clausewitz does, by observing that combat is the phenomenon central to war, and then to inquire how it is that combat affects the behavior of men. There is a great deal of systematic data on this question. The landmark study was conducted by Samuel Stouffer for the American Army during and after World War II. Enlisted men and officers were surveyed to find out the basic facts about what their lives had been like in combat. The results were striking but hardly surprising. U.S. Army troops were surveyed in the spring of 1944. The survey begins its review of the data by observing that "the one all-pervading quality of combat which most obviously marks it off as the subject of special interest is that it was a *situation of stress*." This condition was the result of physical danger, discomfort, loss of comrades, and many other factors, including the lack of privacy. But among all of the stress-inducing factors, lack of sleep was cited more often than any other as a factor affecting combat performance. In the European theater, 71 percent of the company-level officers surveyed said that they were fatigued from being too long in combat, and that fatigue was having a negative effect on their performance. In the Pacific theater, the figure was 72 percent. Fatigue was mentioned as a problem affecting battle performance about three times as often as complaints about lack of training, poor care of personal needs, or the lack of necessary weapons.

What did fatigue mean? Some 31 percent of the infantry reported that they had received four hours of sleep or less per night in the prior weeks. An additional 54 percent reported that they were getting by on four to five hours of sleep a night. It should be noted that the infantrymen were commenting on the sleep received during a *quiet* period; soldiers in combat were worse off.[20] Nor was the phenomenon of fatigue unique to the infantry. Between 60 percent and 65 percent of the enlisted bomber crews that completed a tour of duty in the Mediterranean or the Pacific were observed to have anxiety-related "disturbances." Among medium bomber crews that flew 60–69 missions, 52 percent reported chronic insomnia. In heavy bomber crews, sleep loss, anorexia, weight loss, and tremors were reported, along with a loss of efficiency, depression, seclusion, and increased alcohol consumption.[21] Among bomber crews who went on missions over enemy territory every day for weeks in the spring of 1944, men appeared to age ten years for every six months of missions.

Data has also been obtained under lab conditions. Beginning in the 1960s, experiments were conducted to assess the effects of simple sleep deprivation. The assumption at that time was that all stimuli, called stressors, such as pain, loud noises, and flashes of light, that disturbed the equilibrium of human beings triggered the same general physical response, called stress. Sleep deprivation was easy to create in lab settings and did not injure subjects, and so sleep deprivation was used to understand the general phenomenon of stress. However, when college students were deprived of sleep simply by asking them to stay awake, the results, in terms of the changes in their behavior, were not of much interest. The response time when doing simple physical tasks increased after thirty-six hours without sleep. Scores of subjects performing simple problem-solving tasks declined, but not greatly, and it was observed that if sleep-deprived people concentrated hard, they could, for brief periods, perform normally. Subjects experienced episodes of "microsleep" when they would fall asleep for periods short enough that they would not notice that they had fallen asleep. Short-term memory loss and some performance degradation was observed in real-world settings when antisubmarine warfare sailors, for example, got less than three hours of sleep a night.[22]

Sleepy people dozed off, were forgetful, and made mistakes unless they concentrated hard. They also recovered quickly if given two nights of normal sleep. This did not suggest any surprising or major shift in the way in which people made decisions in wartime. But in the course of the work on sleep deprivation, scientists discovered that their initial assumption, that sleep deprivation induced the same stress response as all other stressors, was not correct. Clinical psychologists noted that some depressed patients experienced some relief from depression when deprived of sleep. Since stress was thought to be associated with depression, this was a puzzle, if sleep deprivation was a stressor like other stressors. Analysis of the blood chemistry of the patients showed that sleep deprivation, in fact, produced bodily responses that were not the same as other stress responses. In particular, animals and humans subjected to threats, pain, and disorientation experienced rapid increases of one chemical, cortisol. Sleep-deprived patients who stayed awake simply because doctors asked them to try to stay awake did not experience increases in their cortisol levels. One team concluded, "From our data we cannot support the hypothesis that TSD [total sleep deprivation] acts through a stress response," since neither cortisol nor endorphin levels went up in response to TSD.[23]

Scientists began to look more closely at the differences between sleep deprivation, fatigue, and stress. The results were more interesting for our purposes. Fatigue, the weariness that sets in after performing a task for long periods of time, had complex effects on human thinking and behavior. Subjects were fatigued by giving them repetitive tasks and were then presented with a problem to solve. They were offered three different ways of solving the problem that required recognizably different amounts of work, but where increased effort was balanced by increased probability of success. The low-effort strategies, for example, led to low probability of success, and the reverse. To quote the report, "a key feature of the task is that the expected amount of work would be the same, regardless of whether one opted to start with a path high in effort and in probability of success, or low in effort and in probability of success." That is, the choice of strategy would not be affected by differences in the expectations of the total costs and rewards. Yet the fatigued subjects consistently opted for the low-effort strategies. Subjects who were fatigued also lost the ability to distinguish between complex, difficult problems and simple problems, judged them all to be easy, and so did not expend more effort to gather information and solve complex problems. Air traffic controllers who were fatigued were observed to associate less information with each airplane, and to plan simpler and shorter routes for airplanes as their workload and traffic density increased. Controllers also paid less attention to peripheral goals as they grew more fatigued.[24]

More study revealed that two very different bodily responses were associated with stimulation that might produce sleep deprivation—noise, light, workloads—and stimulation associated with an unpredictable and uncontrollable environment. Briefly, noise and such triggered the release of catecholmines, hormones such as adrenaline and noradrenaline. Sleep deprivation in particular was associated with increased noradrenaline levels. But a particular kind of stressor—uncertainty—produced an entirely different reaction:

> By contrast with the general response of the catecholamines, corticosteroids are produced by conditions of novelty, strangeness or unfamiliarity—in which uncertainty is paramount. In general, novel, unfamiliar situations produce feelings of uncertainty or anxiety—often associated with an anticipation of stress—which in turn trigger the secretion of cortisol. Cortisol levels are found to be particularly high in anxious or depressed patients, and in phobic reactions. . . . However, environmental predictability and controllability—or at least the feeling of being in control—lead to suppressed corticosteroid production.[25]

The differences between sleep-deprivation, general stimulation, and the response to uncertainty are crucial to our inquiry, because they are crucial to the differences in the condition between the people winning and losing a battle or war. Both belligerents in a battle will be short of sleep, and both will be subjected to high levels of stimulation. But, by definition, the side that is winning battles is doing more to control the environment. The victor is achieving the goals he set for himself or herself. The environment is less unpredictable for the winner, since the plans are working. The opposite is true for the loser, whose plans fail, resulting in a lack of control of the environment. The loser is uncertain about what will happen next because it is apparent that he or she does not control events. If subjects feel that they are in control, the presence of stressors in the environment creates high levels of adrenaline, but not high levels of cortisol, and is associated with the subjective feeling of excitement and arousal, without anxiety. It is the losing side in a war that is subject to stressors in the environment that cannot be predicted or controlled. The condition that this induces is called distress. The observable, physical correlate of distress is an elevated level of cortisol measured in urine or saliva samples.

What are the cognitive effects of elevated cortisol levels? Subjects were told that they had to give a complex speech in front of a large audience the next day, and their cortisol levels were measured. Those subjects with higher cortisol levels were less able to remember the next day what they were taught while their cortisol levels were elevated. The part of the brain that is associated with transferring short-term memories into long-term memories, the hippocampus, shrinks in response to elevated cortisol levels. Vietnam veterans who suffered from posttraumatic stress disorders and who died and were autopsied were found to have atrophied hippocampi.[26] Stressors in the environment combined with uncertainty also result in the production of two sets of brain chemicals—one that enervates portions of the brain known to be involved in anticipation of events and general cognition, and another associated with the activation of the amygdala, which is involved in creating fear-learned responses, and recalling fear-learned responses. In depressed patients with chronic stress system activation, a state is produced in which "cognition, memory, and attention are focused obsessively on depressive ideas, adversely influencing the ability of the individual to remember and focus on learning and solving practical everyday, or pertinent problems. In this disease, assertiveness is often transformed into excessive caution and anxiety."[27]

People who are depressed display stress response and elevated cortisol levels and experience certain changes in their thinking. People exposed to an uncontrollable environment display elevated cortisol levels. This does not necessarily mean that people who have elevated cortisol levels in response to environmental factors will behave like chronically depressed people. A link is missing in the argument. Patients who are chronically depressed have chronic stress system activation, either because of some physical condition that affects their ability to regulate their cortisol levels, or because of some past experience. They are not responding to an environment that is actually uncontrollable. They may have something else wrong with them that causes both elevated stress levels and depression. If people who go to doctors because they are depressed are different from people in general, it might be the case that people who do not begin as chronically depressed patients will not respond to an uncontrollable environment by developing the same patterns of behavior as people who are chronically depressed. So we must next look to see if people, on average, react to uncontrollable levels of stressors in the environment by becoming depressed.

The answer is some people do, but not all.

Stress, Distress, and Learned Helplessness

What do we know about the physiological and cognitive effects of sustained stress caused by environmental uncertainty on individuals who are not selected because they come in for treatment for depression? Studies of the physiological response of general populations to environmental stressors can begin with animal models. The study of primates in natural conditions is less constrained than the study of humans. These studies of nonprimates are suggestive—people may behave the way other primates do, but they may not. Subsequent studies of humans may, however, be suggested by the research on nonhuman primates.

One of the best studies of primate populations in the wild that were subjected to environmental uncertainty is the series of studies done by

Robert Sapolsky of baboons in the Serengeti.[28] Sapolsky began his work by carefully observing the social behavior of these primates. The males that had preferential access to food and to females for mating were identified as the high-status males. Sapolsky wanted to understand the differences in the physiological response of high-status and low-status male baboons to stress. To do so, he shot baboons with tranquilizer darts, at the same time each morning (body chemistry varies during the day), immobilized them, and extracted a blood sample. The effects of the anesthetic had been studied on animals in the lab, and it had been established that the tranquilizer by itself did not affect body chemistry. Similarly, the pain of being shot was determined to be insignificant.

What did the blood samples reveal? The levels of cortisol in the baboons were measured immediately after capture, and then at intervals thereafter. The initial measure revealed the base cortisol level; the subsequent measures indicated the cortisol levels produced in response to stress. As nearly as could be determined, it was the disorientation that the baboons experienced as the result of being anesthetized and then handled by humans that caused the stress reaction. This condition— being drugged, immobilized, and handled by strange creatures—is reasonably characterized as the condition of helplessness or lack of control over the environment. High-status baboons had low basal rates of cortisol, which peaked in response to their capture but then declined rapidly. Low-status baboons had high basal cortisol levels, which did not go up much in response to capture and did not decline over time.

Were low basal cortisol levels the result of high status or did baboons who began with low basal rates engage in behavior that led to high status? It turned out to be a combination of variations across individual baboons and of variations in environmental conditions. Baboons were injected with a synthetic, cortisol-like drug in the lab. Since this was done in a lab, it kept environmental factors constant. Low-status baboons, it was discovered, did not stop producing cortisol when they were injected; high-status baboons did. Low-status baboons had differences in the feedback mechanisms that measured levels of cortisol in the blood and regulated the production of cortisol in response. High-status baboons shut down production of cortisol rapidly when levels went up. So some baboons had different brain/endocrine physiologies.

But, in addition, more groups of baboons were studied. Not all high-status males, it turned out, had low basal cortisol levels. In newly formed groups in which the status hierarchy was unstable, or in groups that were in flux because of large demographic shocks, even high-status males had high basal cortisol levels. In groups with stable social hierarchies, the finding of high status/low basal cortisol levels was replicated. So an unstable, unpredictable social environment also led to high cortisol levels. But social setting did not account for all differences. Personality, or the general style of behavior displayed by the dominant baboons, was also important. One kind of dominant male reacted to many forms of behavior by other baboons as a threat. Such males were prepared to fight all of the time. After fighting, they were still acting as though they were preparing to fight again. Another kind differentiated more precisely between threatening and neutral interactions. They initiated a fight when actually challenged by a rival, thereby controlling the situation, and then they quickly reverted to a resting state after winning a fight. If they lost a fight, they attacked some other baboon. If humans displayed this behavior, we would say they were displacing aggression. The first group of dominant males had high basal cortisol levels; the second, low basal cortisol levels. So while social turmoil could lead to elevated cortisol levels, high status by itself did not confer low cortisol levels. Sapolsky concluded that "this finding indicates that the number of social stressors to which an individual is subjected is less important to physiology than is the emotional style with which one perceives and copes with the stressors."

This study of primates suggested that while environmental or social instability and uncertainty could produce stress reaction in humans, there might be differences among humans in their response to similar levels of stressors in the environment. Those differences might be differences in their inherited characteristics or the result of differences in their prior experiences. So chronically depressed people might, in fact, not be like average people. Some people did not react to uncontrollable environments by displaying chronically high levels of cortisol. What was producing the difference in emotional style or personality was not clear.

Beginning in the mid-1960s, Martin Seligman was studying the behavior of animals and people subjected to environmental stressors under a particular set of conditions. Those conditions were, essentially, ones in which the behavior of the animal had no effect on the level of stressors to which it was then exposed: what the animal did made no difference to how much loud noise it heard or how many mild shocks it received. This condition was also one that could be characterized as helplessness or lack of control over the environment. In experiments with dogs that were first exposed to uncontrollable stressors, it was found that approximately two-thirds of them developed a set of responses to subsequent stressors. These dogs would not try to escape the stressors even when an escape was available, whereas control animals that had not been exposed to stressors they could not escape quickly sought and found the way out. The condition displayed by the dogs who had been exposed to uncontrollable stressors was called "learned helplessness," and it was discovered that the same kind of behavior could be induced in a wide variety of animals, that learned *not* to make an effort when presented with an environmental challenge. Donald Hiroto found that many human students, when exposed to loud noises which they could not control, would subsequently learn less well to perform simple finger maneuvers that would turn off the noise, relative to members of a control group. They performed worse on general problems solving tests as well. Some students, however, did not display learned helplessness, even after being subjected to uncontrollable noise. Before the test, students were given questionnaires that assayed their personality. Those who said that their success in life was a matter of chance or otherwise not under their control subsequently displayed a higher incidence of learned helplessness than did students who answered that they were in control of their lives.[29]

"Men and animals are born generalizers," Seligman concluded, and they could learn enduring lessons from experience that their effort did not matter, even when information to the contrary was subsequently available. Uncertainty about what would happen next in the environment contributed to the feeling of uncontrollability. He speculated that uncontrollable stimuli from the environment could initially induce fear, and he noted elevated levels of norepinephrine in animals initially experiencing uncontrollable environments. Subsequent studies showed that the release of stress hormones such as norepinephrine directly stimulated the amygdala, the part of the brain that links observations of the internal physiological experience of fear to observations of the external world in ways that produce long-term memories of the fearful experience. Additional studies showed that neurons in the amygdala were much slower to reverse their learned responses than the neurons in the cortex, which are responsible for conscious thought—fear learning in the presence of opportunities for conscious learning.[30] These neuro-physiological findings are consistent with Seligman's speculation. He further speculated that if the uncontrollable stimuli persisted, depression could set in. In support of his speculation he noted that there were some physiological responses that depression and learned helplessness shared, such as depletion of norepinephrine in the blood, and a set of shared cognitive/behavioral characteristics: lowered initiation of voluntary responses, difficulty learning that responses affect outcomes, lowered aggression, competitiveness, and loss of appetite for food and sex.[31]

With this perspective, people re-examined available studies for cases in which there were stressors in the environment that individuals could not control or do anything about. They discovered a study of hospitals admitting patients with stomach ulcers in London and the surrounding suburbs during the German bombing of 1940 and 1941. In London, the bombing was intense, but regular. Every night when the air-raid sirens went off, people would go down into the shelters, hear the anti-aircraft guns, and re-emerge with the all-clear signal. In the suburbs of London, the bombing was much less intense, but it was irregular. A given area might go a week or more without attack, and then be bombed, or re-bombed. The per capita incidence of patients admitted to hospitals with ulcers was higher in the suburbs than in London, and after a few months, the incidence of ulcers in London and in the suburbs receded to peace-time levels.[32] It seemed to be the case that when people knew what to ex-pect, and when they had routines for coping with the stressors, they dis-played fewer stress reactions, such as developing ulcers, than they did when there was a high level of uncertainty about when the stressors would occur, and what to do about them, even when the incidence of stressors was higher.

Studies performed after Seligman's work was published collected data from subjects in natural settings that included stress and environments that were, to varying degrees, uncertain or uncontrollable. For example, parachute trainees were studied. Those who mastered jump techniques experienced high adrenaline levels and low cortisol levels. Presumably, they were able to cope with their stressors by taking appropriate action. Trainees who failed the course were unsuccessful in responding to the stressors and experienced high cortisol and adrenaline levels. Increased cortisol levels were observed to be associated with a decrease in attention to the task.[33] Another study used data from firefighters who were being trained for "smoke-diving," putting out fires in smoke-filled tunnels. The firefighters were asked to "think aloud" on their radios about what they were encountering and what they thought they should do. In the tunnel, the firefighters could not see anything and could not find their way by touch. Again, it is reasonable to assume that this induced a feeling in the trainees that they could not know what to expect next, or how to control the situation. As stress reactions mounted and were maintained, as mea-sured by heart rates telemetered back to a receiver, the firefighters would display less and less task-focused problem-solving activity. This was con-sistent with after-the-fact reports by rescue workers working on an oil rig fire at sea that, as the fire continued, they lost the ability to search for in-formation relevant to their problem.[34]

All of this is evidence that stressors in the environment plus an inabil-ity to take constructive action lead in some people to what was termed "distress." Distress produced a condition in many people that was, at a minimum, very similar to chronic depression that was not environmen-tally induced. Yet, there were still questions. Sapolsky noted that not all baboons reacted to stressors in the environment in the same way. In Seligman's lab, not all people developed learned helplessness. In real life, everybody at one time or another experiences events they cannot control, but not everyone develops learned helplessness. Helplessness itself, in people and perhaps in other primates, was not simply the result of physical helplessness, but the subjective perception of helplessness. People who were told that they had a button they could push that could control the unpleasant noises they heard did not develop learned helplessness, even if they never pushed the button, indeed, even if the button, in fact, controlled nothing. How we interpret an experience affects what general lessons we extract.[35] Our mental representations of our experiences must be intermediate between our experiences and learned helplessness or the opposite. Learned helplessness was not a universal, automatic response.

Pushed by these questions, Seligman then developed the concept of "stress immunization" as a phenomenon parallel to learned helplessness. If people or animals learn that they can develop effective responses to stressors, the next time they experience stressors they are less likely to give up, even when in the case at hand there is no effective response, and they are less likely to develop learned helplessness after the helpless experience. Richard Lazarus pointed out that how we appraise or interpret a situation or an experience will affect whether we think that an experience is representative of the kind of events that we will later encounter, and this affects our stress response.[36] A person who dwells on the negative aspects of a situation, at the time and thereafter, experiences and relives an experience that is subjectively different from that of a person who emphasizes the positive aspects. Differences in prior experience or inherited differences might account for the variable response to stressors and helplessness.

There was one set of questions that Seligman could not answer. In lab settings, subjects could not be exposed to stressors that were comparable to the stressors that were presented to men and women in real-life military settings, nor could he render them helpless while exposing them to those military stressors. There was not a compelling reason to do so that would override the obvious ethical objections to exposing subjects to violent, painful stimuli. Would those more powerful stressors have the same physiological and cognitive effects as subjecting people to unpleasant loud noises in a controlled laboratory setting? Unless it could be established that responses in real-world settings to violent stressors were similar to lab responses, it would remain conjectural that the phenomenon of distress and depression as observed in the lab was also produced by failures on the battlefield. There were, however, military training institutions that did have compelling reasons to inflict high levels of physical discomfort—fear, physical exhaustion, and pain—under conditions in which the trainees were deliberately rendered uncertain about whether their actions were controlling the environment. American Army Special Forces enlistees and officers do not face conventional battle problems in the course of their military operations. They are inserted far behind enemy lines and try to operate cooperatively with potentially friendly or hostile local populations. Often, little is known beforehand about what might be the appropriate ways to respond to the environment, or what needs to be done to accomplish a mission. Thus teams are left to define their own tasks. As well as physical strength and stamina, Special Forces teams need to be able to operate under conditions of extreme uncertainty. For that reason, Special Forces training is designed to exhaust trainees, but more, to induce high levels of distress by combining stressors with uncertainty about what to do. Trainees are not told, for example, what constitutes failure or success in the training program, how long a march will be, what the proper rate of advance is, how to behave toward an actor who is playing the part of a local guerrilla chief whose assistance the team needs, and so on. This helps the trainers identify those trainees who will not break down on a real mission, and prepare the trainees for the real-world settings they will face.[37]

Special Forces trainers at the John F. Kennedy Special Warfare Center and School at Fort Bragg, North Carolina, were asked to describe in detail how they created conditions of great stress in their trainees, and what successful strategies trainees developed for coping with uncertainty. Their answers were quite consistent with the findings in the lab and in other real-world settings. The trainers replied that lack of predictability in the environment was the factor that caused the greatest problems for the trainees. When asked if it was the lack of food or sleep that caused trainees to give up, the reply was no: the trainees received adequate calories and hours of rest, but they did not know when they would receive them. One trainer summarized the problem by saying, "People fold because they are taken out of their routine." One trainer took away the watches of his trainees. He had been a trainee and knew from his own experience that he had tried to impose order on the chaotic training environment by regularly noting the time, measuring how much more time till night, and when events occurred, for example. Another noted that giving the trainees one big job to do, however difficult, led to fewer people giving up than constantly switching the trainees from one small job to another. One big job could be organized into subtasks, and people would then know what to do and when to do it. A trainer summarized this observed response: "They [the trainees] will try anything to establish a routine." One portion of the training involved meeting with a man playing the part of a local guerrilla chieftain. He was instructed to be as difficult and as opaque as he could be. The trainees confronted the chief after engaging in physically exhausting activities. The chief did his best not to be controllable. In these circumstances, some trainees displayed the patterns of behavior observed in other settings that induced distress. They ceased being observant with regard to their surroundings, and they stopped processing external information for problem-solving purposes.

Instead, they reverted to memorized routines and attempted to execute predetermined checklists of tasks, ignoring the cues and signals from the chief that indicated that the approach was not working. When asked why some trainees did better than others, the trainers did not use the word "stress immunization," but it was clear that this was what they were talking about. If trainees had had prior successful experiences with subsisting in forest environments, they did better in the course. If they had some failures early in the course, even a small failure, they were less likely to do well subsequently in the course, but small initial successes led to subsequent success. If they were part of a team in which a stable informal social hierarchy did not emerge, they did worse in the course. If a trainer stepped in and selected a competent member of the group to be its leader, morale and performance would improve almost at once.[38]

In addition to the Special Forces training programs, the JFK Special Warfare Center had another program designed to expose trainees to environmental stressors under conditions of helplessness. The Survive, Evade, Resist, and Escape (SERE) program creates a simulated POW camp where personnel at high risk of capture (pilots, Special Forces, some diplomatic personnel, etc.) are exposed to the conditions they might encounter if captured. The trained psychologists who run the program explicitly refer to the objective of the program as stress immunization.[39] The SERE program includes "soft" and "hard" interrogation involving verbal and then physical abuse, after which the subject has a black hood placed over his or her head, and has his or her arms immobilized behind the back. Actors playing POW guards verbally and physically intimidate and menace the trainees. It is hard to imagine a setting short of real war that is more likely to induce distress. Successful completion of the course provides trainees with the knowledge that they can cope with such an experience if it occurs for real. The program has been credited with helping at least one pilot handle capture by Serbian forces in 1998. Techniques that help potential prisoners cope with imprisonment are, for obvious reasons, not publicized, but in general, the trainees are encouraged to find ways of achieving even small amounts of control over their environment and guards, and to interpret what happens to them in ways that emphasize the positive elements of control. All of this is derived from an understanding of the phenomenon of learned helplessness and how to avoid it.

In 1999 a Yale Medical School psychologist, Charles Morgan, in collaboration with United States Army Major Gary Hazlett, obtained permission to get saliva samples from subjects as they went through the SERE course. Consistent with earlier studies, they found that being subjected to stressors and helplessness leads, on average, to radically lower levels of testosterone, and elevated levels of cortisol. But some individuals did better at devising ways of coping with the course. Independent observations of the subjects in the course revealed that Army Special Forces officers better retained the ability to acquire new information while being subjected to harsh interrogation, and to develop new strategies for coping with their situation. Their levels of cortisol did peak in response to stressors, but then they declined. What was equally important was that blood samples indicated that, relative to soldiers who were not Special Forces officers, they were producing more of a substance called Neuropeptide-Y (NPY), a naturally occurring opioid synthesized in the brain that tranquilizes the amygdala. NPY reduced the incidence of ulcers and other anxiety-related effects in rats that were chemically distressed with yohimbine, and it is hypothesized that deficiencies in NPY are associated with chronic depression. At SERE, what appeared to be happening was that some individuals, for unknown reasons, reacted to the presence of stressors and helplessness by producing a chemical that tranquilized the fear-learning part of the brain. With the amygdala tranquilized, instead of responding with fear and fear-linked reactions, they were able to look at their environment more calmly and thus had a better chance of developing strategies that could cope, at least in some measure, with the stressors. Successful coping, in turn, diminished the feeling of helplessness and prevented distress. These same soldiers were also tested twenty-four hours after the course ended. Their NPY levels had returned to normal, while the NPY levels of other subjects had stayed low, a condition of NPY exhaustion. Thus, the Special Forces officers not only were observed to produce more NPY and to be better able to handle stress, they also recuperated quickly so that they were prepared to handle any subsequent stressors that followed the immediate stressful environment.[40]

Individual Distress and Group Behavior

Until this point, we have been dealing with the behavior of individuals, in laboratory or real-world settings. Military and political behavior occurs in social settings, and what we see people do in isolated settings may be very different from what they do when subjected to the same stimuli in social settings. Social institutions and dynamics may inhibit or reinforce the tendency of individuals to react to any stimuli in a given way. In the case of military personnel who may be distressed and depressed, we clearly have to deal with the issue of military discipline and the social dynamics of groups. It is not news to military officers that soldiers may become depressed and wish to give up when things go wrong on the battlefield. That is one reason why there are sergeants and other commissioned and noncommissioned officers to maintain discipline. All of the phenomena noted above may be real, but military discipline may create a set of external incentives and punishments such that even distressed soldiers will continue to perform in the way that their organizations require. In a different way, the phenomenon of unit cohesion, the willingness of soldiers in combat to sacrifice themselves for their task and their comrades, is deliberately created in order to counteract the natural tendency of those subjected to the stresses of combat to give up and do nothing. How might these social factors interact with the individual phenomenon of battlefield distress?

The question of discipline versus distress was the subject of a natural experiment created by the reaction of the German military in World War II to what it had observed in World War I. The causes of and cures for "shell shock," the general term given to the tremors, loss of speech, and other disorders suffered by soldiers on the Western Front, were much debated during and after the war. A Harvard physiologist, Walter Bradford Cannon, came close to the explanation of distress advanced in this chapter. Small, ductless glands, what we now refer to as the endocrine system, he hypothesized, became involved in the emotions of rage and fear by mobilizing the body for fight or flight. He observed that animals so aroused had higher levels of sugar in their blood, in order to provide fuel to the muscles. He noted the presence of adrenaline, but not cortisol, although he came close, since cortisol is involved in the metabolism of sugar in the muscles. What would happen, he and other researchers in this field asked, if these fight or flight mechanisms were activated under conditions in which neither fighting nor fleeing was possible, as in the case of soldiers in the trenches under heavy artillery bombardment? How long could the body withstand this state of mobilization without action and not suffer damage? No one was sure, and it was not clear what could be done to help the soldiers, even if it were true.[41]

In practice, the German Army, after some unsuccessful experimentation with electro-shock therapy, tended to treat shell-shock by means of therapy, either hypnosis or Freudian, and seclusion in clinics. Thousands of soldiers from the German Army were so treated. This was the result of prewar studies of victims of railway and industrial accidents who then suffered the same kind of tremors, and, of course, the influence of Freud and his students.[42] With the rise of Hitler, the aspects of German psychiatry that favored biological and hereditary factors and eschewed "Jewish" science grew in influence. To this was added the retrospective judgment that the lenient treatment of "war neurosis" had been part of the "stab in the back" that produced the defeat of 1918. German doctors had helped to bring down the Wilhelmine Empire, in this view. This led to the prewar atrocities inflicted on those deemed to be psychologically unfit. During World War II itself, this attitude led to a ferocious enforcement of disci-

pline on the battlefield. In contrast with the German Army in World War
I, which executed only forty-eight soldiers, the Wehrmacht in World War
II executed about ten thousand soldiers in the period 1939–1944, and
perhaps another five thousand in 1945, most for desertion or "subverting
the will of the people to fight." The effects seemed to be dramatic: of the
Wehrmacht units operating in the southern portions of the Soviet Union,
Army Group South, numbering over 500,000 men who were in combat in
the period March–June 1943, only eleven soldiers were diagnosed with
"primary fear neurosis following enemy action."

This seems to support the point that whatever the problems of cortisol
and helplessness, external incentives, if they are strong enough, can determine the behavior of soldiers. But as Ben Shephard points out, the of-
ficial Wehrmacht figures for "neurosis" must be treated with extreme
caution. Many soldiers who were cracking may have been shot summar-
ily, and one report from this period notes 364 executions of German
soldiers in eight days. Further, the ideological hostility to psychological
disorders of course led soldiers to discover physical problems with themselves that could be presented to German Army doctors. British doctors
examining German POWs in Normandy in 1944 found many patients
with psychological disorders identifying themselves as suffering from or-
ganic diseases. One way to estimate the level of severe psychological
trauma in the Wehrmacht is to estimate the number of soldiers who inflicted wounds on themselves or killed themselves outright, in order to
escape the war. One such estimate is that twenty-three thousand German
soldiers sought refuge in this way. And finally, the number of German
soldiers who were admitted to hospitals with "abnormal reactions" increased during the 1943 Battle of Kursk to 14 percent of all hospital ad-
missions, despite the fact that the leading military psychiatrist in the
Wehrmacht specialized in electro-shock therapy at levels of electricity ten
time higher than what doctors had judged to be "unbearably painful."[43]

The only reasonable judgment appears to be that while external discipline is a necessary and useful part of all military organizations, it cannot
and does not eliminate at the level of individuals the neuro-psychological
behavior induced by uncontrollable levels of stressors in the environment. On the other hand, if some soldiers will suffer from distress, not all
military organizations experience collapse on the battlefield. Under what
conditions might the distress of individuals be transformed into group-
level military disintegration?

First, and most obviously, uncontrollable levels of stress might be applied to all of the members of a military organization, all of the time, and
not just some of the front-line troops, some of the time. If uncontrollable
levels of stress are experienced by only some, and then only intermit-
tently, troop rotation policies will help the most distressed soldiers with-

draw from the stress while fresh troops take their place. The knowledge that such rotation will happen is itself useful for coping with stress.

But even if uncontrollable levels of stress are inflicted on military units on a sustained and general basis, some units will hold out longer than others, and some will not crack at all. The individual distress of soldiers is not transformed into group behavior. We have some sense that units that break down may experience the spread of the sense of helplessness from one individual to another. That is, one soldier may evaluate his or her own position, and own resolve, and decide that he or she can hold out. But if the next soldier panics or gives in to despair, the steadfast soldier may reconsider his or her own position. If, in fact, this is part of what occurs in military organizations experiencing collapse, then the general ideas we have about information cascades may be relevant to the problem at hand.

Information cascades have been clearly described by economists such as A. V. Bannerjee and have been used by Timur Kuran to explain rapidly shifting political dynamics.[44] Information cascades take place when individuals make decisions on the basis of their own private information, but also on the basis of what they see others doing, and when such decision making is sequential. Bannerjee's model can be put in plain language: I know what I think is the right thing to do, on the basis of what I know, but I also care about what other people do, because what they do reflects what they know, and they may know something I do not. So, suppose "everyone knows" that doing A is a little more likely to be better than doing B, but I also have my own private knowledge of the situation that everybody may not have, and I think that it is better to do B than A. Left to myself, I will choose to do B. But now suppose somebody else decides before I do, and I observe the decision. That person chooses A. The choice, I assume, reflects what he or she knows, and what he or she knows is probably as good as what I know. So my own special knowledge is different. What should I do? I should go with what "everybody knows and choose A, not B. Now suppose there are one hundred people, and ninety-nine of them privately prefer doing B to A, but the one person who prefers A chooses first. The whole group, deciding one by one in sequence, chooses A, not B, even though they preferred to do B, and even if the private information of the first actor is wrong.

Alternatively, in Kuran's formulation, I may feel better simply doing what everybody else does, though I do value my own independence to some extent, at least if I am not alone. If everybody does the same thing, I will feel better if I go along. If, however, a few people who are more independent than I am stand up and go against the group, then so will I, though I will have earlier publicly declared that I favor the group decision. My independent stand, added to the independence of the first few

renegades, will in turn embolden people who were independent, but a little bit less so than me, to go against the group.

This dynamic clearly captures what happens with fads and financial
bubbles. It also explains why public acceptance of a dictatorship unrav-
els as fast as it does once a sufficient core of people stands up against it,
though public acceptance for the dictatorship appears solid up until the
moment it cracks. It can also explain why some units crack when individuals are distressed while some do not. The cascade rests on the key
point that the special, private knowledge of one person is as good, or as
bad, as anyone else's, or on the fact that a small group of people acting
together is enough to embolden me to go with my internally preferred
strategy and against the larger group. If there are people whose actions I
believe are more likely to reflect accurate information than the actions of
others, or if there is a small group of people who act in concert and contrary to the group, I will go with the small group. To make this relevant
to the military problem, let us call the people who are more credible
sources of good information and who act in concert against the actions
of the larger group "officers." If I am a soldier in a bad situation, and a
fellow solder gives in to distress and cracks, I will take in that information. But if an officer or officers whom I trust tell me that the situation is
not so bad, and there are concrete ways to deal with the situation, I will
not follow the example of the distressed soldier. Even if there is a mass
military panic, if a few steady officers stand fast, they will reverse the
panic by rallying one, then many, soldiers. This is completely consistent
with the writings of military practitioners such as Field Marshall William
Slim, who noted that even when military conditions were horrible,
troops would not mutiny if officers they trusted stood by them.[45] Distress
at the individual level will be confined to the individual level as long as
the officer corps itself is solid, is trusted by the rank-and-file soldiers, and
is in contact with the rank-and-file soldiers.

A Model of Stress, Distress in War

How can we summarize these findings? Uncontrollable, unpredictable
stressors in the environment do produce in many people the condition of
distress, which is characterized by cognitive behavior that is indistinguishable from chronic depression. Distressed people display lowered
initiation of voluntary responses, difficulty in or lack of interest in learning about their environment caused by the expectation that their responses will not affect how they are treated, and, finally, lowered levels
of aggression and competitiveness. In extreme cases, they cease to be active. Distress does not occur in people who are stress immunized by prior

successful experiences with stressors, or who, for other unknown reasons, were able to focus on what they could do about their situation to control it, at least in part, and who, afterwards, focused on the more positive aspects of their experiences. Individual distress does not become group distress if there are ways for the distressed troops to withdraw from combat, and if the example of the distressed soldiers is counteracted by a steady and trusted officer corps.

We now have a model, derived from observations of men in combat, and from men and women experiencing distress under controlled circumstances, of how losing a war might affect the soldiers on the losing side by affecting their decision-making process and willingness to end the war. If conditions are created in which those fighting on one side of a war are subjected to stressors in their environment that they perceive they cannot control, they will, over time, become distressed. This means they will become pessimistic about the outcome of their actions, lack energy to perform their tasks, and perceive and understand less information from their environment that is relevant to the solution to their problems. This lack of energy and cognitive attention can contribute to a self-reinforcing cycle, in which lack of attention and action further decreases the ability of those fighting to control their environment. If this condition of distress is unrelieved by outside circumstances, and if a new challenge is presented to the distressed belligerent, the soldier is likely to respond ineffectively and then give up. If the officers do not stand fast or if they lose the trust of the soldiers, individual-level distress will be translated into group failure.

Who might be the victims of this induced depression, and how might their depression lead to war termination? In the first instance, the targets might be troops in battle. If enough of them become unwilling to fight, the capacity of the leaders of the state to continue the fighting will be affected, even if the leaders themselves are willing to continue the fighting. At the same time, or as an alternative, the leadership of a nation might itself be the victim of a state of induced helplessness and depression, and it might decide to end the war. Findings from the SERE psychologists and Special Forces trainers suggest that helplessness is more likely to be induced if there is no way to predict the occurrence of stressors in the environment, no way to avoid the attacks, and no way to establish a routine that enables the target to cope with the attacks. Multiple, different stressors will increase the difficulty of developing coping strategies.

This theoretical pathway to enemy surrender has been foreshadowed in the writings of at least two military philosophers. The ancient Chinese writer Sun Tzu cryptically wrote that all warfare is based on deception, and that the acme of success is not fighting the enemy in battle, but defeating the strategy of the enemy. He presented examples of ruses that confused the enemy and caused him to give up. He was terse in explicating his points, and there is disagreement about what he meant, but he could have been arguing that an enemy will give up if he is made to believe that he cannot understand or control a battlefield situation. If so, Sun Tzu could have been referring to the same basic phenomenon that has been reviewed here.

The British writer B. H. Liddell-Hart admired Sun Tzu and developed what he believed to be the correct reading of Sun Tzu in his book *Strategy*, in which he elaborated his theory of the "indirect approach." In that book, he says that "battle is only one of the means to the end of strategy." He wrote that the strategist's "true aim is not so much to seek battle as to seek a strategic situation so advantageous that if it does not itself produce the decision, its continuation by battle is sure to achieve this. In other words, dislocation is the aim of strategy." This psychological dislocation is the product of physical dislocation and "fundamentally springs from the feeling of being trapped." If an adversary does what is unexpected, by taking "the line of least expectation," he can induce this feeling in the enemy.[46] Again, the "indirect approach" might be the same as inducing cognitive or physical helplessness and subsequent surrender.

However, while Sun Tzu and Liddell-Hart wrote about ways in which one might induce the condition of helplessness and surrender in an adversary, they presented little compelling evidence that the process they posited had occurred. Sun Tzu gave only one or two anecdotes to support his claims (the commander who confuses his enemy by leaving open the gates of his fortress; the commander who feigns the withdrawal of his forces by showing fewer and fewer bonfires at night), and Liddell-Hart presented cases of victorious battles that displayed no obvious common factors. Is it possible to come up with better data that suggests that this mode of inducing surrender has actually worked? To answer this question, we might begin by looking at some battlefield cases. In those cases, we will seek situations of physical vulnerability, combined with the inability to predict, avoid, or respond to physical attacks. Such cases match the laboratory conditions that induce helplessness and correspond to an intuitive conception of helplessness. Such conditions ought to induce distress, depression, and an unwillingness to fight.

The helplessness-depression hypothesis is generally consistent with descriptions of behavior in the losing camp at the end of wars. The soldiers of the Confederacy surrendered in 1865 even though they had the means to go on fighting, and even though they had been highly motivated through 1864. The Confederate States of America had close to 500,000 rations for its men in the spring of 1865, and Robert E. Lee had some 58,000 men under his command. The president of the Confederacy, Jefferson Davis, ordered the Confederate military commanders to continue a guerrilla war when they could no longer meet the Union forces in open battle. But neither the southern battlefield commanders nor the ordinary soldiers were willing to continue fighting. One historian of the final months of the Civil War wrote that "what failed was the structure of command within this mass of men. While some units preserved discipline and morale, many others trudged along more by instinct than conviction. The heart of the Confederate cause had stopped beating long before its military and political leaders acknowledged the fact." It was the judgment of Lee, as he expressed it to Ulysses S. Grant at Appomatox, that "the South was a big country and that we might have to march over it three or four times before the war entirely ended, but that we would now be able to do it as they could no longer resist us." Lee had testified before the rebel senate in June 1865 that the war was lost.[47] The general suffering of the soldiers was accompanied by a cracking of the will of the officer corps. The change between the popular morale observed by Sherman in 1864 and that which prevailed in 1865 did not involve physical so much as mental or emotional exhaustion.

This broad-brush description, while suggestive, does not give us enough information about individual circumstances and behavior to help us understand whether the specified mechanisms of helplessness, distress, and depression were at work. More detailed descriptions of men on the losing side of a battle are, however, available. The German blitzkrieg invasion of France in 1940 is often referred to as a case in which the psychological shock to the defender, rather than physical destruction, produced surrender. Is there evidence that confirms this impression? The historian Marc Bloch recorded his impressions of his fellow French officers during the spring of 1940. Bloch noted, first, that the French officers did feel that they had lost control of their environment because of the unexpectedly rapid pace of the German advances: "The truth of the matter was that the Germans advanced a great deal faster than they should have done according to the old rules of the game." As a result, the Germans were never where the French thought they would be: "We were never quite certain as to his movements . . . due mainly to a persistent failure ever to judge distances correctly," in terms of how long it would take the Germans to traverse them. Second, Bloch noted the mental state of these French officers: "The worst cases of mental paralysis were the result of that mood of outraged amazement which laid hold of men who were faced by a rhythm of events completely different from the kind of thing that they had been led to expect. From this form of psychological shock the officers of front-line formations were certainly not immune, but its ravages were most obvious further back."

Bloch also recorded the observable behavior of the officers:

The first symptoms of this disease were external—haggard eyes, badly shaven chins, a nervous restlessness which showed itself, in the early stages, as fever-ish irritability over small things, and went on to assume a forced calmness which deceived no one. When a high ranking officer started to say "What's the use?" it was time for the fighting troops to keep their eyes skinned. Very soon after that, the tide of despair began to rise, and . . . set them looking for refuge in a sort of nerveless, do-nothing apathy.[48]

Bloch does seem to be describing people suffering from helplessness, dis-tress, and depression. Are there other observations of this phenomenon?

In the 1991 war against Iraq, Iraqi troop morale was not an explicit target of American airpower, but front-line Iraqi Army positions were frequently attacked from the air. Allied forward observation aircraft were overhead more or less all the time, so the Iraqi soldiers knew that air strikes could be called down on their positions at almost any time. There was no way to develop a routine or schedule that minimized expo-sure to attacks. A variety of munitions were used (ordinary high explo-sives, special ten-thousand-pound bombs, fuel-air munitions, A-10 gun-fire), which had different effects and against which different forms of protection were necessary. Subsequent interviews with Iraqi officers taken prisoner were revealing: "One senior officer reported that he could rarely sleep more than two hours at a time and that the constant pound-ing shattered the soldiers' nerves, causing some men, as he put it, nearly to go mad. The bombing produced this strong psychological effect even though it caused the Iraqi officer's division relatively light casualties: per-haps 100 men killed and another 150 wounded." The psychological ef-fects of B-52 strikes were clearly linked to a feeling of physical, but, more importantly, psychological helplessness:

> Even though few Iraqi POWs or line crossers reported that their units were ac-tually hit in B-52 strikes, many had seen B-52s attacking other units in the dis-tance and had felt the ground tremors from B-52 detonations. The sound and vibrations of the B-52 bomb detonations—even when the actual strike zone was as far away as 40 kilometers—spawned suspense and fear because the sol-diers imagined that they would be the next target of attack, and they realized that their bunkers were neither sufficiently deep nor sufficiently hard to pro-tect them.

> An Iraqi officer told his interrogator that he had surrendered because of B-52 strikes. "But your position was never attacked by B-52s," his interrogator ex-claimed. "That is true," the Iraqi officer replied, "but I saw one that was attacked."[49]

Perhaps Iraqi troops were poorly motivated even before the bombing began. The collapse of their will might have been the result of their latent hostility to their own government. Other soldiers with better reasons to fight might not have responded in the same way to this kind of pressure. German and British civilians withstood prolonged bombing and the destruction of major cities, despite beliefs by the opposing forces that their morale would break. What caused the difference? The perspective suggested by this chapter was that the feeling of helplessness was induced in the case of the Iraqi soldiers but not in the British and Germans. The opposing argument is that it was differences in their basic motivation. In order to resolve this, we should look at cases of troops known to have high levels of motivation to see how they reacted to conditions of combat induced helplessness. We have limited evidence that the will to fight of even highly motivated soldiers—North Vietnamese and Viet Cong troops—was shaken when they saw no way of coping with American air power.

Truong Nhu Tang was the Viet Cong "shadow" minister of justice for the communist government that was to be put in place in South Vietnam when the Republic of Vietnam was conquered. He was a veteran of the war against the French and had endured much combat and survival in the field. In his autobiography he wrote that "for all the privations and hardships, nothing the guerrillas had to endure compared with the stark terrorization of the B-52 bombardments." Tang had observed the effects of B-52 strikes, and, on several occasions, he was in an area that was hit by B-52s. "The first few times I experienced a B-52 attack, it seemed, as I strained to press myself into the bunker floor, that I had been caught in the Apocalypse. The terror was complete. One lost control of bodily functions as the mind screamed incomprehensible orders to get out." No physical protection was adequate against the strikes, and, unless hours of warning were available, it was not possible to move far enough away to avoid the killing area.

Some troops would have broken under this pressure. Tang did not. Why? Was it the result of motivation or the ability to avoid helplessness? Tang notes two factors that suggest it was the latter. First, Soviet military intelligence developed the ability to give warning that the B-52s were directed against a specific area while the bombers were in flight, but hours away from their targets. The bombers could then be avoided by rapid flight. Second, multiple exposure to the strikes induced stress immunization, and a sense of fatalism. But Tang observed that many Viet Cong did crack: "Some guerrillas suffered nervous breakdowns and were packed off for hospital stays; others had to be sent home. There were cases, too, of fighters rallying to Saigon government, unable to cope." But when things became too much to endure, there was a way to gain a respite: "Times came when nobody was able to manage, and units would seek a hopeful refuge across the border in Cambodia."[50]

Other cases drawn from the experiences of the North Vietnamese Army are suggestive. In 1971 a special officer was sent to deal with a North Vietnamese transport unit that was near collapse. It had been bringing supplies down the Ho Chi Minh trail at night, but the Americans had introduced AC-130 gunships that utilized electronic signal detection devices and night vision equipment to detect trucks and to aim rapid-fire guns at their targets. The commander of the company said: "I don't think anyone of them fears the enemy. But the AC-130 is really redoubtable. Our drivers call it the 'Thug.' The drivers added, "That's right! The AC-130 is a good marksman and rarely misses its target. . . .' The dangerous thing is that it needs neither flares nor guidance by a recon plane. Moreover, it sticks like a leech." What was unnerving about the new weapon was that its attacks could not be anticipated (ordinary fighter aircraft needed to be guided by forward air observers, whose appearance warned of a possible attack), nor evaded by pulling off the road and turning off the engine. Tactics were changed, and the trucks began to operate again in the day, since methods for handling daylight attacks by fighter-bombers were available. Coping strategies reversed the decline in morale.[51]

Viet Cong troops also faced American ground forces. Beginning in 1964, the RAND Corporation conducted multiple interviews with Viet Cong "hard core" cadres who had been taken prisoner in an effort to assess the factors that might be reducing their morale. However, the interviews indicated that VC morale was not declining at all, and so the focus of the study shifted to the question of why it remained high, despite years of war with a more powerful enemy. In 1967 the first study noted that if the Americans were not going to kill every last enemy soldier, they must achieve effects at the psychological level, that "there must be taking place a gradual destruction of his fighting spirit." This was not happening. The reason why was summarized in the section of the report entitled "The Endurable Battle Experience." Interviews indicated that "despite their high kill ratio, American forces conduct many search-*without*-destroy missions; and on the Viet Cong side, the men, on the whole, move frequently and fight rarely." Viet Cong soldiers faced full-scale action only "a few times a year," 2.3 to 2.8 times a year.[52] They could choose to engage the American troops or not. American firepower, if engaged, was lethal, but they could cope with it by avoiding it. Rather than being helpless, they were quite able to predict and control the levels of battlefield stressors.

This study was followed by another set of interviews with captured Viet Cong and North Vietnamese Army (NVA) troops conducted in 1968 after the two enemy offensives in February and May of that year. Morale was still high, despite a higher frequency of battle and higher casualties. The factor that remained the same was the ability of the Viet Cong and NVA forces to avoid contact with American forces by moving away from them. The need to move now occurred more frequently, and, to that extent, the communist troops were less able to control their environment, and this was reported as a cause of lowered morale.[53]

The RAND analysts noted at several points that the sustained morale of the Viet Cong and NVA troops stood in sharp contrast to the collapse of Chinese People's Liberation Army (PLA) troops in Korea in April and May 1951, when over ninety thousand PLA troops surrendered to the UN forces. The PLA troops sent to Korea were veterans of campaigns fought against the Japanese and the Chinese Nationalists, and were the best in the Chinese army. While the PLA forces were subjected to intense American attack, interviews with Chinese POWs indicated that "the psychoneurosis engendered by UN air attack may actually have outweighed the actual physical destruction done by airpower." Intense battle in the first months of 1951 killed many Chinese soldiers but induced few surrenders. Beginning in April, however, UN tactics shifted. "Previously, when PLA offensives had spent themselves, the communists had been permitted to withdraw beyond artillery range and to reorganize and resupply. In this case, however, the UN Eighth Army launched a vicious counterattack on 22 May, which put the PLA troops to precipitous flight." Sustained ground pressure was accompanied by sustained aerial attack and induced, according to the interviews, a loss of confidence in the POWs in their military and political leadership, doctrine, and ultimate victory.[54] On the basis of these POW interviews, a trained psychologist working for RAND, Herbert Goldhamer, wrote a secret memo in which he stated that by May, the communist forces were on the brink of either collapse or a major military escalation conducted by the Soviet Union: "It is my considered judgment that the cease-fire bid was an imperative necessity for the CCF [Chinese Communist Forces]. This necessity arose not because CCF power had in the ordinary sense been destroyed. . . . A more dangerous development had taken place. The CCF has increasingly lost its capacity to control its troops."[55]

In neither the Iraqi nor the Vietnamese cases did the level of causalities inflicted by American bombing appear to be the main driver of morale. In both cases, initial feelings of helplessness did induce fear and despair. Differences in the ultimate reactions of the troops being bombed or attacked seem, on the basis of reports given by the soldiers, to have been related to differences in their ability to predict, avoid, and ameliorate American attacks, and not due simply to differences in general levels of troop motivation.

Conclusion

Does the phenomenon of distress explain war termination? By itself, clearly not. Chinese troops were distressed and PLA formations collpsed in 1951, but truce talks gave them a respite, and the war went on until the death of Stalin. The collapse in the will to fight can be reversed by able leadership if the actions of the adversary give the distressed troops time to recover or be replaced. As Clausewitz noted, and as modern writers have formally stated, failure in battle tends to propagate, but this is not inevitable. The model of distress, however, may give us a way to explain, for example, the collapse in the morale of the French Army after the failed Nivelle offensives in 1917, and the massive defection from the German Army in the fall of 1918. In both cases, troops at the individual level were distressed, and, at the same time, they lost confidence in their military leadership. The behavior of defeated troops in battle is not irrelevant to war termination.

This approach also supplies a foundation for the traditional military argument that initial success on the battlefield must be ruthlessly exploited by intense pursuit and followup operations: having induced a subjective state of helplessness and depression, enemy troops will be, for a time, more than usually incapable of dealing with additional attacks. The approach suggests why combined arms operations have more value than the independent value of the separate forces because an enemy that is forced to solve multiple problems is more likely to experience a subjective loss of control over the environment. Also, bombing should not be predictable in its timing or in the character of the weapons if maximum distress is to be induced, and sustained bombing that denies the enemy sanctuaries in time and space is more likely to induce distress.

Finally, in the future, as intelligence and long-range precision strike capabilities improve, leadership targets may become the object of direct attacks that have as their objective the creation of distress in the enemy leadership. Currently, the relevant target information is generally not available, but an understanding of distress suggests that obtaining that information may lead to the ability to execute strategies that directly induce the collapse of the enemy leadership even if it cannot be physically destroyed.

Chapter Five_____

Of Time, Testosterone, and Tyrants

How SHOULD we think about states that are ruled by a single, all-powerful leader? This is a difficult question. We are not even sure what to call them. Such states are referred to as authoritarian states, dictatorships, "rogue" states, and "states of concern." Ancient philosophers called them tyrannies. Are such states likely to act rationally, or will they be more likely to behave in ways that we do not anticipate and that lead to wars? How should we deal with such states? If we need to deter them, will we need to do things that differ from what we would need to do to deter a democracy, for example? This chapter will introduce the argument that there are states that we can call, as did the ancient political philosophers, tyrannies. In ancient political philosophy, tyrannies were defined as regimes in which rulers rule in accord with their will, and not with the laws, and against the will of the subjects. Nothing in this definition implies that a tyrant is irrational, but it does suggest that they will, because of the kind of people they are and because of the social setting that they create, calculate differently from other rulers. Tyrants are not crazy, in the sense of acting randomly or without purpose, but, it will be argued, they are more likely than other forms of government to act on the basis of the short-term consequences of their actions. The ability to suppress the desire to gratify impulses in the short term, for the sake of larger, long-term benefits, will be less than in other states. Drawing on arguments made in the chapter on testosterone and dominance, this chapter argues that tyrannies are also defined by the tendency of the tyrant to punish challengers to his position internally. This creates a climate that affects the flow of information to the tyrant. In a social setting in which there is an all-powerful ruler who punishes challenges, few people will be willing to give the tyrant information that policies are not succeeding. Learning and negative feedback will be suppressed. This characterization of tyrannies will suggest how others might best act to deter them.

The specific components of the argument are as follows.

1. Tyrannies have shorter time horizons within which strategic costs and benefits are calculated. Specifically, tyrannies will be shown to be prone to be strongly affected by incentives and disincentives that appear near in time to the moment of choice. Tyrannies will act quickly to pursue what is most in their

interest on the basis of calculations that look at the short-term, rather than long-term, consequences of their actions. In the language of economics, they will severely discount costs and benefits that present themselves far in the future relative to the time of decision. Relative to other governments, they will act "opportunistically." This does not mean that what they want will change, but the means or strategies that they choose can rapidly shift, for example, from pacific to warlike, and then back.

2. Second, tyrants engage in dominant behavior, as defined in chapter 3. They have a predisposition to punish perceived challengers and are unwilling to co-exist with rivals or potential rivals unless the net short-term costs of eliminating the rival is very high.

3. Tyrants who are intolerant of challengers will tend to create a social environment in which the tyrant is feared and hated. The fact that the tyrant is feared and hated will create pressures on the tyrant, in addition to the natural impulses to focus on the short-term need to survive in the dangerous environment, which the tyrant has created.

4. Because the tyrant is feared and hated, subordinates will tend not to provide streams of information containing negative feedback concerning chosen policies. Hence, the social setting of the tyrant will tend to reinforce, rather than correct, the decisions of the tyrant.

5. Tyrants also are more sensitive to information presented in face-to-face settings than by other modes.

6. The policy implications of this understanding of tyrants are that deterrence will fail when communications with the tyrant and available military force are not used in ways that affect calculations about *the short term*. Information about deterrent threats will be most effectively conveyed to the tyrant in face-to-face settings, either by representatives of the deterring power or by direct demonstrations to the tyrant. Deterrent military forces that are in being, but which take weeks or months to be effective, much less military forces that could be created after periods of mobilization lasting some years, will not be effective deterrents to tyrants.

The predictions about the strategic behavior of tyrants have several corollaries that help us to specify forms of behavior characteristic of tyrants in areas other than decisions about war. A man who is less inclined to suppress the short-term impulse to gratify desires for the sake of longer-term gain is likely to be lazy and self-indulgent with respect to his appetites. He will not work hard in the office reading documents, and he will rely on his belief that he can understand a complex situation by meeting with the people involved in it. In addition, while the overall objectives of a tyranny may be quite stable, the policy decisions of a tyrant in general will "jitter" more than that of other governments. Decisions to be hostile or be friendly, to use force or not, will be affected by short-term assessments, and the environments faced by tyrants may change such that the short-term net benefits may shift from negative to positive and back fairly quickly as forces move around and temporary coalitions form and dissolve. Governments that tend to focus on the long-term consequences of their actions will not experience the same perturbations as short-term outcomes shift, if the long-term results stay roughly the same. "Opportunistic" strategies will shift with the short-term opportunities, though external circumstances can lock tyrants into courses of action.

The chapter has six main parts. The first section contains a review of the debate about how to think about tyrannies. It is of primary interest to political theorists. The second, third, and fourth sections, respectively, will develop the arguments supporting the claims that tyrants are people who have shorter-term time horizons (in the sense of acting more on the basis of payoffs that appear near in time to the moment of decision), greater sensitivity to local status issues and less tolerance for rivals than other regimes, and extreme sensitivity to information available in face-to-face settings. The fifth section then looks at tyrannies, not just tyrants. Tyrannies are the product of the personal nature of the tyrant plus the institutions through which the tyrant rules. The sixth section uses the analysis of tyrannies to explain historical behavior of tyrants that otherwise appears anomalous. There is also a brief final section that sketches some of the policy implications of the argument.

The Nature of Tyrannies

Does the behavior of tyrannies, considered as political systems or regimes, differ in any systematic way from that of other states in which the decision-making power of the state is concentrated in the hands of one person? Do tyrants, as individuals, differ in any meaningful way when compared with other political figures? If so, what might those differences be, and can we specify them clearly enough to be able, consistently, to distinguish tyrannies from other forms of government, and to anticipate the particular ways in which tyrannies might react to the behavior of other states? This is a question that has divided political scientists since Machiavelli and is at the heart of current policy debates about nuclear proliferation and the future of deterrence. The abstract questions about the nature of tyranny lie behind our intuitive historical understandings of rulers such as Joseph Stalin, Adolf Hitler, and Mao Zedong, and behind our anxiety about the behavior of rulers such as Saddam Hussein and Kim Chong-Il. We are somehow sure that these are men not like other men, and that men[1] like them have and might in the future behave in ways that are dangerous to us in circumstances in which other rulers, facing the same international conditions, would not behave dangerously. If the spread of democracy tends to hold out the hope that the democratic peace will spread, American policymakers may be concerned with turbulent social and political conditions in countries such as Russia, China, and Iran, conditions that resemble those in Germany, Russia, and China in the first half of the twentieth century, and that led to the emergence of tyrannies in those countries. Given the availability of nuclear and biological weapons of mass destruction, the possibility that tyrannies may use force when we would not expect other governments to do so is particularly worrisome.

For political scientists, the question revolves around whether "tyrants" exist at all as a meaningful analytical category. What is the difference between a tyrant and a king or any other ruler who has all of the authority or decision-making power of the state in his hands? In his book *Discourses on Livy*, Machiavelli referred to some rulers as tyrants, but he referred to the same men simply as "princes" in his book addressed to a ruler who might himself be thought a tyrant.[2] Thomas Hobbes, in book 2, chapter 19, of *Leviathan*, denied the existence of any substantive difference between the two kinds of rulers and claimed that arbitrary and subjective factors were the only reason for the existence of the term "tyranny" at all. The only differences among types of government that could be objectively observed were the differences in the distribution of effective political power within governments. That power, he asserted, resided "in one man, or in an assembly of more than one; and into that assembly, either every man hath right to enter, or not everyone." Following from this structural approach, there could only be three types of government: monarchy, democracy, and aristocracy. "Other kinds of commonwealth there can be none. . . . There be other names of government, in histories and books of policy; as tyranny, and oligarchy: But they are not the names of other forms of government, but of the same forms misliked. For they that are discontented under monarchy call it tyranny."

From the distribution of power within a government, Hobbes deduced several conclusions about the behavior of monarchies and concluded that they were better structured than the other forms of government to acquire and utilize information for the public good, and more likely to act consistently. In all forms of government, the rulers would have their own, private self-interests, which might or might not be consistent with the interests of the commonwealth, "and for the most part, if the public interest chance to cross the private, he prefers the private: for the passions of men are commonly more potent than their reason. From whence it follows, that where the public and private interest are most closely united, there is the public interest most advanced. Now in monarchy, the private interest is the same with the public. The riches, power, and honour of the monarch arise only from the riches, strength and reputation of his subjects." In democracy, on the other hand, "public prosperity confers not so much to the private fortune of one that is corrupt, or ambitious, as doth many times a perfidious advice, a treacherous action, or a civil war."

With regard to the ability of the various forms of government to acquire the information they needed to make decisions for the benefit of the nation, a "monarch can receive counsel from anybody he pleases, and with as much secrecy as he wills," but an assembly can hear only from those who have "a right from the beginning" to be admitted, and secrecy is impossible. Finally, because the decisions of a king were the decisions of a single individual, they were not subject to the inconsistency that shifting coalitions and majorities might generate in democracy or aristocracy, such "that the resolutions of a monarch are subject to no other inconstancy than that of human nature."

The conclusion was that kings and tyrants were the same, and both were better suited to the calculated pursuit of the interest of the nation than other forms of government. Faced with similar international environments, tyrants would be no less inclined to pursue the interests of their nation than democracies, and quite possibly more. If a democracy would not engage in war under a given set of conditions, because the anticipated costs of war to the nation would exceed the benefits, neither would a tyranny. This general conclusion has been picked up by modern political scientists who focused on the different kinds of foreign policy that might be expected from different kinds of government. Jack Snyder has argued, for example, that in societies that contained many powerful groups, each of which participated in government decisions, there would be the problem that well-organized groups with clear-cut interests would be more effective in getting the government to do what they wanted than the general public. The public at large was not well organized and would tend to have less well specified interests, such as "avoid unnecessary wars," that would be hard to turn into specific recommendations to compete with those developed by special interest groups. The general public might well lack the kind of information that would be necessary to show the negative consequences of the policies advocated by particular groups. If this were the case, each special interest group would defeat the general interests of society and could compel the state to adopt its preferred policy. In the aggregate, the state would adopt all of the policies of all of the special interest groups, even if, taken together, the policies constituted an inconsistent or impossibly ambitious national strategy. If different special interest groups had different expansionist foreign policy agendas, the state would adopt them all, and "overexpansion" would result, and lead the state toward a more ambitious foreign policy than it could sustain. If the government, however, was dominated by a tightly integrated "unitary" oligarchy that collectively represented the interests of many groups in society, it could make integrated decisions that took into account the interests of all the groups in society, and that avoided policies that unreasonably favored the interests of one group over another. Similarly, the "encompassing interests of a single dictator should in principle check any inclinations toward overexpansion. But the validity of this hypothesis depends greatly on the dictator's continuing ability to calculate long-run costs and benefits rationally." Snyder, like Hobbes, notes that the king/tyrant/dictator would face no structural obstacles in his pursuit of the foreign policy best for his country, but he would remain heir to the general limits of human nature, and there would be no institutional checks and balances to restrain him if he happened to have idiosyncratic inclinations.[3] On the whole, however, there is no general reason in Snyder's argument to expect tyrants to be less likely than other governments to pursue in a calculated way the interests of their countries on the basis of the opportunities presented to them by the international environment. If anything, he should be more likely so to behave.

Randall Schweller has pursued this line of reasoning to its logical conclusion, arguing that when Hitler declared war on the Soviet Union and then the United States in 1941, he was doing what any rational actor with his goals would have done. He was simply pursuing the best course of action for Germany. Hitler, like many Germans, wanted to revise the international status quo in Germany's favor. He had to take into account the fact that Britain, the United States, and the Soviet Union were likely to oppose Germany's revisionist policies, and what he could know about the international distribution of power. In this situation, it was a rational calculation for Germany to attack the Soviet Union in 1941, because the Soviet Union was generally perceived to be very weak, and then to pursue the defeat of the United States after Germany had incorporated the material resources of the Soviet Union. If Hitler attacked the United States before he had finished conquering the Soviet Union, this was because the United States, by virtue of its support to Great Britain, was already virtually at war with Germany, and so there was nothing substantial to be lost by overtly going to war against it.[4] Hitler attacked the Soviet Union and the United States, not because of the nature of the Nazi government, but because any German government that entertained the goal of reversing the international system that arose after World War I and that had rationally calculated the anticipated outcomes of alternative strategies would also have chosen to go attack those countries at those times. Schweller, like Hobbes, argues that the strategic behavior of a tyrant, if one chose to call him that, was no different than the behavior of other rational actors with revisionist aims.

This view of tyrants, however, is very different from the understanding of ancient political writers such as Plato and Xenophon. Plato discusses the nature of the soul of the tyrant in book 9 of *The Republic* and characterizes it as being dominated by "some love in him—a great winged drone—to be the leader of all idle desires," a love that "purges him of moderation and fills him with madness brought in from abroad. . . . And . . . a man becomes tyrannic in the precise sense when either by nature or by his practices or both he has become drunken, erotic, and melancholic."[5] Xenophon was the author of the dialogue entitled *Tyrannicus*, or *Hiero*, after the name of the tyrant who is the interlocutor of Simonides, the poet, in the dialogue. Tyrannicus is the only work in the ancient corpus devoted entirely and exclusively to a discussion of tyranny. In the dialogue, Hiero, the tyrant, does not refer to the state of his soul, but he does discuss his own desires, remarking, in particular, that "I believe myself that to take from an unwilling enemy is the most pleasant of all things."[6] Xenophon, like Plato, also addresses the nature of the external circumstances in which the tyrant lives by virtue of the nature of his rule. The tyrant, unlike other rulers, lives in constant fear of being killed by his own subjects. Xenophon has Hiero say the following: "The tyrant, Simonides, know well, lives night and day as one condemned by all human beings to die for his injustice." Other rulers might have enemies abroad, but they are safe at home in their own cities. "But the tyrants know that when they reach their own city they are then in the midst of the largest number of their enemies." Nor will they be told the truth, but can expect only flattery, "for no one is willing to accuse a tyrant to his face."[7]

Following Plato and Xenophon, and unlike Hobbes, Leo Strauss defined a tyrant in opposition to a king: "Kingship is such rule as is exercised over willing subjects and is in accordance with the laws of the city; tyranny is such rule as is exercised over unwilling subjects and accords, not with laws, but with the will of the ruler."[8]

Which understanding of tyranny is correct? The claim that a king is the same as a tyrant is easy to understand, but what does it mean to have a soul in which love is a great winged drone? The following sections will use the classical arguments to generate more specific propositions relevant to the analysis of international affairs. If we can decide this issue, we will not then immediately be able to predict the behavior of tyrants. The character of a tyranny is not the same as its decisions. The decisions will depend on how the assessments are performed in particular international settings. But if we can develop a better understanding of the ways in which tyrants make decisions, we will have made a start toward understanding their actions.

Tyrants and Time Horizons

One dimension along which the decision-making behavior of individuals may vary is the time horizon within which they consider the future outcomes of alternative courses of action. Different terms—time preferences, time discount rates, and so on—are used to refer to essentially the same idea and are used almost always to refer to the forward time horizons of individuals, although the concept of time horizons backward, or memory of past gains and losses, is equally important and can affect decision making (as in "don't get mad, get even"). The idea that individuals may be more or less foresighted when making decisions is an old one. Tocqueville, for example, was aware of the dangers of short-term orientations in a democracy and frequently discussed the desirability of institutions in democratic societies that lead individuals to pursue "self-interest properly understood," which seems to be synonymous with the self-interest of an individual that takes into account the fact that the individual lives in a community over a long span of time, and that present actions will affect future environments. Self-interest properly understood leads people to forgo short-term gains and to make small short-term sacrifices for the sake of greater common goods that will arrive in the future.[9] The time horizon of individuals, for Tocqueville, was strongly affected by the nature of local institutions and family, but also by the dominant ideas of the time.

The pathological consequences of radically short-term time horizons were used to explain urban poverty in Edward C. Banfield's *The Unheavenly City*, in which he used differences in time preferences to define social classes: "The individual's orientation toward the future will be regarded as a function of two factors: (1) ability to imagine a future, and (2) ability to discipline oneself to sacrifice present for future satisfaction. The more distant the future the individual can imagine and discipline himself to make sacrifices for, the 'higher' is his class."[10] Persistent urban poverty was, by this definition, a "lower-class" phenomenon, and the product of radical present orientation. In game theory, the importance of time preferences for the emergence of cooperation was highlighted by Robert Axelrod. Briefly put, he showed that if individuals did not look beyond the immediate game or interaction in which they were playing, they would have no reason not to cheat or exploit the person with whom they were dealing. If, however, they did consider many future games in which they would play the same person over and over, or if they knew they would play some other person who knew what happened in the ongoing games, they would modify their behavior and become less exploitive. How much they cared about the future would affect how cooperative they would be in a given game.[11]

Economists, of course, have been confronted with the phenomenon of interest rates for money, which reflect the fact that people prefer to have a given amount of money now rather than the same amount of money sometime in the future, but they have made only intermittent and sketchy attempts to explain why this should be so. They have discussed, for example, the impact of the uncertainty that people have about whether they will be alive at the point in the future when the benefits will arrive, the psychological pain of not being able to consume what is in front of one, and the inability of individuals clearly to envision the pleasure of consuming goods in the future.[12] More recently, economists have tended to argue that the size of the stock of goods we have now affects our interest in giving up some part of that stock in order to get even more later on: poor people, it is reasoned, have less stuff now and so will be less willing to defer the consumption of some of that small stock for the sake of future rewards than will rich people, who have large stocks of goods.[13] But, by and large, economists have been content to note the obvious fact that people must be promised more money in the future to make them willing to defer consumption of a sum of money now, and to quantify that time preference by looking at interest rates in the market. As a result, they have been less interested in exploring why individuals have the time preferences that they do, or to ask whether all individuals have the same time horizons or different ones.

Economist Alan Rogers made one recent effort to think through why people have the time horizons they do. He began by noting that we make decisions with our brains, and that our brains are the product, in part, of our evolutionary history. A key element of that history was having offspring who survived, but having offspring meant that parents had to give up some of what they could consume for themselves for the sake of providing for their children. On the other hand, if parents gave up too much of their current consumption for their children, the parents would suffer and be less able to care for themselves, and thus for their children. Too much or too little sacrifice of present consumption for the sake of the future would decrease the overall chances of having offspring survive to the age where they could have children in their turn. At the point of evolutionary equilibrium, the parents' need for present consumption is balanced against the chances of the future survival of their children. The reductions in the parents' life span that were the result of giving up one unit of present consumption should equal the increase in the life expectancy of the children. At equilibrium, the value to the parents of giving up an additional unit of present consumption, at the margin, will be equal to the marginal increases in evolutionary fitness gained by giving the children that unit of consumption. The concept is refined by acknowledging that at some point in the life of the parents, added years of life for them do not affect their ability to help their children (who are already mature) reach maturity, and so the calculation will yield different results at different points in the life cycle. Given the average number of children families have, the average survival rate of the children, the length of time that it takes children to reach reproductive age, and average life expectancies, one can calculate the time discount rate at equilibrium, which, for people about thirty years old turns out to be about 2 percent a year in constant dollars, a figure that is approximately equal to estimates of the underlying long-term interest rate.[14]

This assumes that if a population has pursued a successful evolutionary course, the population, on average, will have a certain perspective on the future. If the population is genetically homogenous, each individual will have the average time perspective. But what if the population is not homogenous? It is rare, for good evolutionary reasons, for a population to be entirely uniform, so there is likely to be some variation in the time preferences in a population that has emerged through evolution. With regard to time horizons and reproductive strategies, we can see that there are at least two strategies open to parents. They could have many children, and take less care of each of them, if they think that by having lots of children they increase their chances of having at least some of them survive. Or they could have fewer children and take very good care of them. The two different strategies imply two different kinds of time horizons. The first strategy, which could be driven by uncertainty about what the future will bring, is compatible with shorter-term time horizons than the strategy of having fewer children, and betting that they will survive. Both kinds of behavior are observable. Because evolutionary theory does not exclude heterogeneity of time preferences, we still need to ask why and how people might differ with regard to their ability, in Banfield's words, to imagine the future and to discipline themselves to take into account the imagined future consequences of their actions.

One important set of experiments conducted by psychologists suggests a way of understanding this issue. The psychologists began with the observation of an all-too-common form of human behavior. People often realize that something is bad for them in the long run, even though it is pleasant when experienced. They know they should not indulge. But when that something is right in front of them and they must make a decision about gratification that will be delivered in the short term, they cannot adhere to their decision to do what is best for them in the long run. Examples abound. When I go to bed, I set my alarm clock for 4:00 a.m. so that I can work for two hours before breakfast, because I value the long-term benefits of getting the work done sooner. When the alarm clock goes off, however, I turn it off and go back to sleep. I decide not to smoke cigarettes, because of the long-term costs, but when a cigarette is in front of me, I smoke it anyway. Similar examples could be multiplied with regard to encounters with alcohol, narcotics, delicious but fattening food, or attractive but forbidden sexual partners. In all these cases, the action that is good for me in the long run is very different from the action I wish to take when the opportunity to indulge in sleep, food, sex, or drugs is open to me in the short term, defined as a short time interval between my decision to act and the arrival of the reward.

This phenomenon has been studied and its effects quantified by psychologists. In experiments with students, a subject is offered fifty dollars now, or a hundred dollars tomorrow. To make sure that the decision is not biased by issues of uncertainty (how do I know you will keep your promise to pay off tomorrow?), precautions are made to ensure the certainty of future delivery: e.g., the cash is put in a prepaid Courier envelope addressed to the subject and held by the subject over a Courier drop box. In most cases, but not always, subjects choose the fifty dollars today. Depending on how the experiment is conducted, this decision implies an effective annual discount rate of 30,000 percent to 300,000 percent. But then the experimenter offers the following choice: you can have fifty dollars a year from now, or one hundred dollars a year plus one day from now. In this case, the subjects almost always take the one hundred dollars. This is a paradox: if I value A now to B delivered to me one day from now, I should prefer A to B delivered to me one year plus one day from now. But I do not. It is the nearness in time of the payoff to the time of the decision that reverses the choice, just as my preferences shift from the time when I set my alarm clock, when I am not sleepy, to the time when it goes off and the extra hours of sleep are right in front of me. This phenomenon, in which we choose something in favor of another when the payoff is distant in time, but then switch when the payoff is immediate, is different from the steady discounting of the future implied by constant interest rates. When interest rates are constant, if I prefer X to Y now, I prefer X to Y when the choice is offered to me sometime in the future, because both are equally discounted. However, with the kind of discounting familiar in real life and measured in the experiments, I prefer X to Y unless Y is right in front of me.

This kind of discounting lies behind addiction, temptation, regret, and remorse. It is known as hyperbolic discounting, as opposed to exponential discounting. It was analyzed by Richard Herrnstein and is associated with, but distinguishable from, what Herrnstein called the "matching law," which he discovered, in which decisions are made on the basis of average, as opposed to marginal rates of return. With hyperbolic discounting, the value of a reward is inversely proportional to the time delay in its delivery relative to the time of decision. It is this inverse relationship that yields the hyperbolic curve of expected value versus time.[15]

It has a striking implication: that human beings have more than one self inside them. We have one self that is not governed by hyperbolic discounting. This self knows that indulgence is a bad decision, even when temptation is in front of us, and prefers to avoid actions that have negative consequences. But we have another self as well. When options are available that give us immediate access to goods that satisfy some basic appetite, another self becomes dominant and makes the choice. As one set of authors observed after reviewing the literature on this subject, "The pervasiveness and robustness of such observations suggests that the problem may not come from some extraordinary condition that impairs the normal operation of intentionality, but rather from the process by which all people, perhaps all organisms, evaluate future goals. That is, the split ego may not be a freak of nature but the condition of nature itself, uncorrected, in these cases by the learning process that comes to compensate for it at least partially in most people."[16] It also implies that individuals governed by hyperbolic discounting may, in some circumstances, adopt courses of action which, when cumulatively reviewed in retrospect, are clearly undesirable. As Herrnstein wrote, the

> principle implies suboptimality particularly for the class of situations that Prelec and I have characterized as "distributed choices." For distributed choices, the organism does not make a once-and-for-all choice about the alternatives in a choice set. Instead, repeated choices are made over some period of time, and the decision variable is the allocation among alternatives. . . . Most "style of life" questions concern distributed choice. . . . At no one moment in life does one choose, for example, to become promiscuous or a glutton or an alcoholic.[17]

Yet human beings, or at least some human beings, are not ruled by the hyperbolic discounting, or find ways to avoid being governed by the part of themselves that is driven by it. After setting the alarm clock, we put it across the room, so that we will have to get out of bed to turn it off, by which time we will be fully awake. We make sure that there are no cigarettes or alcohol in the house, and we generally avoid temptation. In other words, the part of ourselves that wishes to pursue our long-term interest constructs external constraints on the part of us that wishes to pursue pleasure when confronted with opportunities to indulge. We recognize that there are two selves internal to us in the economic sense of two distinct sets of preferences, one governed by hyperbolic discounting, one not. After discussing this phenomenon, Thomas Schelling reached the conclusion that one of our selves builds external constraints on the other part of ourselves to practice self-mastery or self-discipline.

An important part of the consumer's task is then not merely household management but self-management—treating himself as though he were occasionally a servant who might misbehave. That way we separate the anomalous behavior from the rational; we take sides with whichever consumer self appeals to us as the authentic representation of values; and we can study the ways that the straight self and the wayward self interact strategically.

The conclusion I come to is that this phenomenon of rational strategic interaction among alternating preferences is a significant part of most people's decisions and welfare, and cannot be left out of our account of the consumer. We ignore too many important purposive behaviors if we insist on treating the consumer as having only values and preferences that are uniform over time, even short periods of time.[18]

Another economist has reasoned that we may pursue even more subtle strategies of self-control that involve building internal, as opposed to external, constraints on ourselves. Start with a naïve question. Why do we refrain from doing selfish, deceitful, or dishonest things even when we know that no one is watching? For example, why do we leave tips in restaurants we will never visit again? Robert Frank argued it is because, by nature, we have some reflexes that, at a particular moment, we cannot control. When we lie, for example, we blush or sweat or stammer. This is awkward if we wish to lie, but very useful if we wish reliably to communicate to others that we are telling the truth. Because other people know that we blush when we lie, if we are not blushing, we are telling the truth. People will be more willing to trust us in ways that make possible mutually beneficial cooperation. Those same people will not trust identifiable liars, and so we will gain an advantage over liars, because we can gain the benefits of cooperation, and the liars cannot exploit people. But the problem is more complex. Even though at a given moment we cannot control our physiological reactions, if we tell many lies over long periods of time, we will get used to it. We will no longer blush, and we will be able to tell lies convincingly. But that may not be to our advantage because we will no longer be able reliably to communicate that we are telling the truth when we are telling the truth. So we do not tell lies even when we will not be caught because one of our selves does not want to change or train another part of ourselves to be good at lying.[19] We do so, presumably, because we choose to seek longer-term benefits rather than immediate rewards.

In all of these arguments, we are, of course, abandoning the idea of the self as a unitary actor and returning to the idea of the tripartite division of the soul developed by Plato. In *The Republic*, Socrates discusses the elements of the soul, the appetites, reason, and spirit. He then asks, "Do we act in each of three ways as a result of the same part of ourselves, or are there three parts and with a different one we act in each of the different ways? Do we learn with one, become spirited with another of the parts within us, and desire the pleasures of nourishment and generation and all their kin with a third; or do we act with the soul as a whole in each of them once we are started?"

Socrates then goes on to discuss the fact that some men can master their appetites: "Now, would we assert that sometimes there are some men who are thirsty but not willing to drink?" "Isn't there something in their soul bidding them to drink and something forbidding them to do so, something that masters that which bids?" What is it within us that overcomes our appetites? It is the calculating part of ourselves. "Doesn't that which forbids such things come into being—when it comes into being—from calculation, while what leads and draws is present due to affections and diseases? . . . So we won't be irrational if we claim that there are two and different from each other."

But why do we choose to let reason be the master of the appetites, and why do some men decide not to do so? There must be some part of ourselves that wishes to resist the impulses of our appetites. In the most difficult part of the discussion, Socrates argues that there must be a third element of our soul, which he calls spirit, *thymus*, which is angered by the reactions of our body and wants to master them. It is different from reason, as can be observed by children who wish to fight against their bodies, resisting sleepiness, or insisting on doing things for themselves, for example, without calculating how it is in their interest. Spirit can aid reason, however, and "set its arms on the side of the calculating part."[20] Schelling, while willing to accept the dual nature of the soul, stops short of endorsing the third, adjudicating element, but recognizes that there are other psychologists who do posit the existence of this third component of the soul.[21]

This analysis suggests that there may be differences among individuals with regard to their ability to use their reason to imagine futures and to refrain from satisfying appetites in the short term in order to enjoy greater imagined benefits in the future. Is there any direct evidence that there are individuals who have different, enduring abilities in their abilities to do this? At the statistical level, Jerry Hausman studied the willingness of people to spend more money now on a more efficient but more expensive air conditioner in order to save money in the future by reducing their use of electricity. By studying the purchase of different air conditioners with different efficiencies and prices, and by making some assumptions about the life span of the air conditioners, he was able to infer the implicit ways in which people made tradeoffs between present and future benefits. There were two major findings. First, people, on average, discounted the future much more than would be suggested by market interest rates. On average, they discounted the future at the rate of about 25 percent a year. Second, there were major differences in the implicit time preferences among individuals by class: the poorest people purchased the less expensive but less efficient air conditioners much more often than rich people, and they had implicit discount rates of 89 percent, as opposed to 5 percent for the richest people.[22]

Perhaps this difference in willingness to defer present consumption for future benefits was the result of factors inside people, but perhaps it was the result of the fact that poor people had less money and had to consume more of it every day, and so could not afford to spend a big chunk of it on an air conditioner that would save them a little bit of money every year in the future. Is there any evidence that there are differences in the time preferences of people that are independent of wealth effects, and that are stable over time? There seems to be reliable data that there are. Walter Mischel conducted a series of experiments with a group of children over a period of about twelve years to assess this issue. These experiments were constructed to measure a child's "ability to defer an immediate but less desired outcome for the sake of a preferred outcome contingent on waiting." Specifically, children about four and a half years old were told that their teacher would leave the room, but that the child could ring a bell, at which point the teacher would return immediately and let the child eat a marshmallow that was left behind, in plain sight, in the room. If the child could refrain, "by myself," from ringing the bell and wait until the teacher came back, he or she would receive two marshmallows. Not surprisingly, the children had difficulty rejecting temptation when the desired object was visible, but further experimentation showed that "situational factors, such as the physical exposure of the reward, could be overcome and even totally reversed by self-induced changes in cognition and attention during delay." Preschool children who focused on the "hot" characteristics of the desired object, for example, on the idea of consuming the marshmallow, were unable to wait at all. The children, however, who chose to focus on abstract, "cool" characteristics, for example, the shape of the marshmallow, showed a greater ability to wait. Deciding to direct their attention away from the object altogether produced even longer and easier waiting. What was striking was that some of the children seemed to be aware of these strategies by the age of five and realized they could distract themselves in order to wait.

Eleven years after the experiment with the marshmallows, the now adolescent children were called back. Fifty-nine of the original ninety-five subjects returned. Their parents were interviewed, and the mothers and fathers were independently asked to evaluate their children with regard to ego resiliency (defined as the opposite of ego undercontrol), academic and social competence, the ability to cope with stress, and the frequency of problems with their children. The length of the delay time the children displayed in the first experiment correlated positively and strongly with academic competence for boys and girls, and very strongly with social competence for boys. There was a high positive correlation between the childhood willingness to endure the time delay of gratification and ego resiliency in the adolescent boys and girls. Consistent with that, there was a negative correlation between time delay and ego undercontrol for boys (the less the boys could wait for the marshmallow, the more ego undercontrol they later displayed), but, interestingly, not for girls. Time delay also correlated negatively for frequency of problems with girls, but positively for boys.[23]

Ego resiliency, academic competence, and social competence are not the same as a long-term time orientation, but they do involve impulse control and self-discipline in situations in which there are opportunities to pursue short-term gratification at the expense of longer-term benefits. The Mischel experiments would suggest that there are early and significant differences in the ability of children to delay gratification, to forgo short-term payoffs in favor of larger payoffs in the long term, and that these differences persist into middle adolescence.

Other studies, differently structured, have provided results consistent with the Mischel experiments. In several independent studies, boys in London and Montreal were studied when they were between the ages of six and twelve, and their police records were examined eight to twelve years later. Those children who were impulsive at the early stages in their life were much more likely to be delinquents in later years, when compared with other children of the same age, class, and intelligence.[24] A different set of experiments was designed by Louise Masse to assess whether there were other persistent character traits that could affect the tendency of children to exploit opportunities for gratification present in the short term at the possible expense of long-term benefits. A group of 1,034 ethnically homogenous boys (white, French-speaking, nonimmigrant boys in Montreal, all of low socioeconomic status) were studied with regard to their tendencies to display high levels of novelty seeking and low levels of harm avoidance. These dimensions of personality were drawn from the set of personality dimensions developed by C. Robert Cloninger and have become standard items in personality assessments. These boys, aged six to ten years old, were evaluated by their teachers and then studied again at ages ten to fifteen. The finding was that "high novelty-seeking and low harm avoidance significantly predicted the onset of substance abuse."[25]

Once again, novelty seeking and low harm avoidance are not the same as short-term time orientation, though they do seem to be related to it in obvious ways. Neither the Mischel nor the Masse experiments prove that there are biological factors that influence time horizons, although biological factors could explain variations in behavior that appear early in life and persist through life. However, one benefit of using the novelty-seeking dimension in the Masse study of children is that it permits links to be drawn to the independent studies done by American and Israeli scientists that have linked specific gene loci to levels of novelty seeking. Differences at the level of the genome could account for about 10 percent of the variance in displayed levels of novelty seeking, though these results have been challenged.[26]

If time orientations are, in part, the result of biological inheritance, how might that biological inheritance be made effective? Long-term time horizons were, it will be recalled, associated with the ability to imagine the future consequences of our actions, and then disciplining ourselves to act in accord with the imagined future. Hence, biology might affect time horizons by affecting general intelligence and the ability to control oneself on the basis of the constructed image of the future. The areas of the brain responsible for self-control might or might not be the same as those that are involved in general intelligence. Imagining the future might be the same as doing complicated, multistep calculations, in which case high IQ and long-term time orientation would strongly and positively correlate. There is abundant evidence that somewhere between 40 percent and 60 percent of the variations in general intelligence in a population is associated with biological factors.[27] This, however, might be irrelevant for politics. All political leaders might have to be more or less equally intelligent in order to rise to a position of national leadership. A moment's reflection, however, suggests that some political systems might be more tolerant of low-intelligence leaders than others. A closed political system that has outlawed political competition might eventually fail, but for periods of time measured in decades, loyal but unintelligent leaders might be selected or preserved in power, as was the case in the Soviet Union in the 1970s and 1980s. Monarchies that accepted the royal heir who was most senior might be ruled by less intelligent men. Even democratic elections can yield presidents with less than impressive intellects. So biology might produce variations in the ability of leaders to imagine the future.

What of the ability to discipline oneself in response to the imagined future? In one set of experiments utilizing patients who had suffered partial brain damage, some evidence was found that the inability to act on the basis of imagined future outcomes was associated with damage to the ventromedial prefrontal cortex and was not associated with levels of intelligence as measured by standard IQ tests. A patient, referred to by the code EVR, had suffered such brain damage. Patient EVR, in his life outside the hospital, had repeatedly acted to harm himself and did not seem to be able to learn from his experiences in real-life settings, despite the fact that he scored in the normal range in laboratory tests of general intellect and problem solving. Further tests did not show any impulsiveness or any impairment of short-term or working memory, and he did well when presented with verbally posed social problems. Could his disability be better specified? A test was devised based on rewards and punishments determined by drawing cards from differently structured decks of cards. As the initial cards from some decks were turned over, they yielded large positive payoffs. Later in the deck, as more cards were turned over, the player received even larger negative payoffs, producing net losses. Other decks yielded small negative yields at first, but deep in the deck they began to pay off very well, yielding net benefits. After several rounds of play with all decks, subjects were allowed to choose the decks from which they would draw cards. Forty-four subjects who played with these decks and who had not suffered damage to their prefrontal cortexes quickly learned to choose the decks that yielded short-term losses but higher payoffs in the long term. EVR never did, nor did six other patients with EVR-like brain damage. The games were replayed with the EVR-like patients playing against education-matched control subjects. The decks were restructured to make the early payoffs large and negative instead of positive, but with many small positive benefits later on. The results were that the EVR-like players were sensitive to the early payoffs, negative or positive, and insensitive to later payoffs, negative or positive. In interpreting the results of the experiment, the scientists concluded, "When we combine the profiles of both basic task and variant tasks, we are left with one reasonable possibility: that the subjects are unresponsive to future consequences, whatever they are, and are thus more controlled by immediate prospects." Other tests showed that they remembered the results of sampling the various decks of cards and had the knowledge to make evaluations of future outcomes. "Their defect seems to be at the level of acting on such knowledge."[28]

What can be concluded from these studies? Certainly *not* that all differences in time orientation are biologically determined. Small portions of the variance in novelty seeking could be associated with variations at the level of the gene. The radical present orientation of the patients like EVR was the product of disease-induced trauma. While these experiments help identify areas of the brain associated with self-discipline and connected with imagined futures, brain-damaged individuals are not models of variations in the general population. Beyond that, as we saw in chapter 2, it is almost certainly the case that life experiences and the memories they generate can reinforce or ameliorate the tendencies with which individuals are born. Educational strategies can be designed to ameliorate certain inherited tendencies, and some of the most promising work has been done by scientists who analyze children soon after birth and then in early childhood to try to capture the effects of inherited dispositions and then the way those dispositions are shaped by the first years of life.[29]

Rather, it seems more appropriate to observe that there are differences in individuals with regard to time preferences, and that those preferences can be stable over periods of time beginning in childhood and reaching into adolescence, unless other factors intervene. Those time orientations emerge in early childhood and are probably affected by some combination of inherited characteristics and upbringing. Time preferences of people then tend to change as a function of age, with people, particularly men, under the age of twenty-five being far more likely to engage in present-oriented activity than people over the age of twenty-five.[30]

This is a much more limited conclusion, but it is not unimportant. It suggests that people enter adult life with time preferences that are the result of factors set in their past and not connected with their current environment. People do not freely decide at maturity what time preferences they ought to have, given the kinds of environments in which they find themselves. To be sure, people may not act on the basis of their internal time preferences at maturity if there are external factors that constrain or facilitate the preferred behavior. For the purposes of this discussion, the evidence suggests that if and when political figures achieve power, they may continue to act in ways consistent with the time preferences they displayed earlier in life, unless constrained by external factors.

What does this have to do with tyrants? It would not startle anyone to suggest that at times political leaders in any political system can be short-sighted. It is a commonplace assumption of students of American politics that elected politicians are interested in nothing more distant in time than the next election, and the more frequent their elections, the shorter their time horizons. Military officers are often accused of not thinking beyond the battle they are fighting. Field Marshall Hindenburg was asked what his goal was in his 1918 offensive and is famously quoted as replying, "We'll punch a hole in their lines and see what happens." This kind of time orientation is determined by the nature of the environment, which creates extremely high incentives for succeeding in the short term, and high penalties for failing, such that survival in the long term depends on success in the short term. The behavior produced by environmental pressures is different from the behavior we have been describing, which is behavior driven by a stable, internal disposition to seek short-term rewards, even when the environment does not dictate such behavior. At this stage in the discussion, we would simply develop a hypothesis to be tested later on: tyrants may be people with less ability to discipline themselves when facing an opportunity to make a decision that yields benefits close in time to the decision, even though the longer-terms consequences of the decision make it less than optimal. Determining whether this means that tyrannies have short- or long-term time orientations must wait until the picture of tyrannies is complete. Tyrannies are the combination of the person of the tyrant and the social institutions within which they are situated. Even if tyrants had short-term time orientations, the behavior of tyrannies might display long-term time orientations, if the institutions of the tyranny constrained the tyrant to behave that way. On the other hand, it might be the case that the conditions of tyranny tend to reinforce any personal tendencies a tyrant might have to act on the basis of short-term considerations.

What Do Tyrants Want?

Human decision making cannot be explained simply with reference to time preferences. The goals or preferences of human beings must be specified before we can say how an individual will try to maximize what he or she wants within a given time horizon. Short-term time orientations in the contemporary world may be associated with acquisitive behavior, but this is not a necessary truth. People could be radically short-sighted but altruistic so that, to modify Rousseau slightly, they would give away a blanket to a stranger in the morning because they did not give thought to the next night. Political leaders could want wealth, and if they were short-term-oriented, they could become venal, even though that would reduce their electoral prospects. In international relations, it is commonplace to say that leaders will seek power or security, but it is notoriously difficult to say what constitutes power and security in the abstract, and so almost any activity can be explained after the fact by saying, after the fact, that it was motivated by the search for power, which took a particular form in the given instance.

Thus, when it comes to tyrants, it may be helpful to specify something ahead of time about the goals or preferences of tyrants, beyond saying that they seek power. Given the discussion that we have just concluded, it might be thought that tyrants will try to satisfy the appetites governed by hyperbolic discounting: the appetites for food, sex, drugs, and sleep. Why would a tyrant not simply use his absolute power to indulge in animal pleasures? A tyrant has all the domestic political authority there is to be had, and his only task is to avoid having his position forcibly taken away. In international politics, war is always risky and could bring the tyrant down. Perhaps tyrants are peace loving for that reason. But this question cannot be resolved without some discussion of what tyrants want. Xenophon discussed the desires of tyrants at some length in *Tyran-nicus* and made some distinctions that may be useful.

The poet Simonides, having been called to see the tyrant Hiero, starts off the discussion by asking Hiero how the pleasures and pains of tyrants differ from those of men in private life. Simonides then answers his own question by saying, that private men get pleasure through the body, but also through the soul. Hiero says, yes, so do tyrants. Simonides then says that with regard to bodily pleasures, tyrants must be well off because they can have the best feasts every day, they can go look at the most beautiful sights, and people are always saying pleasant things to them, so the senses of taste, sight, and hearing are always being gratified. Hiero says not at all, a tyrant gets tired of that pretty quickly, and people are al-ways trying to overthrow him, so he dares not go out of the house to see sights. Furthermore, he knows full well that people are lying to him when they flatter him, because they are afraid of him. Even silence is dis-pleasing because he knows that the silent men hate him.[31]

Simonides tries again. Well, he says, you can enjoy a lot of sex, and "it is probable that the enjoyment of sex comes dangerously close to pro-ducing desires for tyranny. For there it is possible for you to have inter-course with the fairest you see."[32] Hiero responds to this statement. He says no, even that is no good because a tyrant cannot make a good mar-riage, because every woman is beneath him, and "because it is never pos-sible for the tyrant to trust that he is loved,"[33] for the same reasons he can never trust flatterers. In addition, slaves are incompetent. This is an interesting response. Hiero does not really say that he cannot have lots of sex with beautiful people, he says he cannot have a good marriage and love, which is different. His response also indicates that he does have lots of sex. Historical analysis shows that, in many different societies, despots did have enormous numbers of children by multiple partners, a repro-ductive strategy that, as noted above, is consistent with shorter-term time horizons.[34] Hiero himself remarks in passing what he likes best: "I be-lieve myself that to take from an unwilling enemy is the most pleasant of all things."[35] Again, he does not deny that he has sex, but he adds an-other element: the desire for domination.

In the next section, Simonides tries another tack. Forget about bodily pleasures, he says. Using the words "real men," Simonides says they are not ruled by their desires for food, drink, and sex, but endeavor to do great enterprises. Hiero, the tyrant, can do more, and can do more quickly—the kind of great enterprises that private men aspire to. Si-monides seems to be shifting from bodily pleasures to pleasures of the soul, or what we might call mental pleasures, in particular, the pleasure from accomplishing great things. He also says that a tyrant will have more of "the superfluous things of life," which seems to mean luxury, and "you are the ones most capable of harming your private enemies and benefiting your friends." Hiero again gives an interesting response. He repeats that a tyrant, unlike private men, must always be afraid that some one will try to kill him, and that makes it impossible to experience peace, even if he does not leave his own city. He then discusses one very great enterprise, possibly the greatest, which is war. In time of war, the city must be on its guard, like the tyrant, but citizens at least find peace and safety at home. In war, men pursue victory on the battlefield, and it gives them great joy: "It is not easy to express how much pleasure [the men] get from routing the enemy; how much from pursuit; how much from killing their enemies; how they exult in the deed; how they receive a brilliant reputation for themselves; and how they take delight in believing they have augmented their city."[36] But a tyrant can never find peace at home, and he must mistrust all praise, so he can have none of the glory that private men find at home.

What can we make of this? First of all, this discussion suggests that there may be two types of tyrants. The first might be called "petty tyrants," interested only in pleasure. A petty tyrant might simply use his power to gratify his appetites. This kind of tyrant would not be very ambitious and might live out his days in self-indulgence, a blight on his country, but generally of no concern to other countries. This type is familiar to us and seems to be common in small countries whose size, sometimes but not always, limits the aspirations of their tyrants: the Duvaliers, Batistas, Somozas, Marcoses, and the like seem to fit into this category. Or the tyrant might be a "real man." He is of greater interest to his neighbors because he pursues the pleasures of the soul by engaging in great enterprises. Those enterprises, however, cannot bring him peace or good reputation that he can value. What is left is the element of pure domination: routing the enemy, pursuing him, killing him. Either from the standpoint of bodily pleasures or pleasures of the soul, the one pleasure the tyrant is free to enjoy and of which he never tires is domination.

Domination is a concept we explored in chapter 3. It was not the same as aggressiveness but was defined as the tendency to punish challengers or rivals, even when doing so brought no benefit to the punisher. It was associated with elevated levels of testosterone in high-status males living in unstable social environments, but also with a particular personality type, one that saw threats everywhere, and that could not relax when not threatened. What might this have to do with tyrants? All that we wish to do at this stage of the discussion is to suggest that, along with a disposition to act on the basis of incentives that appear to be close in time to the moment of decision, "great" as opposed to petty tyrants may be characterized as having unusually high tendencies to engage in dominant behavior among the people and countries with which they are in contact. It seems unnecessary to review, for example, the ways in which, from the 1920s on, Hitler was intolerant of any rivals within the Nazi party or his associates and managed the party and German state apparatus when in power to give him absolute authority over all decisions.[37]

In the case of Stalin, it may be less clear that, before the period of the purges in the 1930s, he had a personal disposition oriented toward dominating his personal surroundings. To be sure, in the 1930s he murdered all of his rivals, real and imaginary, and rewrote party history to make himself Lenin's righthand man, but this might have been the result of absolute power, not his personal disposition. However, personal accounts do exist of his early sensitivity to status considerations and of his ability and willingness to dominate those around him, when he had local autonomy and was free to exercise his will.[38] He always had the goal of complete personal dominance, as one famous quote from an old associate of Stalin, Serebryakov, suggests. Stalin was talking with his friends about what plan each of them would have if they could plan a perfect day. When Stalin's turn came, he said, "Mine is to plan an artistic revenge upon an enemy, carry it out to perfection, and then go home and go peacefully to bed."[39] But Stalin was able to control his desire for dominance when the short-term consequences made it necessary to do so. There were no short-term penalties associated with Hitler's pursuit of dominance within the Nazi party , whereas there were many such obstacles confronting Stalin in the Bolshevik party until 1930. Hitler, himself, was capable of showing great personal control when the short-term payoffs for doing so were high, as was shown by his public deference to President Hindenburg at the ceremony when Hitler first became chancellor.[40] The decisions by Hitler and Stalin not to seek immediate gratification with regard to dominance were the result of seeing that the net results of seeking dominance in the short term would lead to very great losses close in time to the moment of decision. In this they were very much like the Sicilian Mafia leader Tomasso Buscetta, who had great power and was widely admired within the Mafia until he decided to assist the Italian government investigation after internal warfare had produced chaos within the Mafia. Buscetta's actions clearly revealed a man insistent on personal respect. Yet, when Buscetta was in prison together with a man whom he intensely disliked and who had killed one of his friends, he displayed no animosity and even invited his enemy to dine occasionally in his cell. Buscetta knew that to kill this man in prison would have immediate and negative consequences, and he also knew that his enemy had already been sentenced by the Mafia council to be executed upon his release from prison.[41]

Great tyrants want to punish challengers and will do so unless the short-term costs of doing so are high. This tendency will have social consequences, as people learn what are the consequences of appearing to be a challenger to the tyrant.

What Information Do Tyrants Receive?

Decisions are made on the basis of the information available to individuals, but not all the available information. Psychologists, for example, have noted that people, particularly people experiencing some stress, make far less use of the information available to them than they claim and tend to make decisions on the basis of preconceptions and information available early in the process, and then interpret subsequent information in ways that make even discrepant information consistent with the original decision.[42] Academics and government bureaucracies often proceed on the assumption that information is conveyed by words on paper, and that it is possible to recapture the flow of information available to decisionmakers by knowing what paper was put in front of them, or, absent that, by knowing what the most basic material facts about the world were available in print and were generally known. At another level, practitioners of real-world politics know that this assumption is flawed. Many key decisions, about whom to trust and to believe, for example, are made on the basis of factors that are often not expressed in words, written or otherwise. This is because human brains have evolved to be sensitive to human faces and to things that look like human faces, as was discussed in chapters 1 and 2.

What has this to do with tyrants? All people who are adept in social settings are sensitive to the nonverbal communications of others. Tyrants, who are defined as being people who tend to be inclined to short-term gratification, may be even more inclined to use such nonverbal information because they are less inclined to spend time at their desk reading lengthy memos. It is striking in the case of Hitler, Stalin, and Mao just how little time they spent in their offices and in formal work settings, and how much time they spent simply talking to people, even during intense periods such as the Munich crisis and the 1948 Berlin crisis.[43]

What is also striking, certainly in the case of Hitler, though less clearly in the case of the others, is how good he was at using the nonverbal information available in face-to-face settings to understand what people believed and wanted. Hitler was a sporadic and careless reader, but a careful student of people. Examples abound from people who interacted with Hitler, and from him himself. Hitler explained his ability to influence a crowd in terms of his ability to read the crowd while he spoke to it: "An orator receives continuous guidance from the people before whom he speaks. . . . He will always be borne along by the great masses in such a way that from the living emotions of his listeners the very words come to his lips that he needs to speak to their hearts. Should he make even a slight mistake, he has the living correction before him." Alan Bullock noted that Hitler's practice of speaking to the crowd at length before getting to his explicitly political message was his way of sounding the crowd out so that he could say what it wanted to hear. Otto Strasser gave the following account, which also emphasizes Hitler's ability to extract nonverbal information from a crowd: "Adolf Hitler enters a hall. He sniffs the air, feels his way, senses the atmosphere. Suddenly he bursts forth. His words go like an arrow to their target, he touches each private wound on the raw, liberating the unconscious, exposing its innermost aspirations and telling it what it most wants to hear."[44] Hitler displayed this ability in smaller settings as well, though he was unable to use it to form any lasting emotional bonds. Hitler's associate Ernst Hanfstaengl gives this account of Hitler in the 1920s:

> As soon as some person of interest—and there was no one he did not find interesting for a time—joined his company, you could almost see him mobilizing his internal machinery. The asdic pings of inquiry would go out and within a short time he had a clear image of the wavelength and secret yearnings and emotions of his partner. The pendulum of the conversation would start to beat faster, and the person would be hypnotized into believing that there lay in Hitler immense depths of sympathy and understanding.[45]

Hitler would then use this nonverbal information to transmit nonverbal messages to his interlocutor. Hitler's staged rages are well known. Less prominent is the way he would self-consciously prepare the nonverbal cues that he needed in a given setting. Rudolph Hess described how Hitler prepared for a meeting with a person he had not met before:

Hitler: What does he expect?
Hess: Authority, of course. You can speak at length. Your will is unshakable. You give laws to the age.
Hitler: Then I'll speak in a firm voice.

"Hitler would then try a few sentences. Hess would listen carefully and comment. 'No, not like that. Quiet. No passion, commanding. It is Destiny that is speaking. . . .' Hitler would try again, with a firmer voice. After seven or eight minutes he would stop, already somewhat moved by his own acting. 'Good, now I think we have it, he would say.'"[46]

Although fewer firsthand accounts have survived of Stalin's face-to-face interactions, some evidence has come out. One Russian history describes Stalin as "an actor. He was *litsedei*, a man of many faces, as Khrushchev and others recalled. He could be a charming host, a modest, almost self-effacing Old Bolshevik, a magnanimous pontiff, and a vicious, yellow eyed tyrant."[47]

Although the same kind of historical material is not yet available for more recent tyrants, it is striking that the Gulf War Air Power Survey commissioned by the secretary of the air force reported that U.S. intelligence knew that during the Iran-Iraq war, Saddam Hussein relied on face-to-face meetings with his subordinates, visiting them at the front, or calling them back to Baghdad in order, in the words of William Arkin, "to assert his personal control and intimidations."[48]

The Rise of Tyrants to Power

Assume that there are distinguishable personality types who score high along the dimensions we have discussed. First, they are sensitive to immediate rewards and punishments, and they react quickly to opportunities that are favorable on balance to them in the period that is close in time to the decision. Second, they punish challengers and seek dominance over the people and actors with whom they interact. Third, they are receptive to the nonverbal information that is available to them in face-to-face settings. Under what condition would people like this achieve political power? Are these people who will prosper in all social and political settings? A society and its political institutions might well have stable, politically attentive populations who can observe and recall the acts of political figures. The general public might face modestly difficult short-term problems and have reasonably high hopes that they would be able to enjoy the rewards of decisions made for the sake of the long-term future. That society might also have political institutions that rewarded and punished political actors on the basis of their loyalty to institutions over long periods of time, and that required new political figures to sacrifice some of their personal, short-term ambitions in return for support in the future from the institution—that new politicians must "pay their dues." In those conditions, we would not expect an individual with the characteristics we have described to prosper politically. People who were not excessively concerned with short-term problems will not want to pick leaders who promised to resolve short-term problems by means that had ambiguous or possibly negative long-term consequences. Political institutions that rewarded loyalty over long periods of time would weed out those figures who were visibly out for themselves, who were lone wolves. Attentive publics would remember the past actions of politicians that turned out, over the long term, to be "rash."

But suppose the conditions were the reverse of those just described? Suppose there was a great deal of turbulence in the society. The membership of the politically attentive public and elites would be constantly shifting, erasing institutional memories. Urgent, short-term problems would not only be dominant, but overwhelming, and planning for the long-term future would seem an impossible luxury. What if general instability created a general preference for order that followed from general deference to a single authority? These are the conditions under which our hypothesized figure might expect to do much better. His ability to handle the short-term problems would be appreciated by the political public, and his vices, his willingness to do whatever the moment called for, his rashness, would be obscured. They are, of course, also the conditions described by Plato in the aftermath of the breakdown of a democratic political order in which a man with a tyrannical soul would be more likely to come to power. Such a man would be ready to say whatever he needed to say to obtain the allegiance of any particular group. He would lie, he would take advantage of the popular longing for leadership, and the prevailing environment would reward him. In power, he would dismantle any remaining laws that constrained him, and remove any political figures who might challenge him, even those able men who aided him in his rise to power.[49] They are also, of course, the conditions under which Stalin, Hitler, and Mao rose to power. The only major difference existed in the case of Stalin. The relatively small group of politically active people with whom Stalin had to deal after the limited success of the Bolshevik revolution before he rose to total power meant that his weakness as a speaker to mass audiences was not a crippling handicap.

In other words, without the conditions favorable to the political rise of such personality types, they will remain minor figures. If conditions favor them, however, tyrannical personalities may rise to power. If they do achieve political power, tyrants must then exercise that power. The tyrant has no regard for the law if the short-term consequences are not negative and will disregard the basic law, the constitution. It is the general purpose of political constitutions to constrain the behavior of powerful political actors whose good personal characters cannot be guaranteed. Constitutions can be written at times, as Jon Elster has noted, when there are no overwhelming short-term crises, so provisions that increase the general alacrity with which decisions can be made and executed are excluded. This is done to build barriers against decisions that could be made in close time proximity to the delivery of rewards.[50] These are provisions that are necessary because political figures with tyrannical dispositions may seek and gain power. If these constitutional provisions are absent or have been destroyed, tyrannical personalities will be less constrained.

Once in power, unconstrained by the law and intolerant of rivals, the tyrant will concentrate all decision-making authority in his own hands, but he cannot concentrate all political power in his own hands. Although the tyrant has no regard for the laws, he cannot rule by himself. He will need subordinates, some of whom must be armed. He will have his political party, the bureaucracy, and the general distribution of power in society to contend with. There will be a general public that will be subjugated, at least to some degree, but which must still retain some degree of independence in order to make intelligent private decisions that provide the state with the wealth and power it needs. There will be a constant tension between the desire of the tyrant to rule according to his will, to be dominant in all his encounters, and the need of the tyrant for subjects who remain, to some degree, free, and who will necessarily fear him for his unconstrained power, and who will hate him for seeking immediate, personal dominance over them, that is, for being a tyrant. This hatred will never be totally impotent, because a tyrant is a single individual, and, as Hobbes remarked with regard to the ability to kill each other, all men are equal. The tyrant at the center of his tyrannical institutions will, because of what he is, always live in fear of those who will try to kill him. He will live in a state of war with his subjects, a state of war that is of his own making.

This is the picture of tyranny—the tyrannical personality living in the political surroundings that he has created—that Xenophon portrays. The tyrant lives in constant fear of being killed by one of his subjects. In his discussion of love, Hiero has already told Simonides that "we know as a matter of course that those who serve through fear try by every means in their power to make themselves appear to be like friends by the services of friends. And, what is more, plots against tyrants spring from none more than from those who pretend to love them most."[51] The tyrant will uncover plots and murder the plotters, but that will not solve his problem, because "when they whom he feared are dead, he is not any bolder, but is still more on his guard than before. So, then, the tyrant spends his life fighting the kind of war which I myself am showing you."[52] Tyrants must always extract more wealth from their societies, because they always need a larger security apparatus to protect themselves, so that "the tyrants are compelled most of the time to plunder unjustly both temples and human beings, because they always need additional money to meet their necessary expenses. For, as if there were a perpetual war on, [tyrants] are compelled to support an army or perish."[53] The end result, Hiero concludes, is that the tyrant lives in a perpetual state of fear and war:

> To fear the crowd, yet to fear solitude; to fear being without a guard, and to fear the very men who are guarding; to be unwilling to have unarmed men about me, yet not gladly to see them armed—how could this fail to be a painful condition?

Fear, you know, when in the soul is not only painful itself, it is also the spoiler of all the pleasures it accompanies. If you, too, have the experience of war, Simonides, and have ever before now been posted near the enemy line, recall what sort of food you took at that time, and what sort of sleep you had. The kind of pain you suffered then is the kind tyrants have, and that more terrible. For the tyrants believe they see enemies not only in front of them, but on every side.[54]

The first and major institutional consequence of tyranny is that the tyrant lives in a state of internal war. What does the condition of war do to the time horizons of rulers, even those who in time of peace are disposed to defer current gratification for imagined future benefits? It is generally observed that it focuses the attention of rulers on the short term and encourages exploitive, "spoiling" behavior. As Margaret Levi has pointed out, in a state of war, the ruler will extract as much revenue as he can in the short term, without regard for the larger revenue that could be extracted in the long term if short-term extraction were moderated. Endemic internal war creates the same effects as endemic external war.[55] Rather than moderating the personal disposition of the tyrant, the institutional conditions of tyranny exacerbate the tendencies we have postulated for him.

What happens to the flow of information when subjects live in fear of their rulers? Xenophon has Hiero note that no one will tell a tyrant that he has done something bad because all fear him.[56] The flow of information in modern tyrannies is not easy to trace, but more information has emerged from the time of Hitler, Mao, and Stalin. Zachary Shore, for example, has traced the decision of Hitler's foreign minister not to provide Hitler with intelligence about the French unwillingness to fight in 1936 at the time of the German remilitarization of the Rhineland.[57] The degree to which Mao's subordinates hid from him the disastrous consequences of his decision to launch the Great Leap Forward has been widely reported. Several incidents from Stalin's rule indicate how, in practice, bad news, in the form of information that contradicted the wisdom of Stalin's decisions, was either ignored or deliberately kept away from Stalin. Stalin's lack of receptivity to information about Hitler's impending attack in 1941 is well known, but the systematic way in which the KGB failed to report to Stalin on policy failures is only now coming to light. One history done jointly by former CIA and KGB officers about intelligence reporting on Germany in the period immediately after World War II through the Berlin crisis gives concrete examples of how the Western reaction to the Berlin blockade was misinterpreted and how factual evidence on the success of the airlift was provided to Molotov but not to Stalin during the crisis, in ways that probably encouraged Stalin to prolong the blockade.[58] Another historical study confirmed, first, that Stalin went on an extended vacation after initiating the Berlin blockade and received only brief and intermittent reports about the crisis. Furthermore, as a result of an intelligence reorganization that Stalin had ordered, there was a small committee that had to review *all* incoming raw intelligence before it could be passed up to Stalin. This, of course, created enormous delays in the internal transmission of intelligence to Stalin.[59]

Thus, in addition to the personal tendency a tyrant might have to be particularly receptive to certain kinds of information, there is the institutional factor that his subordinates will be fearful and unwilling to present him with information that shows his errors. It may be presumed that they would be particularly unwilling to present bad news in face-to-face settings with the tyrant. This suggests that tyrants may enter into interactions with outside powers and then not be clearly presented with or attentive to information that punitive or deterrent measures to block his policy are underway. Strategic information actually received by the tyrant may be biased to a greater extent than in other political systems. The implication is that tyrannies will be disproportionately sensitive to information that confirms what are known to be the pre-existing ideas of the tyrant.

The Strategic Behavior of Tyrants: A Preliminary Historical Assessment

What is the evidence that tyrants in the real world have actually behaved in the ways that the picture of them developed above would suggest? The statistical studies of the outbreak of war that do take into account regime type find that, controlling for other plausible factors that might affect the outcome of war, democracies that initiate war are much more likely to win than oligarchies or anochracies, and somewhat more likely to win than autocracies. To some extent, states that initiate war have more opportunity to evaluate their prospects before choosing to go to war than those states that are attacked by others. Hence, the success rate in wars might be a rough guide to their ability accurately to assess the longer-term implications of their actions. A lower success rate suggests a lower ability to assess the longer-term implications of going to war. The short-term orientation of tyrannies might lead them to lose wars more often than other regimes.

The raw win-loss record of states fighting 197 wars from 1823 to 1982 shows democracies winning 93 percent of the wars that they initiate, anochracies 60 percent, and autocracies 58 percent. When those states were noninitiators, the success rates were 64 percent, 34 percent, and 41 percent. When these rates were adjusted for factors such as military-industrial power and alliances, autocracies did somewhat better than anochracies but still lagged behind democracies.[60] There is some evidence, therefore, that tyrannies are less able successfully to choose when to go to war, and this might be related to the characteristics attributed to them in this chapter.

Though interesting, there are many problems with using a statistical approach to assess the strategic behavior of tyrants. First, autocracy is not tyranny. The definition of autocracy used in the study just discussed focuses on mechanisms for selecting governments and the distribution of power, and not the more subtle concept of the legitimacy of the ruler, or the character of the ruler. In this, the study follows the Hobbesian rejection of the category of tyranny. This has interesting consequences. For example, the government of czarist Russia and Ottoman Turkey are coded as being slightly more autocratic than the governments of Josef Stalin and Adolf Hitler. The government of King Hussein of Jordan in 1967 and 1973 is also coded as being more autocratic than the governments of Hitler and Stalin. The category of autocratic/democratic also does not take into account the issue of constitutional checks, or their absence, on the power of democracies. In addition, it is difficult to determine in a way that is not arbitrary what constitutes genuine versus nominal war initiation (in the coding, for example, the United Kingdom is coded as the initiator of hostilities against Germany in 1939 and Italy in 1940). Finally, the picture of tyranny given in this study does not predict that tyrants will be bad at choosing war or peace, but that they will be bad at assessing the longer-term implications of their actions relative to the short-term payoffs. This might make them bad at understanding the best strategy in wars that become long wars. They might be expected to do well in wars that stay short. Still, with all those reservations, it does appear as if autocracies, which may overlap with tyrannies to some extent, do less well in assessing the outcome of alternative strategies associated with going to war than do democracies, which may overlap with the category of nontyrannies. This is not inconsistent with the picture of tyrannies in this chapter.

If statistical studies are problematic, fine-grained analyses of the behavior of tyrannies could show how tyrannies used information as they decided military courses of action. This argument in this chapter would suggest that tyrannies would act on the basis of costs and benefits that would be felt by the tyranny near in time to the moment of decision, and that this tendency might lead to shifting policies as the near term situation shifted, and to preemption. In longer wars or crises, the argument would suggest a lack of ability to alter or reverse courses of action because negative data would not reach the tyrant. To examine whether the historical record is at all consistent with this picture, we can study episodes in the foreign policies of two tyrants: the behavior of Hitler in the 1936 remilitarization of the Rhineland, the decision by Hitler to declare war on the United States after Pearl Harbor in December 1941, the behavior of Stalin in the Berlin crisis of 1948, and the behavior of Stalin in the Korean War, 1950–1951.

Hitler is generally characterized as behaving in opportunistic ways, saying and doing whatever best seemed to fit his needs given the domestic or international political problem before him, even if those statements and actions were inconsistent with each other.[61] In private domestic political practice, he handled the contradictions that this might have caused by keeping his communications with each of his interlocutors separate and secret from the others.[62] In foreign policy, his policy inconsistencies and reversals were more visible. One of his first major foreign policy actions was to flip flop on the question of the June 1934 Nazi coup in Austria, first supporting the coup, then disowning it when it failed. This and his inconstant policies toward Great Britain led Alan Bullock to comment, "Hitler was a thorough opportunist in both tactics and timing, as his fluctuating attitude towards Great Britain . . . demonstrates."[63]

The question with regard to Hitler's actions to remilitarize the Rhineland in 1936 is not so much why he acted in that year, but why he acted then and not in 1934 or 1935. Hitler's strategic objectives always included the conquest of France, but he refrained from invading the Rhineland in 1935, but not in 1936. The objective balance of power cannot explain the timing of Hitler's action. Germany was weaker militarily than France in 1936 as well as in the earlier years. Though Germany was growing stronger, the consequences of French military action were understood as being catastrophic for Hitler in any of those years. Hitler's assessment of the basic political weakness of the Western democracies did not vary with time, and rested on his understanding or misunderstanding of their nature. Why was Hitler deterred from remilitarizing the Rhineland in 1935, but not in 1936? Why did he not wait until Germany was even stronger?

Hitler, in private meetings with his cabinet, showed that he was amply aware of Germany's military weakness in 1933 and 1934, and aware that it would not be until 1938 or 1939 that the German people would be ready to fight. On 3 February 1933, Hitler discussed his fear that France would attack Germany in a preventive war before the German military was ready. The minutes of Hitler's cabinet meeting on 8 February 1933 record that Hitler said that "Germany was now negotiating with foreign countries about her military equality of rights. But Germany could not content itself with that. . . . The next five years in Germany had to be devoted to rendering the German people again capable of bearing arms. Every publicly sponsored measure to create employment has to be considered from this point of view." In his military budget plans of April 1933, Hitler told the leaders of the German Navy to replace its one-front mobilization plan against Poland with a two-front mobilization plan. But the ability to act on two fronts was scheduled to be available in five years. Furthermore, Hitler was able to restrain his foreign policy consistent with this appreciation of the shifting military balance. He dropped the remilitarization of the Rhineland from the list of issues presented by the Germans to the British in the summer of 1934. In October 1934, Gerhard Weinberg wrote, Hitler was intent on avoiding "a major crisis before Germany was ready to face it, [and so] the foreign ministry restrained the pressures from the military for remilitarization of the Rhineland," and Hitler delayed reintroduction of conscription.[64] But toward the end of January 1936, Hitler was raising with his closest advisers the possibility of remilitarizing the Rhineland. By 19 February he was drafting speeches to be given *after* Germany had marched into the Rhineland.[65] On 2 March Hitler issued orders to the German military to prepare to march. What had happened?

Who would act if Germany invaded the Rhineland? The demilitarization of the Rhineland was guaranteed under the terms of the Locarno Treaty by Great Britain and Italy, and they would be called upon first to give their response. Without their intervention, France, it was generally assumed, would not take military action alone. What happened in January 1936 that might have affected Great Britain and Italy? Gerhard Weinberg argues persuasively that the crisis over Ethiopia created a fleeting, tactical window of opportunity for Germany to act. The Italian offensive in Ethiopia in January 1936 was going well. In response, Britain and France were preparing to offer an oil embargo against Italy for consideration by the League of Nations. This would lead, the Italians told the British, to a rupture between Italy and the Western democracies. Britain was focusing on the Ethiopian crisis, and Italy was not likely to participate in joint action with Britain against Germany while this dispute was active. If Germany acted quickly, it could take advantage of a temporary rupture among the powers that were most directly linked to the status of the Rhineland. If Germany waited, however, the Italian offensive was expected to succeed, and Britain and France would quite possibly accept Italy's fait accompli and restore the working relations with Italy that had prevailed before the Ethiopian crisis and that were still an important part of British European diplomacy.[66]

After Hitler ordered the invasion, there were at least three moments when he came close to reversing his policy. On the day of the invasion, 7 March, Hitler is described as having an attack of nerves, and coming close to canceling the invasion. Then, after the German troops marched in, the British issued their first protest. They asked Hitler to reduce the

German troop presence in the Rhineland, or at least not to increase it, and Hitler's first reaction was to offer concessions, and he did order a halt in the deployment. When the British finally issued a stiff warning on 12 March and the German attaché in London warned that war was possible, Hitler again wavered, but within a day, by 13 March, it was clear that the British would not go to war alongside France, and Hitler stood pat.[67]

What can be understood from this episode? We cannot easily read Hitler's goals and time preferences from the events, but we can observe the following. Hitler's shift from a policy of avoiding active intervention in the Rhineland to a decision to invade was, by the available evidence, made and executed very quickly, within a month at most. The balance of military forces in Europe had not shifted by January 1936 so as to favor Germany in a war with France. The factors that had, until February 1936, been sufficient to deter Hitler from invading the Rhineland, were no longer sufficient in February, and the only thing that appears to have changed was a diplomatic rupture in the coalition that would have responded to the invasion, a rupture that occurred quickly and might have disappeared quickly. Hitler then wavered in his decision despite no objective changes in military capabilities, in reaction to perceived changes in events anticipated in the near term.

At a minimum, it seems reasonable to infer that Hitler reacted to an opportunity that appeared to yield rewards that would be favorable on balance to him close in time to his decision to act. It is hard to understand this action as motivated by long-term considerations. Hitler could not have been thinking that he was paying a short-term price to achieve a long-term gain—if he had been wrong about France, the loss would have precluded any long-term gains. We can conjecture that he saw a situation in which the powers that would block him were distracted and at odds with each other, and if they acted at all, they would act only after some delay; that is, the costs of his action, if there were any, would be incurred at some longer period of time into the future, some months perhaps. His irresolution might have been the result of a weak commitment to his goal of German expansion, but this seems unlikely. It seems more probable that he was strongly affected by what was in front of him at the moment, and as it changed, he changed.

Hitler also reacted in the same rapidly fluctuating way in the Munich crisis in 1938. Interestingly, his decision to make demands on the Czechs was made in May 1938, at the same time that his fears that he had cancer led him to write his will. The fear of personal death in the near term might be expected to increase an emphasis on actions and rewards in the near term. Hitler initiated the crisis with the hope of provoking a war, but the diplomacy of the British gave Hitler an immediate payoff with no cost to Germany, and Hitler changed gears and accepted the offer.[68] What is striking was his reaction to the outcome of the crisis. He was furious for having given in to himself, and he blamed his diplomats for having allowed him to negotiate with the British. Then, in the preparations for war with Poland, he constructed constraints to prevent the same thing from happening. Weinberg described his actions:

> To avoid the risk of becoming entangled in last-minute diplomatic negotiations, the German ambassadors in London and Warsaw were recalled from their posts and not allowed to return to them in the final critical weeks. Demands on Poland designed to influence public opinion inside Germany for war and outside Germany against it were formulated, but Hitler would take no chance on these demands being either accepted or made the basis of new negotiations. He personally instructed his Foreign Minister not to let them out of his hands.[69]

What was Hitler afraid of? He could always say no to any diplomatic offer. He was afraid that he would accept such an offer again, that he would go for the short-term payoff, and so constructed external constraints that would make it harder for him to do so.

During the world war itself, much of Germany's behavior was easily understood in terms of the nature of Hitler's goals, unmoderated by any consideration of time horizons and information flows. There is, however, the issue of Hitler's decision to declare war on the United States. Hitler's assessment of the power of the United States went up and down in the 1920s and 1930s. In the 1920s he was impressed by the power of the continental economy of the United States and sought a similar geographic base for Germany. After the onset of the Great Depression, he shifted to believing that the United States, dominated by Jews and Negroes, would be unable to stand in his way.[70] He remained convinced that, at some point, Germany would have to defeat the United States in war. The precondition, in Hitler's mind, for a successful war with the United States was the creation of a German fleet that could defeat the United States Navy in the Atlantic. He pursued the goal of a powerful German trans-Atlantic fleet in fits and starts. The naval construction program began in the 1930s but was put on hold when the war with Poland and France diverted German production to those ground and air wars. Hitler then met with Admiral Raeder in July 1940 to order the resumption of the naval building program. The defeat of Norway was followed by the start of a program to build a massive German naval base on the Norwegian coast, complete with construction and repair facilities and a set of roads linking that base back to Germany. The Channel Islands were to become part of the base for the German trans-Atlantic Fleet, and bases on and off the North Atlantic coast of Africa, and the Canary

Islands, owned by Spain, were considered as part of the infrastructure to support the trans-Atlantic German fleet. All these projects were delayed or put on hold by the invasion of the Soviet Union.[71] They were never near completion. Because Germany was not ready for war with the United States, Hitler was careful to avoid incidents and confrontations with the United States in 1940 and 1941.

Yet Hitler declared war on the United States in December 1941, before Germany had consolidated the European base that would make possible the construction of a fleet to challenge the United States, and certainly before anything like that fleet and its support structure had been created. The only plausible answer that has been given is that Hitler believed that the Japanese attack on the United States gave the German fleet naval supremacy in the Atlantic because the attack on Pearl Harbor would divert the American fleet into the Pacific.[72] Suppose this was true. What else must have been true in order for Hitler to conclude that it was in his interest to declare war on the United States? In December 1941, Hitler believed he was near victory against the Soviet Union, which could permit the restarting of the German naval building program. The short-term pressures for the United States to divert Atlantic Fleet assets to the Pacific would be enormous. It would be many months, maybe years, before the United States could complete its military mobilization and take military action against Nazi Europe. The American Victory Program was a massive military construction program, with a large naval component. Hitler was aware of it, and mentioned it in his 11 December speech declaring war.[73] There does appear to have existed a short-term tactical opportunity open to Germany in the Atlantic, which would be appealing only if one heavily discounted the longer-term consequences of fighting a fully mobilized United States.

Did Hitler really plan to win a near-term victory in the Atlantic against the United States? Hitler had indicated his willingness to seize and hold the Canary Islands against Spanish opposition, if necessary, and the German military presented plans on 14 December 1941 for terminating the war with the Soviet Union, driving the British Fleet out of the Mediterranean, and seizing and using other Atlantic ports and islands to prevent the United States fleet from coming near Europe.[74] These attacks did not occur because the war with the Soviet Union did not end with the expected quick German victory, and Hitler would not accept a defensive position in the Soviet Union.

Putting the pieces together, Hitler's declaration of war on the United States does seem to have been the result of an orientation that emphasized the importance of a near-term opportunity to deal with the American problem. Hitler lacked the ability to follow through on the declaration of war and to take advantage of the window of opportunity by striking the United States because events in the Soviet Union did not go according to expectations. Hitler was not irrational, in the sense of acting without an appreciation of costs and benefits, but he was short-sighted. He was aware of the military potential of the United States but was not deterred from going to war by that potential, because that potential would materialize only in the long term, and in the short term there was an opportunity to strike and gain a decisive advantage.

What of Stalin? People who are generally prepared to accept that Hitler was in some ways different from other leaders argue that Stalin, when compared to Hitler, was less inclined to aggressive behavior, more pragmatic, and more in control of himself.[75] There is, of course, the issue of the fascinating private interview between Stalin and a prominent Russian neuro-pathologist, Vladimir Bekhterev, initiated by Stalin in 1927, which ended with Bekhterev telling his assistant that Stalin was a classic case of severe paranoia, and then suddenly dying in his Moscow hotel.[76] One observation does not establish a diagnosis. But it is also not correct to infer from the absence of openly aggressive foreign policies that Stalin was the same as other leaders. One cannot simply observe the actions that a leader takes and then assess the ways in which he makes decisions. It is necessary to look at the behavior of a leader given the opportunities that present themselves to him. A serial killer who refrains from killing because police are watching him remains distinguishable from average people. The picture of tyranny that has been developed in this book does not assert that the tyrant will lose control of himself or commit aggression without thought, but that he will seek dominance on the basis of the rewards and punishments that are available in close proximity to the time of decision. This characterization generates a prediction of opportunistic pursuit of short-term benefits.

Did Stalin display this type of orientation? To begin with, there is the counterargument that Stalin had a very long-term orientation and built up the industrial power and military strength of the Soviet Union in the 1930s before there was an immediate military threat to his regime. This seems to be quite different from seeking short-term rewards. Stalin's policy of rapid industrialization is indisputable. It is equally indisputable, however, that Stalin saw himself at war with the Russian peasantry, that is, the great bulk of the Russian people, as well as with the officials of the Communist Party of the Soviet Union, and the officers of the Red Army. Stalin's vision of enemies everywhere inside the Soviet Union, it is also clear, reflected the conditions that he created, rather than pre-existing attitudes. Stalin's relationship to the Soviet peasantry was characterized by him and by others as a state of war. His relationship to his subordinates was similarly dominated by mutual fear of death. If the condition of internal war creates short-term time preferences, no one should have had a

shorter-term orientation than Stalin, regardless of his underlying personality. Moreover, although there was little in the way of objective factors
that would justify a belief in the existence of an external military threat
to the Soviet Union at the time that Stalin initiated his program of rapid
industrialization, his stated attitude toward external powers indicated
that he saw himself permanently at war with them. As Vojtech Mastny
wrote, Stalin's constant refrain in the late 1920s and 1930s, during the
anti-Trotsky campaign, the collectivization of agriculture, and the
purges, was "that war was imminent. While the war scare Stalin raised
was deliberately exaggerated, it was not totally disingenuous. He was in-
ordinately concerned about war."[77] His actions to liquidate all political
figures not completely submissive to him, to crush the independent peasantry, and to build up Soviet industrial and military power might well
have been efforts to deal with dangerous threats Stalin saw to himself in
the short term, not sacrifices of short-term benefits to prepare for future
contingencies. Milovan Djilas, among many others, came to that conclusion. "What my visits to Stalin taught me was that these men regarded
themselves as appointed to rule over and against the will of the people.
They acted like a group of conspirators . . . in a conquered land, not
their own. Power for Stalin was a plot with himself as chief plotter as
well as the one cast to be plotted against."[78]

It is also arguably the case that Stalin pursued a policy that did aim at
Soviet territorial expansion before the German invasion of the Soviet
Union. He did dissolve the Communist Party of Poland in 1938, and this
was possibly his signal to Hitler that he was willing to make a deal to
partition Poland with Germany. He did invade the Baltic states, contrary
to the provisions of the Hitler-Stalin treaty, as well as Finland, and
pushed Hitler to grant the Soviet Union greater control over southeast
Europe.[79] Given the apparent inability of France and Great Britain to
check the expansion of Germany in that period, Stalin's actions have usually been portrayed as making the best of both the long- and short-term
conditions facing the Soviet Union. Those decisions were certainly in the
short-term interest of Stalin and proved to be disastrous in the long term,
but this does not prove that Stalin acted on the basis of short-term considerations.

During World War II and the 1945–1951 period, conditions changed
in ways that made Stalin's time preferences somewhat more visible. Once
the German Army had been halted at Stalingrad, complete German conquest had been avoided, but neither was victory clearly in sight. The German Army showed that it was still capable of effective offensive military
action against the Soviet Union in the spring of 1943, and the Allies were
not yet engaged in a land war in Europe against Germany. A short-term
orientation should have inclined Stalin to make the best deal that would

yield immediate benefits. A longer-term orientation would have accepted present sacrifices in return for future gains. If Stalin had a short-term time orientation, an effort to reach a separate peace with Hitler in 1943 would be expected.

There is considerable evidence that Stalin did investigate the possibility of such an agreement. Agents of the Soviet Union and Germany met in Sweden that spring, while Stalin liquidated the Comintern and instructed members of the German, Italian, and Hungarian Communist parties to organize their fellow nationals who were POWs in Soviet hands and to signal their compatriots back in their respective countries that if the fascist governments were overthrown, the Soviets were willing to accept negotiated peace agreements with those countries short of total victory.[80] The Allies were probably aware of these overtures, and this may have been one of the reasons they were so forthcoming about the postwar distribution of territory to the Soviet Union at the Tehran conference. The logic of the argument about tyranny suggests that Stalin's government would be predisposed to consider a separate peace, but the Western constitutional democracies would not, and this is consistent with the observed behavior. But Hitler also rejected the possibility of a separate peace, and it is not clear why his tyranny did not also seek an opportunistic settlement in 1943.

In addition to opportunistic behavior, shorter time horizons also suggest that there will be frequent shifts in policy in response to incentives presented in the near term. Governments with leaders who had longer-term time horizons and who were operating from within institutions that inhibited impulsive behavior would display less sensitivity to shifting short-term incentives. In the period 1945–1951, Stalin had far greater freedom of action in his foreign policy than he had in the 1930s, because the power of the Soviet Union relative to its European neighbors was greater. Given greater freedom of choice, he might have displayed greater inconstancy of decision in reaction to changing opportunities and penalties. Did Stalin's behavior in this period display the predicted sensitivity? In 1947 Stalin did shift the policy of the Soviet Union from limited cooperation with the United States and Britain to open hostility and back, within the span of approximately six months. Before 30 June 1947, Stalin had restrained the Communist government of Yugoslavia, the most openly aggressive Communist government in the east bloc, and the Communist parties of Europe. Tito was instructed to respect British interests in Greece, to give up his territorial ambitions, and to refrain from organizing an openly anti-American-British Communist Balkan coalition. The Greek Communist Party was ordered not to push its internal struggle, and the Communist parties of West Europe were ordered to pursue power legally through electoral and parliamentary strategies. The Soviet

Union itself participated in the initial discussions of how Marshall Plan aid was to be distributed to European countries, including those in East Europe. On 30 June, at a Marshall Plan conference, Molotov was handed an intelligence report based on information obtained from spies in the British government. This report stated that the Marshall Plan was understood by the U.S. and British governments to be part of a general strategy to protect West Europe against the Soviet Union. Molotov, after reading the report, abruptly left the conference, and Stalin subsequently ordered the other East European governments to do so as well. On 22 September 1947, the Communist parties of West Europe were ordered by Stalin to abandon parliamentary strategies and to promote open mass struggles designed to destabilize their governments. In December, the Greek Communist Party was given permission to capture the city of Salonika, and on 17 December, Stalin told Tito that he had permission to absorb Albania. Bulgaria and Romania were authorized to form an anti-Western Balkan League. On 22 January 1948, however, Foreign Minister Ernest Bevin gave a speech condemning the actions by Communists in the Balkans, invited the Low Countries to accede to the Franco-British Dunkirk Treaty, and asked the United States to defend West Europe. Starting on 26 January, orders were given by Stalin to the leaders of the Balkan governments to reverse their policies. Stalin told Enver Hoxha in a meeting that he must not provoke the British. Soviet officers assigned to occupation duty in Berlin who had been putting pressure on the United States were removed from their positions in January.[81]

Stalin also seems to have rapidly shifted his basic policy toward Korea at least twice in response to short-term shifts in the environment. On 24 September 1949, Stalin reiterated his position to Kim Il-Sung, that a North Korean attack on the South was out of the question because of North Korean weakness. By 4 January 1950, the Soviet government had shifted to a more hostile orientation toward Japan, praising the Chinese revolutionary model to the Japanese Communist Party and reprimanding it for following a parliamentary strategy. On 5 January President Truman ended all military assistance to South Korea, and on 12 January Secretary of State Acheson gave his famous perimeter speech, a translated version of which Molotov is said to have read out loud to Mao. On 30 January Stalin sent word to Kim that he would be willing to receive him and that a North Korean attack would take great preparation and that Korea would have to pay for weapons with Korean raw materials.

The biases in receptivity to different streams of information in Stalin's government were visible in this period. Stalin clearly believed that foreign governments had links to his enemies inside the areas he controlled. Soviet intelligence officials refused to pass on to Stalin reports from Kim Philby that there were no British spies in the Soviet Union.[82] On the other hand, Stalin was highly sensitive to information that there were contacts between foreign intelligence services and the subjects of Communist governments. Mastny notes that the Soviet defense budget increased 20 percent in 1949 after the signing of the Brussels Treaty creating NATO, but the massive East European military buildups of 1950 follow the reports of the American and British effort to introduce agents into Albania as part of a larger strategy to utilize internal opposition to Communist governments to keep the Soviet Union in check. Western efforts to exploit internal opposition to East European Communist governments may have also led Stalin to his conclusion that the United States might send forces into Czechoslovakia as part of its response to the invasion of South Korea.[83]

Stalin's decision to support Kim Il-Sung's invasion closely followed the public actions and statements of the United States distancing itself from the defense of South Korea. Stalin had already embarked on a more active campaign of pressure against Japan. Given the opportunity that appeared to be presented to him by the United States, his decision does not seem to be hard to understand. What recent research has revealed, however, is not only how closely his decision to invade followed the actions of the United States, but how quickly Stalin reversed his basic course of action in Korea after the war began. The position of Mao with regard to the United States military response in Korea and the crossing of the 38th parallel has been debated. Stalin's actions, however, are clear and do fit the pattern of action predicted for tyrants: he did react very sharply and made decisions closely following the presentation of incentives and disincentives near in time to his decision. Up through the end of August 1950, Stalin adopted a hard line at the United Nations, opposing both a cease fire in Korea and any conciliatory negotiations over the future of Germany. He even, according to Marshall Zhukov, considered the idea of airborne operations against Yugoslavia. He does not appear to have moderated his position at all in response to the July dispatch of B-29s to the Pacific. Once the United States conducted its amphibious landing at Inchon, Stalin did bring more pressure to bear on Mao to intervene militarily in Korea, although there is debate about whether or not Stalin promised Mao Soviet military air cover for Chinese military operations in Korea. The Soviet Union also called for a cease fire in Korea. Then, on 7 October, U.S. troops crossed the 38th parallel, and on 8 October, American fighter aircraft accidentally strafed a Soviet airfield sixty-two miles from the border with Korea, in broad daylight, and destroyed numerous aircraft. Zhou Enlai then met with Stalin at his Black Sea resort on 10 and 11 October. According to Chinese accounts, at this point Stalin went back on his promise to provide Soviet air cover to the Chinese troops when they entered Korea, and told the Chinese not to intervene. What is clear is that Stalin and Zhou cabled back to Beijing that the Soviet Union would not be able to take military action for two and one half months, and Stalin ordered Kim Il-Sung on 12 October to evacuate his government and the remnants of his army across the border into China. Mao then temporarily suspended his decision to intervene, but on 13 October he decided to go ahead, at which point Stalin reversed his order to Kim, and the war continued.[84]

Stalin's vacillation is consistent with a decisionmaker who responds strongly to shifting incentives presented near in time to his decisions. Stalin was afraid of near-term American attacks. Khrushchev's judgment was pithy: Stalin "showed cowardice. He had his nose to the ground. He developed fear, literally fear, of the US."[85] The longer-term consequences, in terms of his relations with China, of vacillation, and the longer-term costs of losing the Communist regime in Korea, were not sufficient to justify a decision that seemed to be very costly to Stalin in the short term.

Mao, in contrast, did decide to go ahead with his intervention. Mao was also a tyrant. If Mao and Stalin were both motivated by an orientation toward near-term costs and benefits, why did Mao not behave as Stalin did? Assume both tyrants were concerned with the survival of their regime. Stalin may have viewed war, possibly nuclear war, with the United States to have been a real short-term threat to the survival of his regime. He sacrificed longer-terms gains to the short-term need to survive. The United States had crossed the border into prewar North Korea and bombed the Soviet Union. Stalin was facing an immediate war with the United States.

Mao, on the other hand, considered the prospects of war with the United States in a telegram dated 2 October that may or may not have been sent. He proposed the quick destruction of the United States Eighth Army in Korea and accepted the possibility of American air attacks on the mainland of China. But he was also, according to Chinese accounts, assuming Soviet air protection of some kind, that is, if war came with the United States, it would be in the context of a U.S.-Soviet war, in which, presumably, the bulk of U.S. forces would be engaged with the Soviet Union. What is crucial is what Mao thought would be the consequences of Chinese intervention without Soviet air support. Mao expressed his belief in two telegrams to Zhou Enlai that the Chinese military sent to Korea would *not* engage U.S. forces, but only those of the "Wonsan puppet" regime, and this would avert the near-term threat to the regime and war with the United States. The Chinese military intervention, Mao telegraphed to Zhou Enlai on 13 October, "in the first period" could "focus on attacking the puppet forces; our troops countering the puppet forces is [sic] certain [of success]; we can open up a base in Korea in the large mountain region north of the Wonsan-Pyongyang line." That is, the Chinese would fight only South Korean troops and would establish a defensive position north of the American line. Alternatively, "if we do not send troops, allowing the enemy to press to the Yalu border, and the arrogance of reactionaries at home and abroad to grow . . . then this will be disadvantageous to all sides; above all, it will be most disadvantageous to Manchuria; all of the northeastern border defense forces will be absorbed, and south Manchurian electrical power will be controlled [by the enemy]." In his telegram to Zhou on 14 October, Mao summarized his orders to the Chinese military commander Peng Dehuai, stating that the Chinese troops under Peng's command were to cross the border, establish a defensive position, and then wait to see if the Americans or Koreans attacked that position. What would the Chinese do if attacked? Mao wrote, "Currently, we have resolved ourselves to attack the puppet armies; we may also attack some isolated American forces." The plan was to build up the military strength of the Chinese in Korea for six months. Then, "when our forces are fully equipped and trained, and after in the air and on the land we enjoy a state of overwhelming superiority over enemy forces . . . we will then discuss the issue of attacking." For the time being, however, "American forces are still stopped at the 38th parallel; their offensive to Pyongyang will require time. . . . [T]he Wonsan puppet forces will probably have difficulty advancing alone; this will give our force time to move in and construct defenses"[86] As far as can be determined, Mao was not deciding to engage the United States in war in the short term. He was preventing an immediate threat to his regime by keeping enemy troops away from the Yalu, while avoiding a military engagement with the United States. While Mao did consider the possibility of destroying American armies and American air attack on China in the context of a US-Soviet war, his telegrams after the withdrawal of the promise of Soviet air support are noticeably reserved about attacks on American forces, and silent on the subject of air attack on China. Reconstructing Mao's decision, he appears to have been dealing with the most immediate threat to his regime, just as Stalin did, but on the basis of his assumption that the United States would not go to war with China if China did not engage U.S. forces in Korea.

Conclusion

To be analytically complete, this chapter would need to address the comparative question. If the claim is made that tyrannies are more short-term oriented, more focused on considerations of local status, and more receptive to information presented in face-to-face settings, the question must be posed, "Compared to what?" Democracies are alleged to be short-sighted, everyone cares to some extent about status, and politicians in general may be predisposed to assimilate information in face-to-face settings. The competing explanation of tyrannies is that it is the centralization of power in one man that explains all the relevant behavior. If, as this chapter argues, it is the personal characteristics of tyrants combined with the institutional character of tyrannies that produces the alleged orientation, one relevant comparison may be with leaders who did not emerge through the pathways associated with the rise of tyrants, but who are given something like the power of tyrants. The wartime leaders of democracies, such as Lincoln, Clemenceau, Lloyd-George, Franklin Roosevelt, Churchill, and Ben Gurion, had supreme authority centralized in their persons to a great extent. Their decision-making behavior should be distinguishable from that of tyrants. If centralization of power matters more, then their decision making should resemble that of tyrants. A surface inspection would suggest that such a comparison might support the argument of this chapter, but a closer examination is still necessary.[87]

From the perspective of policymakers, the picture of tyrannical decision making presented in this chapter is not sufficient to make predictions of behavior, but it may be useful nonetheless. Anticipating and affecting the behavior of a tyrant, in this argument, means affecting his imagined image of the near-term future. It means being sensitive to the tyrant's sensitivity to status, and his limited receptivity to information. But this limited insight may not be without use, even if its application to specific problems requires auxiliary information and analysis.

Chapter Six_____

Where Do We Go from Here?

THE INTENTION of this book was to conduct a preliminary investigation into the role that inherited biological factors may play in shaping human strategic behavior, by examining what is known about the operation of those factors, and by generating some propositions about what kind of behavior we should see, if and when those factors affected real-world decision making. The book has not given definitive proof of those propositions. It began by saying that our understanding of human cognition was still incomplete, and that some leaps would have to be made in order to construct arguments about what impact inherited biological factors might have on international relations. Many questions were left unanswered. In each chapter, suggestions were made as to how standard forms of social science research might be employed to test the propositions advanced in the book. But might more be done? If this book is on the right track, the most important question to ask now is how new kinds of research could be conducted to prove or disprove the ideas set forth, and perhaps move beyond them. Some readers will judge that no further effort in this field is warranted. But for those who remain interested, what kind of work might usefully be conducted? Such work, broadly speaking, falls into two categories. Researchers can conduct more controlled experiments with various subjects to collect and analyze information about the biological factors that may be affecting their behavior in the experiments, and more biological data about real-world actors can be collected.

Controlled experiments are routinely conducted that investigate the possible impact of psychological factors on decision making in laboratory settings. Some of them involve decision making about questions of international relations. Typically, American college students are presented with simulated international situations and are asked to make choices about the courses of action they would adopt. Alternatively, they are given roles to play in a simulated international interaction. The conditions of the simulation are then varied to see, for example, if the subjects respond in ways that might be attributed to certain psychological tendencies. If the subjects behave in the ways predicted by the psychological theories, this is taken as evidence that those theories might be correct. One additional step could be taken. In the case where the biological sciences suggest that human body chemistry will vary in ways that could affect decision making, painless tests to assay blood chemistry could be conducted on the subjects engaged in simulations of international relations. As noted in the chapter on testosterone, Rose McDermott has conducted experiments to see what psychological factors lead some subjects to engage in arms race competitions when presented with a fictitious scenario about an international incident. Presented with exactly the same scenario concerning an ambiguous incident on an international border, some subjects immediately began to engage in bellicose rhetoric and to spend fictitious dollars on their armies, while others initiated diplomatic exchanges to resolve the "crisis."

The chapter in this book on testosterone and dominance argues that players with base levels of testosterone that are higher than the norm of the group should be more inclined to respond to perceived challenges by punishing the challenger. If saliva tests are used to assay base-level testosterone, this proposition could be tested. The chapter on testosterone also argued that among winners of social interactions, those who perceive themselves as having won by virtue of their effort will experience a subjective sense of well-being and will have levels of testosterone that are elevated, relative to their own base levels. Again, saliva tests administered at the appropriate points in the simulation could test this proposition. Finally, the chapter on testosterone argued that the process of winning in a social interaction provided its own reward, independently of the external payoff given to the winner. This would make the winner more likely to engage in subsequent social conflicts. Repeated or iterated plays of this game could investigate this. With sufficiently large numbers of subjects, statistical controls could be established to ensure that the findings were not the result of chance. Continuing with the issue of testosterone, the next step would be to engage subjects who more closely resembled real-world participants in international relations. There are schools operated by the American government that are attended by active duty foreign service, military, and intelligence officers. The arms race simulation could be conducted with them, and their blood chemistry could be similarly assayed.

Computer simulations would also be useful ways of running controlled, if artificial, experiments. In what is called agent-based modeling, brief sets of simple rules govern the behavior of the computer-generated agents.[1] These rule-governed agents react to their environment and the other actors. They can be given different thresholds that govern their willingness to go to war. Typically, they will go to war when they face a balance of power in which they have a two-to-one advantage or better. Conceivably, the willingness of an agent to go to war could be made conditional on its sensitivity to challenges. An agent might be programmed to attack if other actors "challenged" it by approaching its territorial domain. Such actors would simulate high-testosterone individuals in oligarchies, as argued in the chapter on testosterone. Other players would be more tolerant and would simulate democracies. The computer simulation could be run many times. The following question could then be posed. Did the frequency of war in simulations populated by many oligarchies resemble the frequency of real wars in real historical settings populated by many oligarchies? When democracies are added to the simulation, did the simulated change in the incidence of war resemble the actual historical changes that accompanied the real spread of democracy?

If the physiological and psychological impact of stress were of interest, other experiments could be conducted. In the chapter on distress, the observation was made that officers in a simulated prisoner-of-war camp reacted to interrogation by displaying different cortisol levels and neuropeptide-Y (NPY). Levels of cortisol that were high and stayed high were said to be associated with psychological depression, reduced willingness to engage problems, and, at the extreme, despair. High levels of NPY were said to be associated with less fear-induced behavior, and better ability to engage the environment. While investigators in the university world cannot and should not run simulated prisoner-of-war camps, professors, for example, do routinely administer oral examinations to graduate students, presenting them with cognitively complex tasks, perhaps not less taxing than those that real-world decisionmakers face, in a relatively high-stakes, time-urgent environment. Consenting graduate students could be asked to provide saliva samples at appropriate intervals before, during, and after oral examinations, to test the proposition that distress is caused by elevated cortisol levels and affects the ability to deal with complex problems.

Controlled experiments of this sort could establish whether some of the mechanisms discussed in this book are visible in simulations with students. The other set of tasks would involve investigations whether and to what extent the biological factors in question were or are present in real world decisionmakers. In many ways, this is a set of tasks more suitable to government than academic research. The U.S. government went to a great deal of trouble to arrest and confine the leader of Panama, Manuel Noriega. Convicted felons lose many of their rights, one of which is to decline certain medical examinations. In the United States, they are routinely subjected to DNA testing. If there are genetic markers of certain cognitive characteristics, Noriega's DNA could be analyzed with the objective of understanding his genetic inheritance and its possible impact on his behavior. Other foreign government officials occasionally become the prisoners of friendly governments and could also be examined.

What would be more desirable is knowledge of the biological state of government officials while they are still in power. Governments already go to some trouble to obtain information about the biological state of world leaders. The Israeli government, for example, is said to have run an operation, the purpose of which was to obtain a urine specimen from the leader of Syria, Hafez al-Assad, in order better to determine his health and expected life span. A new kind of intelligence, biological intelligence, could be developed that might give governments, in near real time, information concerning the biological state of foreign leaders of concern.

But even with more such work, we will not even be able to come up with theory that makes good general predictions about human behavior in international relations, for two very different reasons. First, this book has examined the role of emotion and memories, testosterone and dominance, stress, and time horizons. Assume, for the sake of argument, that these are the only factors that matter, and that we can reduce these complex factors into simple indicators. And, finally, assume that we can assess whether a given individual has a low, medium, or high score, on testosterone, for example. We would then have three possible values for our four indicators. This, of course, means that we would have three to the fourth power (3^2) or eighty-one different personality types. To this we would have to add the variations in the nature of the political environment in which the individual operates, variations that this book has argued to be essential in understanding group, as opposed to individual, behavior. We would end up with several hundred types of decision-making processes to be understood. A general theory that has to deal with that much complexity would not easily generate general predictions that could be tested with the limited number of real-world cases available for us to study.

Second, this book has made arguments that assume that there are certain cognitive tendencies that derive from our biological inheritance, and that those tendencies are relatively hard to change in the time span of the active professional life of political leaders. This was never completely true, and it will be less true over time. People have always been able to modify their decision-making processes, by drinking coffee or alcohol, most commonly. Now they can take Prozac. It is very likely that by 2010 there will be a number of drugs available to individuals that will enable them to modify their cognitive profiles at will. We might have full knowledge of the DNA of an individual, but if we did not have adequate pharmacological intelligence, we still might not be able to anticipate his or her behavior.

Nonetheless, an understanding of the factors investigated in this book could still be useful, in specific situations. As Isaiah Berlin noted many years ago, practical political judgment is not the same as political science. Political scientists seek general explanations that, on average, use a small number of factors to predict behavior across a wide range of cases, and across time and space. Political leaders do not wish to be right, on average, about hundreds of cases. They wish to be right about one case, the case that they are faced with. They are willing, and able to look at many factors to help them understand what to do in this one case.[2] To better understand the leader with whom we might be dealing in a particular crisis involving questions of war and peace, we might be able and motivated to learn as much as we could to anticipate his or her behavior. We might be able to deploy the assets of an intelligence organization to improve the accuracy of our predictions about this one person. One of the kinds of intelligence we could seek would be biological and pharmacological intelligence, to be added to the other kinds of intelligence we want to have when trying to anticipate the behavior of a leader. Political scientists could perform analogous studies of particular leaders, at particular moments in time, to understand the detailed nature of the biological issues that may have affected their decisions.[3] This would be a more modest form of political science that made less sweeping generalizations. It would be willing to work hard to understand people the way they are, and not adopt models that were easy to work with even if they were known to be seriously unrealistic. It might also be more useful. This book is meant to be a small contribution to that more modest form of political science.

Notes

Chapter One
Introduction

1. Daniel Kahneman, Paul Slovic, and Amos Tversky, eds., *Judgment under Uncertainty* (Cambridge: Cambridge University Press, 1982).

2. Thomas C. Schelling, "Self-Command in Practice, in Policy, and in a Theory of Rational Choice," *American Economic Review* 74, no. 72 (May 1984): 1–11.

3. In response to the publication of the book *The Bell Curve* by Richard Herrnstein and Charles Murray, the Board of Scientific Affairs (BSA) of the American Psychological Association "concluded that there was an urgent need for an authoritative report" on the issue of the inheritability of intelligence. A task force was commissioned to write such a report, and its results were published in the February 1996 issue of *American Psychologist*. With regard to the observed variations in intelligence across populations in the ordinary range of modern, Western societies, the heritability (h^2) of intelligence is about 0.35–0.45, and by adolescence heritability increases to 0.75. The impact of environments within a family (c^2) is also about 0.35–0.45 for children, declining to 0 by adolescence. The report was careful to note that these figures referred to traits of a population, not an individual, and that a trait that was heritable could be changed by environmental factors. See Ulric Neisser, "Intelligence: Knowns and Unknowns," *American Psychologist* 51, no. 2 (February 1996): 77, 85–86.

4. Thomas Hobbes, *Leviathan*, ed. C. B. MacPherson, pt. 1, chaps. 11 and 12 (Baltimore: Penguin Press, 1971), pp. 169–70.

5. Jean-Jacques Rousseau, *The First and Second Discourses*, ed. and trans. by Roger D. and Judith R. Masters (New York: St. Martins, 1964), "Discourse on the Origin and Foundations of Inequality among Men," pt. 2, pp. 143, 149.

6. John Locke, *An Essay Concerning Human Understanding* (London: Penguin Books, 1997), bk. 2, chap. 21, pp. 238, 242.

7. Michael S. Gazzaniga, Richard B. Ivry, and George R. Mangun, *Cognitive Neuroscience: The Biology of the Mind* (New York: W. W. Norton, 1998).

8. Philip E. Tetlock, "Social Psychology and World Politics," chap. 35 in *Handbook of Social Psychology* (New York: McGraw Hill, 1998), pp. 870–72.

9. David O. Sears, "College Sophomores in the Laboratory: Influences of a Narrow Data Base on Social Psychology's View of Human Nature," *Journal of Personality and Social Psychology* 51, no. 3 (September 1986): 515–30.

10. The new abundance of computational power, however, does make it possible to rerun simulations of world history to see how outcomes vary as we vary the character of the rules governing the actors. Lars-Erik Cederman, *Emergent Actors in World Politics: How States and Nations Develop And Dissolve* (Princeton: Princeton University Press, 1997); Joshua Epstein and Robert Axtel, *Grow-*

ing Artificial Societies: Social Science from the Bottom Up (Washington, D.C.: Brookings Institution Press, 1996).

11. Bruce Bueno de Mesquita and David Lalman, *War and Reason* (New Haven: Yale University Press, 1992); Bruce Bueno de Mesquita, *The War Trap* (New Haven: Yale University Press, 1981).

12. D. Scott Bennett and Allan C. Stam III, "Is Instrumental Rationality a Universal Phenomenon?" ms., October 1997, pp. 25–27, 36.

13. Bruce Bueno de Mesquita, David Newman, and Alvin Rabushka, *Red Flag over Hong Kong* (Chatham, N.J.: Chatham House, 1996), fig. 6.6 and accompanying text, pp. 117–18.

14. As quoted in John Tooby and Leda Cosmides, "The Psychological Foundations of Culture," in *The Adapted Mind: Evolutionary Psychology and the Generation of Culture*, ed. Jerome Barkow, Leda Cosmides, and John Tooby (New York: Oxford University Press, 1992), p. 24.

15. Noam Chomsky, *Syntactic Structures* (The Hague: Mouton, 1957).

16. For an excellent recent review of the debate, see Charles T. Snowdon, "From Primate Communication to Human Language," in *Tree of Origin: What Primate Behavior Can Tell Us About Human Social Evolution*, ed. Frans B. M. deWaal (Cambridge: Harvard University Press, 2001), pp. 195–227, esp. pp. 210–13.

17. Richard Byrne and Andrew Whitten, "The Machiavellian Intelligence Hypothesis," and "Taking Machiavellian Intelligence Apart," in *Machiavellian Intelligence: Social Expertise and the Evolution of Intellect in Monkeys, Apes, and Humans*, ed. Richard Byrne and Andrew Whitten (Oxford: Clarendon Press, 1988), pp. 1–10, 50–52.

18. Tooby and Cosmides, Introduction, to Barkow, Cosmides, and Tooby, *The Adapted Mind*, p. 5.

19. Tooby and Cosmides, "The Psychological Foundations of Culture," p. 34.

20. John Allman and Leslie Brothers, "Faces Fear and the Amygdala," *Nature* 372 (15 December 1994): 613–14. For additional discussion of the role of the amygdala in emotional memory and learning, see Larry Cahill et al., "The Amygdala and Emotional Memory," *Nature* 377 (28 September 1995): 295–96; Antoine Bechara et al., "Double Dissociation of Conditioning and Declarative Knowledge Relative to the Amygdala and Hippocamus in Humans," *Science* 269 (25 August 1995): 1115–18; and Antonio R. Damasio, *Descartes' Error: Emotion, Reason, and the Human Brain* (New York: Grosset/Putnam, 1994).

21. Charles Darwin, *The Expression of the Emotions in Man and Animals* (London: Julian Friedman, 1998 reprint of 1879 edition); James A. Russell, "Is There a Universal Recognition of Emotions from Facial Expression? A Review of the Cross-Cultural Studies," in *Human Facial Expression: An Evolutionary View*, by Alan J. Fridlund (San Diego: Academic Press, 1994), pp. 194–268; Erika L. Rosenberg, "Facing the Facts," *Nature* 373 (16 February 1995): 569–70.

22. Simon Baron-Cohen, *Mindblindness: An Essay on Autism and Theory of the Mind* (Cambridge: MIT Press, 1995), p. 142.

23. Richard Byrne, *The Thinking Ape: Evolutionary Origins of Intelligence* (New York: Oxford University press, 1995), pp. 111–17 and 25.

24. Alan R. Rogers, "Evolution of Time Preferences by Natural Selection," *The American Economic Review* 84, no. 3 (June 1994), 460–481.

25. Stephen Jay Gould, *Wonderful Life: The Burgess Shale and the Nature of History* (New York: W. W. Norton, 1986), pp. 292–323.

26. C. Robert Cloninger, "A Systematic Method for Clinical Description and Classification of Personality Variants," *Archives of General Psychology* 44 (June 1987): 573–88; A. C. Heath, C. R. Cloninger, and N. G. Martin, "Testing a Model for the Genetic Structure of Personality: A Comparison of the Personality Systems of Cloninger and Eysenck," *Journal of Personality and Social Psychology* 66, no. 4 (1994): 762–75.

27. C. Robert Cloninger, Dragan M. Svrakic, and Thomas Przybeck, "A Psychobiological Model of Temperament and Character," *Archives of General Psychiatry* 50 (December 1993): 975–90.

28. Robert Plomin, Michael J. Owen, and Peter McGuffin, "The Genetic Basis of Complex Human Behaviors," *Science* 264 (17 June 1994): 1733–39.

29. C. Robert Cloninger, Rolf Adolfsson, and Nenand M. Svaric, "Mapping Genes for Human Personality," *Nature Genetics* 12 (January 1996): 3–4. The supporting studies were Richard Ebstein et al., "Dopamine D4 Receptor (D4DR) Polymorphism Associated with the Human Personality Trait of Novelty Seeking," *Nature Genetics* 12 (January 1996): 78–80; Jonathan Benjamin et al., "Population and Familial Association between the D4 Dopamine Receptor Gene And Measures of Novelty Seeking," *Nature Genetics* 12 (January 1996): 81–84.

30. Studies that found no support for the Cloninger hypothesis or that could not replicate his findings include C. Gebhardt et al., "Non-Association of Dopamine D4 and D2 Receptor Genes with Personality in Healthy Individuals, *Psychiatric Genetics* 10, no. 3 (September 2000): 131–37; J. H. Herbst et al., "Do the Dimensions of the Temperament and Character Inventory Map a Simple Genetic Architecture?" *American Journal of Psychiatry* 157, no. 8 (August 2000): 1285–90; M. Pogue-Geile et al., "Human Novelty-Seeking Personality Traits and Dopamine D4 Receptor Polymorphism: A Twin and Genetic Association Study," *American Journal of Medical Genetics* 81, no. 1 (7 February 1998). Studies supporting the Cloninger hypothesis include Y. Okuyama et al., "Identification of a Polymorphism in the Promoter Region of DRD4 Associated with the Human Novelty Seeking Personality Trait," *Molecular Psychiatry* 5, no. 1 (January 2000): 64–69; R. P. Ebstein et al., "Additional Evidence for an Association between the Dopamine D4 receptor (DRD4) Exon III Repeat Polymorphism and the Human Personality Trait of Novelty Seeking," *Molecular Psychiatry* 2, no. 6 (October–November 1997): 472–77; G. Gerra et al., "Neuroendocrine Correlates of Temperamental Traits in Humans," *Psychoneuroendocrinology* 25, no. 5 (July 2000): 479–96; Y. M. Hur and T. J. Bouchard, "The Genetic Correlation between Impulsivity and Sensation Seeking Traits," *Behavior Genetics* 27, no. 5 (September 1997): 455–63.

31. Russell Hardin, *One for All: The Logic of Group Conflict* (Princeton: Princeton University Press, 1995), pp. 91–95. The point concerning the relatively low odds of dying in a duel is made on p. 95.

32. Kevin McAleer, *Dueling: The Cult of Honor in Fin-de-Siecle Germany* (Princeton: Princeton University Press, 1994), pp. 34–35, 57, 65–66.

33. Kenneth Waltz, *Foreign Policy and Democratic Politics: The American and British Experience* (Boston: Little, Brown, 1967).

34. Timur Kuran, *Private Truths, Public Lies: The Social Consequences of Preference Falsification* (Cambridge: Harvard University Press, 1997), esp. pp. 64–77.

Chapter Two
Emotions, Memory, and Decision Making

1. Ernest R. May, *Strange Victory: Hitler's Conquest of France* (New York: Hill and Wang, 2000), pp. 117, 129.

2. Robert Jervis, *Systems Effects: Complexity in Political and Social Life* (Princeton: Princeton University Press, 1997).

3. Howard Margolis, *Patterns, Thinking, and Cognition: A Theory of Judgement* (Chicago: University of Chicago Press, 1987), pp. 1–4.

4. Antonio R. Damasio, *Descartes' Error: Emotion, Reason, and the Human Brain* (New York: Grosset/Putnam. 1994), p. 173.

5. Ken Nakayama and Julian S. Joseph, "Attention, Pattern Recognition and Pop-Out in Visual Search," in *The Attentive Brain*, ed. Raja Parasuraman (Cambridge: MIT Press, 1998), pp. 280–84.

6. Tor Nørretranders, *The User Illusion*, trans., Jonathan Sydenham (New York: Viking, 1998), pp. 124–25, 137–39.

7. Charles Darwin, *The Expression of the Emotions in Man and Animals*, with commentary by Paul Ekman commentator (New York: Oxford University Press, 1998), p. 340.

8. Joseph LeDoux, *The Emotional Brain* (New York: Simon and Schuster, 1996), pp. 38–41.

9. John H. Krystal, Stephen M. Southwick, and Dennis Charney, "Post Traumatic Stress Disorder: Psychobiological Mechanisms of Traumatic Remembrance," in *Memory Distortion: How Minds, Brains, and Societies Reconstruct the Past*, ed. Daniel Schacter (Cambridge: Harvard University Press, 1995), pp. 150–51, 154, 156–60, 174.

10. Daniel Schacter, *Searching for Memory: The Brain, the Mind, and the Past* (New York: Basic Books, 1996), pp. 198–201, 209.

11. Larry Cahill et al., "The Amygdala and Emotional Memory," *Nature* 377 (28 September 1995): 295–96.

12. Antoine Bechara et al., "Double Dissociation of Conditioning and Declarative Knowledge Relative to the Amygdala and Hippocampus in Humans," *Science* 269 (25 August 1995): 1115–18.

13. LeDoux, *Emotional Brain*, p. 48.

14. Stanislas Dehaene et al., "Imaging Unconscious Semantic Priming," *Nature* 395 (8 October 1998): 597–600.

15. John F. Kihlstrom, "The Cognitive Unconscious," *Science* 237 (1987): 1445–52, cited in Nørretranders, *User Illusion*, p. 171.

16. R. B. Zajonc, "Feeling and Thinking: Preferences Need No Inferences,"

American Psychologist 35 (February 1980): 154–55. I am grateful to Jonathan Mercer for bringing the exchange between Zajonc and Lazarus to my attention.

17. LeDoux, *Emotional Brain*, p. 59.

18. Richard S. Lazarus, "Thoughts on the Relations between Emotion and Cognition," *American Psychologist* 37 (1982): 1019, 1021–22.

19. R. B. Zajonc, "On the Primacy of Affect," *American Psychologist* 39 (1984): 118.

20. Sigmund Freud, *Civilization and Its Discontents*, ed. and trans. James Strachey (New York: Norton, 1961), p. 15.

21. LeDoux, *Emotional Brain*, pp. 73–74, 98–101.

22. Ibid., pp. 152, 154, 158, 163, 165, 168, 169, 188–92, 198, 203, 214–16.

23. Damasio, *Descartes' Error*, discussions of patient "Elliot," pp. 35–45, and patient "A," pp. 54–56.

24. LeDoux, *Emotional Brain*, p. 207.

25. Antoine Bechara et al., "Deciding Advantageously before Knowing the Advantageous Strategy," *Science* 275 (28 February 1997): 1293–95.

26. Benjamin Libet et al., "Control of the Transition from Sensory Detection to Sensory Awareness in Man by the Duration of a Thalamic Stimulus," *Brain* 114 (1991): 1731–57, cited in Nørretranders, *User Illusion*, pp. 219–21, 232, 241.

27. LeDoux, *Emotional Brain*, pp. 236–38.

28. This is the essential argument developed by Richard Byrne in numerous research articles and summarized in his book *Machiavellian Intelligence: Social Expertise and the Evolution of Intelligence in Monkeys, Apes, and Humans* (Oxford: Clarendon Press, 1988).

29. Zajonc, "Feeling and Thinking," p. 153.

30. John Allman and Leslie Brothers, "Faces, Fear, and the Amygdala," *Nature* 372 (15 December 1995): 613–14.

31. Ralph Adolphs, Daniel Tranel, and Antonio R. Damasio, "The Human Amygdala in Social Judgment," *Nature* 393 (1998): 470–74. This raises the issue of whether the facial expression of human emotions, as opposed to human social gestures, is universal and biological in origin, as opposed to being culturally determined. For a review of that debate and what appears to be conclusive evidence, see the afterword by Paul Ekman, in Darwin, *Expression of Emotions*, pp. 363–93.

32. Yuen Foong Khong, *Analogies at War: Korea, Munich, Dien Bien Phu and the Vietnam Decisions of 1965* (Princeton: Princeton University Press, 1992), pp. 25–28, 35–36.

33. See, for example, the discussion of the way in which storytelling helps children attach emotional meaning to social events by adults who experience emotion when telling or reading stories to children in Nørretranders, *User Illusion*, p. 147.

34. Richard A. Posner, *Aging and Old Age* (Chicago: University of Chicago Press, 1995), pp. 67–69, 101–4.

35. Howard Schuman and Jacqueline Scott, "Generations and Collective Memories," *American Sociological Review* 54 (June 1989): 359–81.

36. Gideon Rose, "Victory and Its Substitutes: Foreign Policy Decisionmaking at the Ends of War," Ph.D. diss., Harvard University, 1994, pp. 212, 312.

37. Dan Reiter, *Crucible of Beliefs: Learning, Alliances and World Wars* (Ithaca: Cornell University Press, 1996), pp. 21–24, 92.

38. Barbara Farnham, *Roosevelt and the Munich Crisis: A Study of Political Decision-Making* (Princeton: Princeton University Press, 1997), pp. 107–16.

39. Deborah W. Larson, *Origins of Containment* (Princeton: Princeton University Press, 1985), pp. 196–97.

40. Deborah Shapley, *Promise and Power: The Life and Times of Robert McNamara* (Boston: Little, Brown, 1993), p. 290.

41. Alexander Fursenko and Timothy Naftali, *"One Hell of a Gamble": Khrushchev, Castro, and Kennedy, 1958–1964* (New York: Norton, 1997), p. 203.

42. Ernest R. May and Philip D. Zelikow, eds., *The Kennedy Tapes: Inside the White House during the Cuban Missile Crisis* (Cambridge: Harvard University Press, 1997), pp. 54–56.

43. Fursenko and Naftali, *"One Hell of a Gamble,"* p. 225.

44. James G. Blight and David A. Welch, *On the Brink: Americans and Soviets Reexamine the Cuban Missile Crisis* (New York: Hill and Wang, 1989), pp. 194–95, 215–16, 352n.64.

45. Marc Trachtenberg, *History and Strategy* (Princeton: Princeton University Press, 1991), pp. 245–47.

46. Fursenko and Naftali, *"One Hell of a Gamble,"* p. 205.

47. Ibid., p. 131.

48. May and Zelikow, *Kennedy Tapes,* p. 39.

49. Blight and Welch, *On the Brink,* p. 367n.92. Richard Neustadt is mentioned as one source for this quote.

50. Richard K. Betts and Leslie Gelb, *The Irony of Vietnam: The System Worked* (Washington, DC: Brookings Institution, 1979).

51. Larry Berman, *Planning a Tragedy: The Americanization of the War in Vietnam* (New York: Norton, 1982), pp. xii, 6–7, 145–47.

52. John P. Burke and Fred I. Greenstein, *How Presidents Test Reality: Decisions on Vietnam, 1954 and 1965* (New York: Russell Sage Foundation, 1989), pp. 173, 234–35, 298–99.

53. Robert Dallek, *Flawed Giant: Lyndon Johnson and His Times, 1961–1973* (New York: Oxford University Press, 1998), pp. 99–100, 103.

54. Michael R. Beschloss, ed., *Taking Charge: The Johnson White House Tapes, 1963–1964* (New York: Simon and Schuster, 1997), pp. 364, 368–69.

55. Ibid., 401–3.

56. Robert Dallek, *Lone Star Rising* (New York: Oxford University Press, 1991), pp. 323–25.

Chapter Three
Status, Testosterone, and Dominance

1. Paul W. Schroeder, *Austria, Great Britain, and the Crimean War: The Destruction of the European Concert* (Ithaca: Cornell University Press, 1972), p. 405.

2. For an excellent discussion of the ways in which concerns for status affected British behavior in the 1956 Suez crisis, see Louise Richardson, *When Allies Differ: Anglo-American Relations in the Suez and Falkland Crises* (New York: St. Martin's Press, 1996). For a statistical analysis of how status discrepancies have an independent effect on the outbreak of war, see Manus I. Midlarsky, *On War: Political Violence in the International System* (New York: Free Press, 1975), pp. 94–132. For a game theoretic discussion of how envy will impede the emergence of cooperation in iterated games, see Robert Axelrod, *The Evolution of Cooperation* (New York: Basic Books, 1984), pp. 110–13. For a discussion of how status competition may affect current state behavior, see William Wohlforth, "Status Competition and the Stability of Pax Americana," ms, 20 February 2000.

3. Robert Frank, *Choosing the Right Pond: Human Behavior and the Quest for Status* (New York: Oxford University Press, 1985), pp. 8–9.

4. Robert Powell, "The Problem of Absolute and Relative Gains in International Relations Theory," *American Political Science Review* 85 (December 1991): 1303–20.

5. Barry O'Neill, *Honor, Symbols, and War* (Ann Arbor: University of Michigan Press, 1999), p. xii.

6. Russell Hardin, *One for All: The Logic of Group Conflict* (Princeton: Princeton University Press, 1995), pp. 91–95. The point concerning the relatively low odds of dying in a duel is made on p. 95.

7. Kevin McAleer, *Dueling: The Cult of Honor in Fin-de-Siècle Germany* (Princeton: Princeton University Press, 1994), pp. 34–35, 57, 65–66.

8. Charles Darwin, *The Descent of Man, and Selection in Relation to Sex* (Princeton: Princeton University Press, 1981), vol. 1, pp. 272–75.

9. Ibid., p. 276.

10. Ibid., p. 258.

11. Ibid., volume 2, pp. 239, 314, 326.

12. For an excellent review of the literature on nonhuman and human sexual selection, see Matt Ridley, *The Red Queen: Sex and the Evolution of Human Nature* (New York: Macmillan, 1993), pp. 53–170.

13. Peter Schmidt and David R. Rubinow, "Neuroregulatory Role of Gonadal Steroids in Humans," *Psychopharmacology Bulletin* 33 (1997): 219–20.

14. Donald H. Edwards and Edward A. Kravitz, "Serotonin, Social Status and Aggression," *Current Opinion in Neurobiology* 7 (1997): 812–19.

15. David R. Rubinow and Peter Schmidt, "Androgens, Brain, and Behavior," *American Journal of Psychiatry* 153, no. 8 (August 1996): 974–84.

16. W. Jack Rejeski et al., "Anabolic Steroids and Aggressive Behavior in Cynomolgous Monkeys," *Journal of Behavioral Medicine* 11 (1988): 95–105.

17. Drake Morgan et al., "Predictors of Social Status in Cynomolgous Monkeys after Group Formation," *American Journal of Primatology* 52 (2000): 115–31.

18. Margaret R. Clarke et al., "Social Dominance and Serum Testoserone Concentration in Dyads of Male Macaca Fasicularis," *Journal of Medical Primatology* 15 (1986): 419–32.

19. Rubinow and Schmidt, "Androgens, Brain, and Behavior."

20. Alan Booth and Allan Mazur, "Authors' Response: Old Issues and New Perspectives on Testosterone Research," *Behavioral and Brain Sciences* 21 (June 1998): 386–96; M. Hines, "Adult Testosterone Levels Have Little or No Influence on Dominance in Men," *Behavioral and Brain Sciences* 21 (June 1998): 377.

21. Melford E. Spiro, *Gender and Culture: Kibbutz Women Revisited* (New Brunswick, N.J.: Transaction Publications, 1996), pp. 17, 22–23, 73–80.

22. Lionel Tiger and Joseph Shepher, *Women on the Kibbutz* (New York: Harcourt Brace Jovanovich, 1975).

23. Eleanor E. Maccoby, *The Two Sexes* (Cambridge: Harvard University Press, 1998), pp. 36–37.

24. Ibid., pp. 112–14.

25. James Q. Wilson and Richard J. Herrnstein, *Crime and Human Nature* (New York: Simon and Schuster, 1985), p. 120.

26. Martin Daly and Margo Wilson, "Darwinism and the Roots of Machismo," *Scientific American Presents* 10, no. 2 (Summer 1999): 9–11. See also Laura L. Betzig, *Despotism and Differential Reproduction Rates: A Darwinian View of History* (New York: Aldine Press, 1986).

27. Rose McDermott, Jonathan Cowden, and Cheryl Koopman, "An Experimental Simulation of the Psychological Factors Underlying Military Procurement Decisions in International Conflict," ms., May, 2000.

28. See, for example, the metasurvey done by John Archer, "The Influence of Testosterone on Human Aggression," *British Journal of Psychology* 82 (1191): 1–28.

29. F. Suay et al., "Effects of Competition and Its Outcome on Serum Testosterone, Cortisol, and Prolactin," *Psychoneuroendicrinology* 24 (1999): 551–66.

30. Robert M. Sapolsky, "Endocrinology Alfresco: Psychoendocrine Studies of Wild Baboons," *Recent Progress in Hormone Research* 48 (1993): 437–67.

31. Morgan et al., "Predictors of Social Status."

32. Clarke et al., "Social Dominance."

33. W. J. Jeffcoate et al., "Correlation between Anxiety and Serum Prolactin in Humans," *Journal of Psychosomatic Research* 30 (1986): 217–22.

34. James M. Dabbs, Jr., Elizabeth Carriere Alford, and Julie Fielden, "Trial Lawyers and Testosterone: Blue-Collar Talent in a White-Collar World," *Journal of Applied Social Psychology* 28, 1 (1998): 89.

35. James M. Dabbs, Jr., "Testosterone and Occupational Achievement," *Social Forces* 70, no. 3 (March 1992): 813–24.

36. Allan Mazur and Joel Michalek, "Marriage, Divorce, and Male Testosterone," *Social Forces* 77, no. 1 (1998): 315–30.

37. Dabbs, "Testosterone and Occupational Achievement," p. 811.

38. Julie Atkin Harris, Philip A. Vernon, and Dorret I. Boomsma, "The Heritability of Testosterone: A Study of Dutch Adolescent Twins and Their Parents," *Behavior Genetics* 28, no. 3 (1998): 165–71.

39. Matti Virkkunen, David Goldman, and Markku Linnoila, discussion of "Serotonin in Alcoholic Violent Offenders," Ciba Foundation, *Genetics of Criminal and Antisocial Behaviour: Ciba Foundation Symposium 194* (Chichester, England: John Wiley, 1996), p. 179, referring to the article M. Virkkunen et al.,

"CSF Biochemistry, Glucose Metabolism, and Diurnal Activity Rhythms in Violent Offenders, Impulsive Fire Setters and Healthy Volunteers," *Archives of General Psychiatry* 51 (1994): 20–27.

40. Allan Mazur and Alan Booth, "Testosterone and Dominance in Men," *Behavioral and Brain Sciences* 21 (1998): 353–97.

41. Dan Olweus et al., "Circulating Testosterone Levels and Aggression in Adolescent Males: A Causal Analysis," *Psychosomatic Medicine* 50 (1988): 261–72.

42. Archer, "Influence of Testosterone."

43. Alicia Salvador et al., "Correlating Testosterone and Fighting in Male Participants in Judo Contests," *Physiology and Behavior* 68 (1999): 205–9.

44. Elena M. Kouri et al., "Increased Aggressive Responding in Male Volunteers Following the Administration of Gradually Increasing Doses of Testosterone Cypionate," *Drug and Alcohol Dependence* 40 (1995): 73–79.

45. Harrison G. Pope, Elena Kouri, and James Hudson, "Effects of Supraphysiological Doses of Testosterone on Mood and Aggression in Normal Men, *Archives of General Psychiatry* 57 (2000): 133–140.

46. Jan Volvaka, "The Neurobiology of Violence: An Update," *Journal of Neuropsychiatry and Clinical Neurosciences* 11, no. 3 (1999): 307–14.

47. Dabbs, "Testosterone and Occupational Achievement," pp. 813–24.

48. Dabbs et al., "Trial Lawyers and Testosterone."

49. James M. Dabbs, Marion F. Hargrove, and Colleen Heusel, "Testosterone Differences among College Fraternities: Well-Behaved vs. Rambunctious," *Personality and Individual Differences* 20, no. 2 (1996): 157–61.

50. Richard E. Nisbett, "Violence and U.S. Regional Culture," *American Psychologist* 48 (1993): 441–49. See also the discussion of the impact of pastoral economic organization on Arab society, and the resultant intense and unstable social competition, or *fitmah*, in Ibn Khaldun, *The Muqaddimah*, volume 1, trans. Franz Rosenthal (Princeton: Princeton University Press, 1980), vol. 1, pp. 252, 263–67, 304–5.

51. Theodore D. Kemper, *Social Structure and Testosterone* (New Brunswick, N.J.: Rutgers University Press, 1990), p. 23.

52. Alan Booth et al., "Testosterone and Winning and Losing in Human Competition," *Hormones and Behavior* 23 (1989): 556–71; Mazur and Booth, "Testosterone and Dominance in Men"; Suay et al., "Effects of Competition." *Psychoneuroendicrinology* 24 (1999) 551–566. The results of the last study, which examined judo fighters, was more mixed, and the authors suggested that simple victory was mediated by psychological mechanisms before affecting testosterone levels.

53. Brian A. Gladue, Michael Boechler, and Kevin D. McCaul, "Hormonal Response to Competition in Human Males," *Aggressive Behavior* 15 (1989): 409–22.

54. Allan Mazur, Alan Booth, and James Dabbs, Jr., "Testosterone and Chess Competition," *Social Psychology Quarterly* 55 (March 1992): 70–77.

55. Gladue et al., "Hormonal Response"; Booth et al., "Testosterone and Winning."

56. Gladue et al., "Hormonal Response." See also Kemper, *Testosterone and Social Structure*, pp. 47, 53.

57. Booth et al., "Testosterone and Winning."

58. Tibor Scitovsky, *The Joyless Economy: The Psychology of Human Satisfaction*, rev. ed. (New York: Oxford University Press, 1992), pp. 64–65.

59. Ibid., pp. 130–32.

60. Abraham Lincoln, *The Collected Works of Abraham Lincoln*, ed., Roy P. Basler (New Brunswick, N.J.: Rutgers University Press, 1953), vol. 1, pp. 113–14.

61. Peter Gay, *The Cultivation of Hatred* (New York: W. W. Norton, 1993), pp. 252, 254, 257.

62. David Reynolds, "Churchill and the British Decision of Fight on in 1940," in *Diplomacy and Intelligence during the Second World War*, ed. Richard Langhorne (New York: Cambridge University Press, 1985), p. 167.

63. Winston S. Churchill, *The Gathering Storm* (Boston: Houghton Mifflin, 1948), p. 667

64. Christopher Boehm, *Hierarchy in the Forest: The Evolution of Egalitarian Behavior* (Cambridge: Harvard University Press, 1999), pp. 30–31, 35–37.

65. Baron de Montesquieu, *The Spirit of the Laws*, trans. Thomas Nugent (New York: Hafner Publishing, 1949), vol. 1, bk. 3, p. 22, bk. 4, p. 32.

66. Richard E. Nisbett, "Violence and U.S. Regional Culture," *American Psychologist* 48 (1993): 441–49.

67. Richard E. Nisbett and Dov Cohen, "Men, Honor and Murder," *Scientific American Presents* 10 (Summer 1999): 16–19.

68. Dan Reiter and Allan Stam, *Democracies at War* (Princeton: Princeton University Press, 2002), pp. 19–21, 29.

69. Hein Goemans, *War and Punishment: The Causes of War Termination and the First World War* (Princeton: Princeton University Press, 2000).

70. Jon Mercer, *Reputation and International Politics* (Ithaca: Cornell University Press, 1996), chapters 2–4, pp. 44–153.

Chapter Four
Stress, Distress, and War Termination

1. Carl von Clausewitz, *On War*, ed. and trans. Michael Howard and Peter Paret (Princeton: Princeton University Press, 1976), p. 92.

2. Hein Goemans, *War and Punishment: The Causes of War Termination and the First World War* (Princeton: Princeton University Press, 2000), pp. 11, 13–14, 27.

3. Ibid., pp. 27, 28, 30, 31.

4. Ibid., pp. 35–36.

5. Clausewitz, *On War*, p. 102.

6. Ibid., p. 108.

7. Ibid., p. 90.

8. Ibid., p. 115.

9. Ibid., pp. 254–56.

10. M. A. De Wolfe, ed., *Home Letters of General Sherman* (New York: C. Scribner's Sons, 1909), p. 287.

11. Cited in U. S. Grant Sharp, *Strategy for Defeat: Vietnam in Retrospect* (San Rafael, Calif.: Presidio Press, 1978), p. 258.

12. This argument is often related back to arguments made by James Fearon, that wars begin out of imperfect knowledge of relative capabilities. Fearon himself, however, is careful to note that while states ought to update their information about the power of their adversaries as they interact with them, in political-military crises, for example, he could not find clear evidence that such updating actually took place: "I do not know of a single clear instance of this, even though updating about an opponent's resolve, or willingness to fight, is very common." James D. Fearon, "Rationalist Explanations for War," *International Organization* 49, 3 (Summer 1995): 409.

13. David Reynolds, "Churchill and the British 'Decision' to Fight on in 1940: Right Policy, Wrong Reasons," in *Diplomacy and Intelligence during the Second World War: Essays in Honour of F. H. Hinsley*, ed. Richard Langhorne (Cambridge: Cambridge University Press, 1985), pp. 158, 167.

14. Allan R. Millet, "Cantigny, 28–31 May 1918," in *America's First Battles, 1776–1965*, ed. Charles E. Heller and William A. Stoft (Lawrence: University of Kansas Press, 1986), pp. 180, 185. Battles of Cantigny and Buna "too costly," first battles are "peculiar." John Shy, "First Battles in Retrospect," in ibid., pp. 327, 329.

15. Fred Charles Ikle, *Every War Must End* (New York: Columbia University Press, 1971), pp. 23, 30, 32.

16. Cited in David French, "Sir John French's Secret Service on the Western Front, 1914–1915," *The Journal of Strategic Studies* 7 (December 1984): 436; and Major General Charles E. Callwell, *Experiences of a Dug-Out 1914–1918* (London: Constable, 1920), p. 109.

17. F. H. Hinsley, *British Intelligence in the Second World War* (London: HMSO, 1979), vol. 1, pp. 241, 243; vol. 2, pp. 131, 691–92, 2:134, 136–37.

18. Stephen Peter Rosen, *Winning the Next War* (Ithaca: Cornell University Press, 1991), pp. 145–46.

19. Ikle, *Every War Must End*, p. 96.

20. Samuel Stouffer et al., *The American Soldier* (Princeton: Princeton University Press, 1949), vol. 2, pp. 72, 76, 78.

21. Ibid., pp. 373–75, 450.

22. See, for example, David F. Dinges et al., "Cumulative Sleepiness, Mood Disturbance and Psychomotor Vigilance Decrements during a Week of Sleep Restricted to 4–5 Hours per Night," *Sleep* 20, no. 4 (1997): 267–77. For data on sailors and sleep deprivation, see A. Tilley and S. Brown, "Sleep Deprivation," in *Handbook of Human Performance*, vol. 3: *State and Trait*, ed. A. P. Smith and D. M. Jones (San Diego: Academic Press, 1992), pp. 248–52. Interviews with Thomas Balkin, Walter Reed Army Institute for Research, sleep deprivation, 29 September 1999.

23. D. Ebert et al., "Cortisol and Beta-Endorphin Responses to Sleep Deprivation in Major Depression—The Hyperarousal Theories of Sleep Deprivation," *Neuropsychology* 29 (1994): 64–68.

24. A. Craig and R. E. Cooper, "Symptoms of Acute and Chronic Fatigue," in *Handbook of Human Performance*, vol. 3: *State and Trait*, ed. Smith and Jones, pp. 308–11.

25. Ibid., pp. 313, 319.

26. Paul J. Rosch, "Stress and Memory Loss: Some Speculations and Solutions," *Stress Medicine* 13 (1997): 1–6.

27. George Chrousos, "The Concepts of Stress and Stress System Disorders," *Journal of the American Medical Association* 267 (4 March 1992): 1246–47.

28. Robert Sapolsky, "Individual Differences in Cortisol Secretory Patterns in the Wild Baboon: Role of Negative Feedback Sensitivity," *Endocrinology* 113, no. 6 (1983): 2263–67; Sapolsky, "Stress in the Wild," *Scientific American* 262, no. 1 (January 1990): 116–123.

29. Martin E. P. Seligman, *Helplessness: On Depression, Development, and Death* (San Francisco: W. H. Freeman, 1975), pp. 21–24, 28–33.

30. Chrousos, "Stress," p. 1246; Edmund T. Rolls, *The Brain and Emotion* (Oxford: Oxford University Press, 1999), pp. 48–49: "The amygdala may thus be a somewhat slow and inflexible system, compared with the orbitofrontal cortex which has developed greatly in primates, in learning about which visual stimuli have the taste and smell of food."

31. Seligman, *Helplessness*, pp. 33, 82.

32. D. Stewart and D. Wisner, "Incidence of Perforated Peptic Ulcer: Effects of Heavy Air-Raids," *Lancet* (28 February 1942): 259.

33. N. Bohnen et al., "Cortisol Reactivity and Cognitive Performance in a Continuous Mental Task Paradigm," *Biological Psychology* 31 (1990): 107–16.

34. Mika Kivimaki and Sirpa Lusa, "Stress and Cognitive Performance of Firefighters during Smoke-Diving, *Stress Medicine* 10 (1994): 63–68; L. Weisaeth and S. Ersland, "Stress on Helpers in Mass Death Situations," *Annual Medical Military Fenn* [*sic*] 64 (1989): 12–17.

35. Seligman, *Helplessness*, pp. 46–48.

36. Ibid., pp. 47, 57; Richard Lazarus, *Stress and Emotion: A New Synthesis* (New York: Springer, 1999), p. 92.

37. See, for example, Susan L. Marquis, *Unconventional Warfare: Rebuilding U.S. Special Operations Forces* (Washington, D.C.: Brookings Institution, 1997), pp. 52–55; Anna Simons, *The Company They Keep: Life Inside the U.S. Army Special Forces* (New York: The Free Press, 1997), pp. 57–75, 77–92.

38. Interviews conducted by the author, Camp Mackall, 1/1st, 1st Special Warfare Training Group (A), U.S. Army John F. Kennedy Special Warfare Center and School, Fort Bragg, North Carolina, 4 November 1999. I would like to thank Major William P. Banker for his invaluable assistance in arranging these interviews.

39. Briefing by Major Carla Long, SERE psychologist, JFK Special Warfare Center and School, 5 November 1999.

40. Charles A. Morgan III et al., "Hormone Profiles in Humans Experiencing Military Survival Training," *Biological Psychiatry* 47 (2000): 891–901; Charles A. Morgan III et al., "Plasma Neuropeptide-Y Concentration in Humans Exposed to Military Survival Training," *Biological Psychiatry* 47 (2000): 902–909. For discussions of the effects of Neuropeptide Y, see Markus Heilig and Robert Murison, "Intracerebroventricular Neuropeptide Y Protects against Stress-In-

duced Gastric Strains in the Rat," *European Journal of Pharmacology* 137 (1987): 127–29; Markus Heilig et al., "Anxiolytic-Like Action of Neuropeptide Y: Mediation by Y1 Receptors in Amygdala and Dissociation from Food Intakes," *Neuropsychopharmacology* 8, no. 4 (1993): 357–63; Markus Heilig et al., "Anxiolytic-Like Effect of Neuropeptide Y (NPY), but Not Other Peptides in an Operant Conflict Test," *Regulatory Peptides* 41 (1992): 61–69; Markus Heilig and Widerlöv, "Neuropeptide Y: An Overview of Central Distribution, Functional Aspects, and Possible Involvement in Neuropsychiatric Illnesses," *Acta Psychiatrica Scandinavica* (1990): 95–114. I thank Charles Morgan for providing me with the references to these articles.

41. Ben Shephard, *A War of Nerves: Soldiers and Psychiatrists in the Twentieth Century* (Cambridge: Harvard University Press, 2001), pp. 112–13.

42. Ibid., pp. 99–101, 105–7.

43. Ibid., pp. 305, 307–9.

44. A. V. Bannerjee, "A Simple Model of Herd Behavior," *Quarterly Journal of Economics* 107, no. 3 (1992): 797–817. I thank Randall Nishina for bringing this article and other formal treatments of herd behavior to my attention. Timur Kuran, *Private Truths, Public Lies: The Social Consequences of Preference Falsification* (Cambridge: Harvard University Press, 1997), esp. pp. 24–27, 40–50.

45. For a general discussion of Slim and the problem of mutiny, see Stephen Peter Rosen, "Mutiny and the Warsaw Pact," *The National Interest* 2 (Winter 1985–1986): 74–82.

46. Basil Liddell-Hart, *Strategy*, 2d rev. ed. (London: Faber and Faber, 1967), pp. 339–40.

47. Noah Andre Trudeau, "A Mere Question of Time," in *Lee: The Soldier*, ed. Gary W. Gallagher (Lincoln: University of Nebraska Press, 1996), pp. 549, 552.

48. Marc Bloch, *Strange Defeat: A Statement of Evidence Written in 1940* (New York: W. W. Norton, 1968), pp. 38, 45, 107–8.

49. Stephen T. Hosmer, *Psychological Effects of U.S. Air Operations in Four Wars, 1941–1991* (Santa Monica: RAND, 1996), pp. 164–65.

50. Truong Nhu Tang with David Chanoff and Doan Van Toai, *A Vietcong Memoir* (San Diego: Harcourt Brace Jovanovich, 1985), pp. 167, 170–71.

51. Unsigned article, "Supply Trucks Moving Down the Trail in Daylight," *Vietnam Courier* 5 (1984): 15–16.

52. Konrad Kellen, *A View of the VC: Elements of Cohesion in the Enemy Camp in 1966–1967*, RM-5462-1-ISA/ARPA (Santa Monica: RAND, 1969), pp. 24–25.

53. Konrad Kellen, *Conversations with Enemy Soldiers in Late 1968/Early 1969: A Study of Motivation and Morale*, RM-6131-1-ISA/ARPA (Santa Monica: RAND, 1970), pp. 9–12.

54. Alexander L. George, *Political Organization and Morale in the Chinese Communist Forces*, RM-902-PR (Santa Monica: RAND, 1952).

55. Herbert Goldhamer report of 29 July 1951 to CG HQ FEAF, cited in Kellen, *Conversations*, p. 104.

Chapter Five
Of Time, Testosterone, and Tyrants

1. There are few women who have plausibly ruled as tyrants, and most of those have exercised political power because of their relationship to a husband or father who was the ruler of his country.

2. Leo Strauss, *On Tyranny*, ed. Victor Gourevitch and Michael S. Roth (New York: Free Press, 1991), pp. 24, 64.

3. Jack Snyder, *Myths of Empire: Domestic Politics and International Ambition* (Ithaca: Cornell University Press, 1991), pp. 32–33, 42–45, 52–54.

4. Randall L. Schweller, "Hitler's Tripolar Strategy for World Conquest," in *Coping with Complexity in the International System*, ed. Jack Snyder and Robert Jervis (Boulder: Westview Press, 1993), pp. 208, 211–13, 222–26, 231.

5. Plato, *The Republic*, trans. Alan Bloom (New York: Basic Books, 1968), bk. 9, 573a–c. Being drunk, erotic, and melancholic appear to represent the corruption of the three elements Plato says there are in the soul: reason, the appetites, and spirit.

6. Xenophon, *Tyrannicus*, in Strauss, *On Tyranny*, sec. 1, para. 34 (hereinafter 1:34).

7. Ibid., 7:10, 2:9, 1:14.

8. Strauss, *On Tyranny*, p. 68.

9. Alexis de Tocqueville, *Democracy in America*, trans. George Lawrence, trans., ed. J. P. Mayer (New York: Anchor, 1969), vol. 2, pp. 526–27. See also Jon Elster, "Intertemporal Choice and Political Thought," in *Choice Over Time*, ed. George Loewenstein and Jon Elster (New York: Russell Sage Foundation, 1992), p. 35.

10. Edward C. Banfield, *The Unheavenly City* (Boston: Little, Brown, 1970), p. 47.

11. Robert Axelrod, *The Evolution of Cooperation* (New York: Basic Books, 1984), pp. 110–13, 126–32.

12. George Loewenstein, "The Fall and Rise of Psychological Explanation in the Economics of Intertemporal Choice," in *Choice over Time*, pp. 6–9, discussing the works of John Rae, N. W. Senior, and W. S. Jevons.

13. David Laibson, "Hyperbolic Discount Functions and Time Preference Heterogeneity," draft of 1 March 1997; Christopher Harris and David Laibson, "Instantaneous Gratification," Harvard Economics Department online paper, 30 May 2001, post.economics.Harvard.edu/faculty/laibson/papers/instgrat.pdf; Gary Becker, *Accounting for Tastes* (Cambridge: Harvard University Press, 1996), pp. 10–11, 48–49.

14. Alan R. Rogers, "Evolution of Time Preferences by Natural Selection," *The American Economic Review* 84, no. 3 (June 1994): 460–81. The key assumption is that a population is in evolutionary equilibrium, that is, that evolution has ceased at a single optimum point, an assumption that is disputed in chapter 1 of this book as being inconsistent with the essential nature of evolution, which requires heterogeneity and variety.

15. Richard J. Herrnstein, "Rational Choice: Necessary but Not Sufficient," *American Psychologist* 45 (March 1990): 356–67. This is an article re-

viewing Herrnstein's original work done in the early 1960s and subsequent developments.

16. George Ainslee and Nick Haslam, "Hyperbolic Discounting," in Loewenstein and Elster, *Choice Over Time*, pp. 58, 63–66.

17. Herrnstein, "Rational Choice," p. 363.

18. Thomas C. Schelling, "Self-Command in Practice, in Policy, and in a Theory of Rational Choice," *American Economic Review* 74, no. 72 (May 1984): 1–11.

19. This is a very brief summary of the elegant argument developed in Robert H. Frank, *Passions within Reason: The Strategic Role of the Emotions* (New York: W. W. Norton, 1988), pp. 18–19, 51–53, 66, 74–76, 81–84.

20. Plato, *The Republic*, 436a, 439c–e, 440a, 441a–b.

21. See, for example, Howard Margolis, *Selfishness, Altruism, and Rationality* (Cambridge: Cambridge University Press, 1982).

22. Jerry A. Hausman, "Individual Discount Rates and the Purchase and Utilization of Energy-Using Durables," *Bell Journal of Economics* (Spring 1979): 33–54.

23. Walter Mischel, Yuichi Shoda, and Philip K. Peake, "The Nature of Adolescent Competencies Predicted by Preschool Delay of Gratification," *Journal of Personality and Social Psychology* 54, no. 4 (1988): 687–96.

24. These studies are cited in James Q. Wilson, *The Moral Sense* (New York: Free Press, 1993), pp. 82, 86–87.

25. Louise C. Masse and Richard Tremblay, "Behavior of Boys in Kindergarten and the Onset of Substance Use during Adolescence," *Archives of General Psychiatry* 54 (January 1997): 62–68. The personality elements were taken from the Cloninger personality dimensions.

26. C. Robert Cloninger, Rolf Adolfsson, and Nenad M. Svrakic, "Mapping Genes for Human Personality," *Nature Genetics* 12 (January 1996): 3–4; Richard Ebstein et al., "Dopamine D4 Receptor (D4DR) Exon III Polymorphism Associated with the Human Personality Trait of Novelty Seeking," *Nature Genetics* 12 (January 1996): 78–80.

27. See the discussion in chapter 1.

28. Antoine Bechara et al., "Insensitivity to Future Consequences Following Damage to Prefrontal Cortex," in *Cognition on Cognition* (Amsterdam: Elsevier Science, 1995), pp. 3–11.

29. Jerome Kagan, "On Future Psychological Categories," in *Mind and Brain Sciences in the 21st Century*, ed. Robert L. Solso (Cambridge: MIT Press, 1997), pp. 236, 240.

30. James Q. Wilson and Richard J. Herrnstein, *Crime and Human Nature* (New York: Simon and Schuster, 1985), pp. 127–30.

31. Xenophon, *Tyrannicus*, 1:1, 1:4, 1:7. Then the discussion of the pleasures of the senses: 1:11 Hiero, for tyrants, "it is not safe for them to go where they are not going to be stronger than those who will be present. Nor is what they possess at home secure enough for them to entrust it to others and go abroad. For there is the fear they will at the same time be deprived of their rule and become powerless to take vengeance on those who have committed the injustice." 1:14 Simonides, tyrants hear only praise, no abuse, "for no one is willing to accuse a

tyrant to his face." 1:15 Hiero—what pleasure from those who say nothing bad "when he knows clearly every thought these silent men have is bad for him?" 1:17–1:20 Hiero: people grow tired on what they have in abundance. Tyrants have such abundance that "they admit no possibility of increase at feasts."

32. Ibid., 1:26.

33. Ibid., 1:37.

34. Laura L. Betzig, *Despotism and Differential Reproduction Rates: A Darwinian View of History* (New York: Aldine Press, 1986).

35. Xenophon, *Tyrannicus*, 1:34

36. Ibid., 2:1–2, 2:7–11, 2:15.

37. Ernst Hanfstaengl noted that even when visiting museums, Hitler "simply could not bear not to dominate any situation in which he found himself." *Hitler: The Missing Years* (New York: Arcade Publishing, 1994), p. 60.

38. Alan Bullock, *Hitler and Stalin: Parallel Lives* (New York: Vintage, 1993), pp. 100–101.

39. Ibid., p. 344.

40. Ibid., p. 311.

41. Alexander Stille, *Excellent Cadavers* (New York: Pantheon, 1995), p. 117.

42. Ole R. Holsti, "Crisis Decision Making," in *Behavior, Society, and Nuclear War*, vol. 1, ed. Philip E. Tetlock et al. (New York: Oxford University Press, 1989), pp. 30–31.

43. See, for example, concerning Hitler, Ian Kershaw, *Hitler 1936–1945: Nemesis* (New York: W. W. Norton, 2000), pp. 32–33, 105–6. Stalin was on vacation during the Berlin blockade, as noted below.

44. Bullock, *Hitler and Stalin*, pp. 73, 146.

45. Hanfstaengl, *Hitler: The Missing Years*, p. 266.

46. Robert G. L. Waite, *The Psychopathic God: Adolf Hitler* (New York: De Capo Press, 1993), p. 373.

47. Vladislav Zubok and Constantine Pleshakov, *Inside the Kremlin's Cold War: From Stalin to Khrushchev* (Cambridge: Harvard University Press, 1996), p. 21.

48. William Arkin, "Baghdad: Urban Sanctuary in Desert Storm?" *Airpower Journal* 11, no. 1 (Spring 1997): 15, citing Thomas A. Keany and Eliot A. Cohen, *Gulf War Air Power Survey* (Washington, D.C.: GPO, 1993), vol. 1, pt. 1, p. 69.

49. Plato, *The Republic*, 565d: "when a tyrant grows naturally, he sprouts from a root of leadership and nowhere else." 565e, A tyrant comes out of the leader of a "particularly obedient mob, does not hold back from shedding the blood of his tribe, but unjustly brings charges against a man—which is exactly what they usually do—and, bringing him before the court, murders him, . . . and hints at cancellations of debts and redistributions of land." 566d, "In the first days of his time, doesn't he smile at and greet whomever he meets, and not only deny he's a tyrant but promise much in private and public, and grant freedom from debts and distribute land to the people and those around himself, and pretend to be gracious and gentle to all?" 567b–c, As time passes, those of his associates who helped put him in power, "the manliest among them—speak frankly to him and to one another, criticizing what is happening. . . . Then the tyrant

must gradually do away with them, if he's going to rule, until he has left neither friend nor enemy of any worth whatsoever. . . . He must, therefore, look sharply to see who is courageous, who is great-minded, who is prudent, who is rich. And so happy is he that there is a necessity for him, whether he wants to or not, to be an enemy of all of them and plot against them until he purges the city."

50. Jon Elster, "Intertemporal Choice and Political Thought," in Loewenstein and Elster, *Choice Over Time*, pp. 35, 39–41.

51. Xenophon, *Tyrannicus* 1:39, in Strauss, *On Tyranny*.

52. Ibid., 2:18.

53. Ibid., 4:11.

54. Ibid., 6:4, 6:6–8.

55. Margaret Levi, *Of Rule and Revenue* (Berkeley: University of California Press, 1988), pp. 71, 73, 93, 110, 178–79.

56. "for no one is willing to accuse a tyrant to his face." Xenophon, *Tyrannicus*, 1:14.

57. Zachary Shore, "Hitler, Intelligence and the Decision to Remilitarize the Rhine," *Journal of Contemporary History* 34, no. 1 (January 1999): 5–18.

58. David E. Murphy, Sergei A. Kondrashev, and George Bailey, *Battleground Berlin: CIA vs. KGB in the Cold War* (New Haven: Yale University Press, 1997), pp. 62–63, which has comparison quotes: 30 June 1948, Secretary of State George Marshall: Americans will "remain in Berlin and make maximum use of air transport to supply the civilian population." Soviet KI (GRU/MGB foreign intelligence service) Berlin resident report to Marshal Sokolovsky, 3 July 1948: "The American mood has changed from warlike to dejected. The many American aircraft arriving in Berlin are taking out documents and other property of the American administration." The authors comment: "KI reporting during the Berlin blockade was often startling misleading. No better example can be found of how Cold War reporting from well-placed Soviet sources was filtered and revised until a report was fashioned that was sure to please Stalin. . . . The reports prolonged the blockade by underestimating both Western resolve and how apprehension in the West caused by the blockade led to efforts to enlist West Germany in European defense."

59. Vojtech Mastny, *The Cold War and Soviet Insecurity: The Stalin Years* (New York: Oxford University Press, 1996), p. 52. Stalin takes long vacation after initiating blockade of Berlin, and his subordinates send him only upbeat reports; p. 59: "Although Stalin's spies were capable of penetrating into the inner sanctum of Western governments, he was prevented from making the best use of their information. Impressed by the organizational prowess of his adversaries, the month after launching the Cominform as a response to the Marshall Plan, he had also established a super intelligence agency in response to the recent reorganization of the U.S. intelligence apparatus. The Committee of Information at the Soviet Foreign Ministry, however, was so rigidly centralized that its staff could not effectively process the vast masses of incoming material. Stalin himself was receiving from Molotov only brief digests of what the foreign minister's overworked subordinates considered important, and given the dictator's erratic working habits, he hardly found enough time to read, much less absorb, even that."

60. Dan Reiter and Allan C. Stam, III, "Democracy, War Initiation and Victory," ms., Marc, 1997.

61. Bullock, *Hitler and Stalin*, pp. 79, 145, 155, 157, 221.

62. Hanfstaengl, *Hitler: The Missing Years*, p. 50. "I was almost the only person who crossed the lines of his groups of acquaintants. Normally, he kept them all in watertight compartments and never told them where he had been or where he was going"; p. 359, quoting Hitler to Kurt Ludecke, in the 1920s: "I have an old principle, only to say what must be said to him who must know it, and only when he must know it." Hjalmar Schacht of Hitler: "'He never let slip an unconsidered word. He never said what he did not intend to say, and he never blurted out a secret. Everything was the result of cold calculation.'"

63. Bullock, *Hitler and Stalin*, p. 331.

64. Gerhard L. Weinberg, *The Foreign Policy of Hitler's Germany: Diplomatic Revolution in Europe 1933–1936* (Chicago: University of Chicago Press, 1970), pp. 27, 30, 36, 198, 239–40.

65. Ibid., pp. 247–48.

66. Ibid., p. 246.

67. Ibid., p. 253, 257–58.

68. Gerhard L. Weinberg, *A World at Arms: A Global History of World War II* (New York: Cambridge University Press, 1994), pp. 27–29.

69. Ibid., pp. 33–34.

70. Weinberg, *Foreign Policy of Hitler's Germany*, pp. 22–23.

71. Weinberg, *World at Arms*, pp. 175–77, 181, 239.

72. Ibid., pp. 250–51.

73. Eric Larrabee quotes Hitler's December 11, 1941 speech: "A plan prepared by President Roosevelt has been revealed in the United States, according to which his intention is to attack us in 1943 with all the resources of the United States. Thus our patience has come to the breaking point." Larrabee, *Commander in Chief* (New York: Harper, 1987), pp. 124–25. The Victory Program was secret but had been leaked by its opponents to the isolationist press, and the *Chicago Tribune* ran a story on it on 4 December 1941.

74. Weinberg, *World at Arms*, p. 177; Larrabee, *Commander in Chief*, p. 126.

75. For example, see Bullock, *Hitler and Stalin*, p. 172, and Mastny, *Cold War and Soviet Insecurity*, p. 20.

76. Bullock, *Hitler and Stalin*, 355. In December 1927, an international scientific conference met in Moscow. A Russian neuro-pathologist, Vladimir Bekhterev, spoke and was widely acclaimed. Stalin then invited Bekhterev to come and meet him. The interview took place on 12 December, and Bekhterev told his assistant afterwards that Stalin was a typical case of severe paranoia. Bekhterev then suddenly took ill in his hotel and died while still in the hotel. E. A. Lichko, *Literaturnaya Gazeta*, September 1988.

77. Mastny, *Cold War and Soviet Insecurity*, p. 13.

78. Bullock, *Hitler and Stalin*, p. 471.

79. Mastny, *Cold War and Soviet Insecurity*, pp. 13, 15; Martin Van Creveld, *Hitler's Strategy 1940–1941* (London: Cambridge University Press, 1973), pp. 72, 82.

80. Mastny, *Cold War and Soviet Insecurity*, p. 18; Weinberg, *World at Arms*, pp. 609–11.

81. Mastny, *Cold War and Soviet Insecurity*, pp. 28–41.

82. Murphy et al., *Battleground Berlin*, p. 408 n. 12.

83. Mastny, *Cold War and Soviet Insecurity*, pp. 74, 80–84, 100.

84. Ibid., pp. 102–6.

85. Khrushchev's memoirs cited in Mastny, p. 106.

86. Mao's three telegrams to Zhou Enlai are reprinted in appendix B to Thomas J. Christensen, *Useful Adversaries: Grand Strategy, Domestic Mobilization, and Sino-American Conflict, 1947–1958* (Princeton: Princeton University Press, 1996), pp. 271–75.

87. Eliot A. Cohen, *Supreme Command: Soldiers, Statesmen and Leadership in Wartime* (New York: Free Press, 2002), is very suggestive on this issue.

Chapter Six
Where Do We Go from Here?

1. See the works by Joshua Epstein and Lars-Erik Cederman cited in chapter 1.

2. Isaiah Berlin, "On Political Judgment," *New York Review of Books*, 3 October 1996, pp. 26–30.

3. The book by Rose McDermott that has the working title *Sick and Tired* uses the medical records of elite decisionmakers to understand why these individuals may have behaved the way they did.

Index

Acheson, Dean, 174
adrenal glands, 79
adrenaline, 41–42, 112–13, 118, 123
African states, 14
age differences, 2, 5, 52, 84, 97, 153
agent-based modeling, 180–81
aggression, 73, 76–77, 79, 83, 85–87, 126.
    See also dominant behavior
air traffic controllers, studies of, 112
alliance behaviors, 53–54
alternative strategies decision making. *See*
    rational choice decision making
amygdala, 4, 31, 39, 45–47, 50–51, 57,
    114, 117, 122
analogical reasoning, 51–55
anger, 52, 79, 84, 96
anochracies, 97, 164–65
Arab societies, 193n.50
Archer, John, 84–85
aristocracies, 95, 138–39
Aristotle, 52
Arkin, William, 160
Arrow's theorem, 13
Asian states, 14
al-Assad, Hafez, 182
auditory cortex, 45
auditory pattern recognition, 34
autism, 21–22
autocracies, 70, 97, 164–65
autonomic nervous system reactions,
    39–42
Axelrod, Robert, 142

baboons, studies of, 81, 96, 115–16
backward reasoning, 7, 12–13, 23
Ball, George, 64
Banfield, Edward C., 142, 144
Banker, William P., 196n.38
Bannerjee, A. V., 125
Bekhterev, Vladimir, 171
Ben Gurion, David, 178
Bennett, D. Scott, 14
Berlin, Isaiah, 182
Berlin Crisis (1948), 158, 163–64, 166
Berman, Larry, 64–66

Betts, Richard, 64, 66
Bevin, Ernest, 174
Bismarck, Otto von, 12, 94–95
Blainey, Geoffrey, 102, 106
Bloch, Marc, 129–30
Booth, Alan, 78
brain, the, 3, 5, 18, 32–37, 44; amygdala,
    4, 31, 39, 45–47, 50–51, 57, 114, 117,
    122; content-specialized mental func-
    tions and, 18–23; cortex, 3–4, 45–46,
    48, 117, 151; hippocampus, 4, 39, 45–
    46, 51, 113; Standard Social Science
    Model of, 18–19, 21; thalamus, 31, 45,
    48; trauma studies of, 1, 29, 38, 40, 46–
    47, 50, 151–52
Bueno de Mesquita, Bruce, 14
Bullock, Alan, 159, 166
Bundy, McGeorge, 59, 66
Buscetta, Tomasso, 157
Byrne, Richard, 20, 189n.28

Callwell, Charles, 108
Cannon, Walter Bradford, 123
castration, 76
challengers, punishment of. *See* dominant
    behavior
Chamberlain, Neville, 56–57
China, People's Republic of, 14, 66–67.
    See also Mao Zedong
Chomsky, Noam, 19
Churchill, Winston, 94, 106, 178
Civil War, U.S. (1861–65), 104–5, 128–29
Clausewitz, Carl von, 101–4, 110, 134
Clemenceau, Georges, 178
Clifford, Clark, 64
Cloninger, C. Robert, 150
cognition, 3, 30, 40–44; serial thought
    processes and, 33, 37, 43, 51, 54. *See
    also* pattern recognition, emotion-based
cohesion, military unit, 16, 123
computer simulations. *See* simulation
    experiments
Concert of Europe system, 71
consciousness, 37, 48
constitutions, 161